Spaces of Intensity

3h architects

To Dóra, Júlia, Anna and Péter

Spaces of Intensity
3h architects

Claus Käpplinger (ed.)

Birkhäuser

Basel

Layout, cover design and typesetting
Zalán Péter Salát, Budapest

Editorial supervision and project management
Henriette Mueller-Stahl, Berlin

Translation
Hungarian-English (all texts with the exception of the essays by Olaf Bartels, Claus Käpplinger, Holger Kleine and the interview with the architects)
Katalin Rácz, Bob Dent, Budapest

German-English (essays by Olaf Bartels, Claus Käpplinger, Holger Kleine and the interview with the architects)
Julian Reisenberger, Weimar

Coordination
Ildikó Maár, Budapest

Copy Editing
Catherine Atkinson, Hanover

Production
Amelie Solbrig, Berlin

Lithography
Sándor Rácz, Budapest

Paper
Munken Kristall Rough 120 g/m^2

Printing
DZA Druckerei zu Altenburg GmbH, Altenburg

Library of Congress Control Number: 2020937891

Bibliographic information published by the German National Library
The German National Library lists this publication in the Deutsche Nationalbibliografie; detailed bibliographic data are available on the Internet at http://dnb.dnb.de.

ISBN 978-3-0356-1966-9
e-ISBN (PDF) 978-3-0356-2042-9

P.O. Box 44, 4009 Basel, Switzerland
Part of Walter de Gruyter GmbH, Berlin/Boston
9 8 7 6 5 4 3 2 1
www.birkhauser.com

Contents

The Work of 3h architects – Between Centre and Periphery

Ákos Moravánszky

Intensity of expression is a quality that resonates with the spirit of a place. No-one expects the intensity of flamenco in Scandinavian music. Finnish tango is not the same as Argentinian – but it perfectly fits the mood of Aki Kaurismäki's movies. So, when the Budapest-based architecture office 3h cites "intensity" as the term that best describes their work, we should see this as a reflection of a specific geographical and cultural condition.

Some three decades ago, while writing about the firewalls that still adjoined the vacant lots of war-ravaged Budapest, I had a palpable sense of the intensity of a Central European city.[1] In the capitals of Western Europe the firewalls had long since disappeared, but in cities like Budapest, Dresden or Warsaw they were still omnipresent. [Fig. 1] They had remained through the economic and cultural liberalism of the so-called "long sixties" and its experiments with market mechanisms, and although they slowly disappeared, many could still be seen after the fall of the Iron Curtain. The firewalls marked fissures in the smooth surface of the city, revealing the layers of history and the textures of the past in the fabric of the city like strata made visible by an excavation. Appropriated as children's playgrounds or public markets, these sites became places of energy, spaces of intensity, a promise to the citizens of potential for the future, even as their city, unlike the historical towns of Italy, had not yet been (re)built. The mismatch between these gaps and the dreams of the well-ordered city, until then only present in scattered fragments across Budapest, produced a stimulating frisson. This situation was captured by the sentimentality of Wim Wenders' angels in *Wings of Desire,* but what was really needed, as I thought at the time, was hard, unambiguous answers.[2]

The clarity of 3h's work seems to deliver such unambiguous answers. Gunther's and Csillag's response to the intensity of Budapest eschews the mimetic strategies that perpetuate the characteristic features of Hungarian architecture: expressive, gestural forms evoking oriental or regional architectural vocabularies. To understand their wariness towards such approaches so typical in Hungarian architecture, it helps to consider the office's roots. 3h was not founded in Budapest. Zsolt Gunther and Katalin Csillag, two young architecture graduates from the Technical University in Budapest, established the office in 1994 in Győr, a city in Western Hungary, some 50 kilometres from the Austrian border, and 120 km from Budapest. Twelve years later, they moved to Budapest, a decision that is noteworthy, not least because such relocations from a "peripheral" to a "central" location are quite rare in Hungary.

In a lecture entitled "Common Architectural Space" in 2003, Zsolt Gunther spoke of the specific situation of the periphery. Quoting the Serbian philosopher Radomir Konstantinović and the Hungarian writer Péter Esterházy, he highlighted "the challenges of the province" and reflected critically on the fear of the Other, the lazy traditionalism and also the sense of inferiority that characterise the provinces. [3] One should be careful, however, not to confuse province with periphery. A peripheral situation is always relative: a periphery in one context can be a centre in another. Peripheries are also frequently laboratories for experiments that in turn feed back into the centre. Gunther argued for change, for communicating the goals of new architecture more effectively to the public, for establishing new institutions and initiating cultural exchange with neighbouring countries. The Pannonian Basin had, after all, always been at the crossroads of different cultures. Such reflections on one's own situation and specific geo-cultural context are rare among Hungarian architects. Zsolt Gunther and Katalin Csillag found their ideas echoed in the works of literary authors who connect their peripheral situation with a particular sensitivity towards the city, for example the Turkish writer Orhan Pamuk and the Portuguese novelist José Saramago.

During the Cold War, the border between Austria and Hungary near Győr was also the boundary between East and West where the Iron Curtain in all its concrete (and iron) materiality bisected Europe into twin empires. The frontier region of Burgenland had for centuries been a site of border struggles, territorial disputes, and migration movements. It was a neglected territory, a sleepy but picturesque idyll, in striking contrast to the vibrant worlds of Vienna and Budapest. But the qualities of the villages of Burgenland had been noted long, before the Iron Curtain fell, by intellectuals such as Roland Rainer, one of the most significant Austrian architects of the post-war period. Rainer published a book on the vernacular architecture of the region [Fig. 2] in which he lauded the "admirable consistency and clarity" of these villages as an expression of the prevailing needs, resources, and economic and social relations in an age long before the concept of functionalism had been coined. [4]

With fall of State Socialism in 1989 the Iron Curtain was swept aside. A region previously neglected now received generous European financial support for the economy, culture and architecture, known in Austria as *Ziel-1-Förderung.* It was a turning point for the region, with new investment, a surge in building activity, promoting exchange, tourism and in particular new wineries, a building task that brought many young Hungarian architects international recognition. In 1993 *Architektur Raum Burgenland* was established as a platform to promote exchange, discussions, workshops and study trips. Zsolt Gunther and Katalin Csillag were involved from early on, and participated in a book by the Austrian architecture critic Otto Kapfinger, *Neue Architektur in Burgenland und Westungarn.* [5] In his contribution, Zsolt Gunther outlined the institutional network of architectural design in West Hungary, commenting critically on international trends such as post-modernism and deconstruction, and stressing the importance of "simple buildings that respond to their environments, whose purity resist the waves of fashion". [6]

3h's involvement in mapping the new architecture of Pannonia taught the office important lessons. The discovery of the periphery was a phenomenon that began from the centre. Around 1900, ethnographers and architects in Hungary looked to the villages of Transylvania for inspiration in reforming the architectural culture of the metropolis. Interest in the vernacular had been an underlying strain of the Modern movement everywhere and became particularly strong after

1 Ákos Moravánszky, "Fire Walls. Central Europe's Intensity and Hungarian Architecture", in: *Daidalos* 39 (15.03.1991), p. 50–63, 52.

2 Ibid.

3 Zsolt Gunther, *Közös épitészeti tér* (Common Architectural Space), unpublished lecture manuscript, 10.10.2013.

4 Roland Rainer (Ed.), *Anonymes Bauen Nordburgenland.* Salzburg, Verlag Galerie Welz, 1961; Reprint Vienna, Cologne, Weimar, Böhlau, 1995, p. 6.

5 Otto Kapfinger (Ed.), *Neue Architektur in Burgenland und Westungarn.* Salzburg, Anton Pustet, 2004.

6 Zsolt Gunther, "Nyugat-Magyarország kortárs építészete" (The Contemporary Architecture of West Hungary), in Kapfinger, *op. cit.,* n.p.

World War II when younger generations began to reject the tenets of the functionalist aesthetic. Architects such as Robert Venturi and Denise Scott Brown started to investigate the American periphery and the architecture of suburbia. Kenneth Frampton posited a programme of critical regionalism to counter the global tendencies of Postmodernism and reconnect with local tradition, materials and craftsmanship. Álvaro Siza and Jørn Utzon were among his references, architects who learned from the vernacular but transformed the lessons into modern architecture without formal citation. This notion of regionalism met with great enthusiasm in East-Central Europe, partly because it resonated well with the search for a national language that was particularly strong at the start of the 20th century. But even the Socialist Realism of the 1950s condemned the "cosmopolitan" international style, calling for forms that reflected a national identity.

Gunther and Csillag distanced themselves early on from an interpretation of regionalism that stressed difference over a shared past. But the lessons they had learned in the periphery continue to guide their work in Budapest. Their design method can be summarised as a sequence of three stages leading from the site to a type, from type to construction, and from construction to form.

The *site,* whether urban or rural, is not understood by 3h as a "given context" but as a condition in constant transformation. Writing about the site of the school for children with intellectual disabilities in Csorna, the architects describe the ongoing disintegration of traditional settlement structures. The original plot sizes, long and narrow strips of land running perpendicular to the main street, were giving way to larger buildings that presented a broad façade to the street. They use the term "transcription" to characterise the typo-morphological research that leads them to a proposal that reflects the changing situation rather than "restoring" an earlier situation. [7] And the configuration of their building, with intermediate spaces between the volumes, itself evokes the historical process of transformation. [Fig. 3]

As the Csorna school shows, the architects' definition of *type* is informed by their research into the history of the site. But it is also the product of a careful analysis of the needs of the building task itself. Typological work is not about choosing a pre-existing model but about understanding the local culture. Explaining their housing project for people with intellectual disabilities in Koroncó, the architects point to a traditional typological element of Hungarian vernacular architecture: the arcaded porch. "The link between the interior and exterior is the porch." [8] [Fig. 4] Such covered outdoor spaces are well suited to the Hungarian climate, mediating between the cooler, enclosed indoor spaces and the sunlit, hot open courtyard outside. "A prime example of this is the porch of a peasant's house. It is, to use a modern term, the interface of the house. A key characteristic is that it does not house or enclose, it just defines space rather than closing it off. In contrast to the undefined and unbounded area of the fir grove, it simply marks the cornerpoints of a rectangular space." [9] [Fig. 5] The type connects the form to the culture of inhabiting a place and responds to the climatic conditions and to the topography. The form of the house makes the culture visible through the evocation of a type.

The *construction* is the next stage and mediates between building type and building *form.* In the work of 3h, construction is not about demonstrating technological virtuosity but about the gesture of a building. The Geometria office building, embedded in a densely built neighbourhood of Budapest, asserts its presence through the gesture of stacking. [Fig. 6] The projections and recesses of the façade, glazed with transparent and translucent glass panes, create the impression of a series of boxes piled upon one another. A possible precedent for this chessboard-like solution is the façade of a villa by the Bauhaus architect Farkas Molnár in Budapest (Pasaréti út 7), built in 1936. [Fig. 7] While the obvious presence of a continuous system of vertical supports would undermine the stacking gesture of the Geometria office building, the K4 office building in Budapest derives its strength from the rigorous materialisation of the load-bearing structural system. [Fig. 8] The clear formal identities of these two projects are each the result of the consistent conceptual implementation of a construction idea.

In 3h's work, there is no direct causal relationship between construction and form. In contrast to functionalist dogma, the form is not determined by the construction. 3h speaks of the sculptural qualities of form, hinting that the form is entirely detached from the constraints of construction. The multi-functional pavilion of the Audi car factory in Győr derives its sculptural presence from the figurative motif of the ramp leading onto the roof. [Fig. 9] The dramatic effect is further heightened by the red colour of the object embedded in a lush green park. Zsolt Gunther points to the work of the British sculptor Antony Gormley, who develops his objects from a systematic investigation of the relationship of the human body and its movements to the surrounding space. [Fig. 10] Other sculptors whose works interact in a similarly complex spatial manner with their surroundings are István Haász, Eduardo Chillida and Anish Kapoor. [10] [Fig. 11] Gunther also speaks of alienation as a method for sidestepping one's received response to a known situation and as a key concept of formalist aesthetics: the act of "making strange" turns the familiar into a form that demands attention. [11] According to Otto Kapfinger, the ambiguity of the "intimately known" and the "unfamiliar" is central to understanding the work of the office. [12]

"The tension created by tradition and its alienation is also manifest in the use of materials," writes Gunther, explaining the office's use of brown-coloured stucco and raw concrete as the materials for the façade of the Csorna school. [13] [Fig. 12] Architectural history uses the term *decorum* to differentiate between architectural form and mere construction. Decorum denotes the appropriateness of form, the way in which a construction translates fulfilling the needs of function and construction into architecture. This applies to the architectural work of 3h in general. Ornament, on the other hand, is added decoration, and has only begun to feature in more recent projects. [Fig. 13] While working together with John Pawson on remodelling the interior of the medieval Benedictine Archabbey at Pannonhalma, they juxtaposed the new minimalist design against the colourful 19th-century neo-historicism of Ferenc Storno – a solution that not all were enamoured to the same degree. [Fig. 14] Today, they see "ornamentation as a historical demand" for contemporary Hungarian architecture. [14] This statement reflects perhaps the office's increasing involvement in restructuring and remodelling projects for historical monuments, a field that was long regarded as the realm of conservation specialists but is now increasingly being undertaken by architects with a freer, more experimental approach. As the "Bilbao effect" strategy of inserting spectacular signature buildings into the urban fabric begins to wane, architects are increasingly beginning to work with the historical substance of the cities, modifying and injecting buildings with new uses and meaning, rather than placing them under the bell jar of preservation. This approach stands in stark contrast to the practice of rebuilding historic monuments in a supposedly authentic form, even when the result is pure fiction.

3h's move to Budapest exemplifies how thinking about the periphery can fertilise architecture and architectural debate in the centre. It can be characterised as a certain realism, one that is not overly spellbound by the historic city and its monuments as objects of worship. Their experience in dealing with a range of different situations ranging from the industrial to the historical, for prosperous clients or for people with disabilities, has enabled 3h to successfully navigate a path within the diverse and varied context of modern Central Europe and its new political, economic and cultural realities – on the one hand, the Postmodern cult of monuments, as seen in Budapest's public squares and the rebuilding of war-destroyed palaces, and on the other, the "starchitecture" of international offices. Gunther and Csillag do not insert ready-mades into the existing urban fabric. They tread carefully on the patterned, palimpsest-like ground of the city, accepting its contradictions and allowing it to inform their projects and contribute to their meaning. Today, the intensity of Central Europe appears to be even stronger than before, and the need for hard, unambiguous responses as important as ever.

7 Katalin Csillag, Zsolt Gunther, 2 épület. Building in the Province / Hungary. (Győr), 2004, p. 28.
8 Ibid., p. 6.
9 Ibid., p. 6.
10 3h website: http://3h.hu/about-us/index.php
11 Csillag, Gunther, op. cit., p. 36.
12 Otto Kapfinger, "Intimately Unfamiliar: On the Construction of the School in Csorna by 3h office for architecture", in Csillag, Gunther, op. cit., p. 46–54.
13 Ibid., p. 36.
14 3h website: https://3h.hu/about-us/index.php accessed on 25.01.2020.

[Fig. 1] Firewall in Budapest, Dessewffy utca

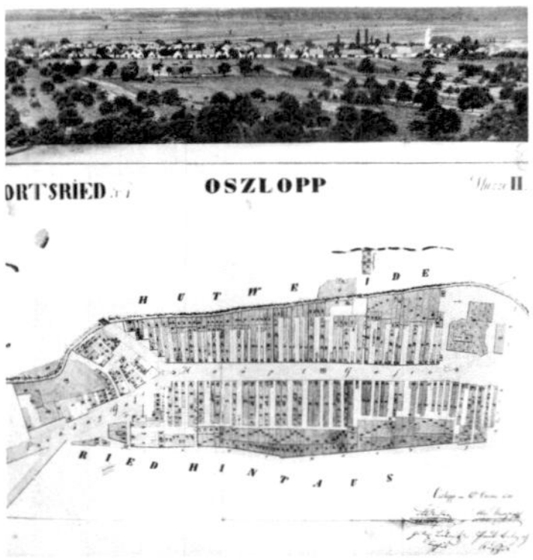

[Fig. 2] Plan and bird's eye view of the village Oszlopp/Oberrabnitz, from Roland Rainer (ed.), *Anonymes Bauen Nordburgenland.* Salzburg: Verlag Galerie Welz, 1961

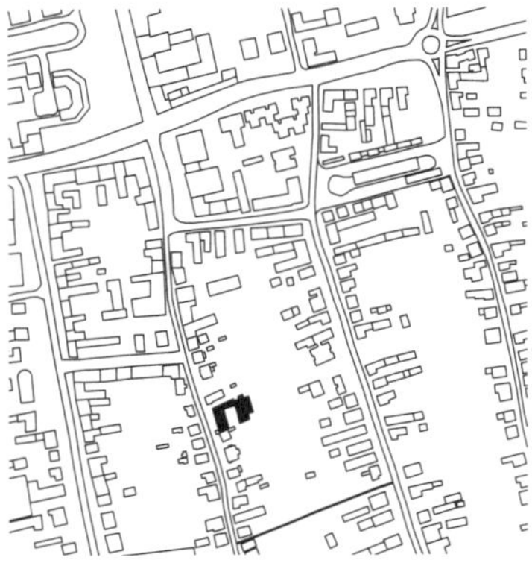

[Fig. 3] Special school for children with intellectual disabilities, Csorna, site plan

[Fig. 4] Accomodation for 22 people with intellectual disabilities, Koroncó, porch

[Fig. 5] Porch of a peasant house, Fertőszéplak

[Fig. 6] Geometria office building, Budapest

[Fig. 7] Farkas Molnár, villa in Budapest, Pasaréti út 7 (1936), from *Tér és Forma,* 1937

[Fig. 8] K4 office building, Budapest

[Fig. 9] Multifunctional pavilion of the Audi car factory in Győr

[Fig. 10] Sculpture by Antony Gormley

[Fig. 11] Eduardo Chillida, Comb of the Wind, San Sebastián

[Fig. 12] Brown-coloured stucco and raw concrete as façade materials of the Csorna school

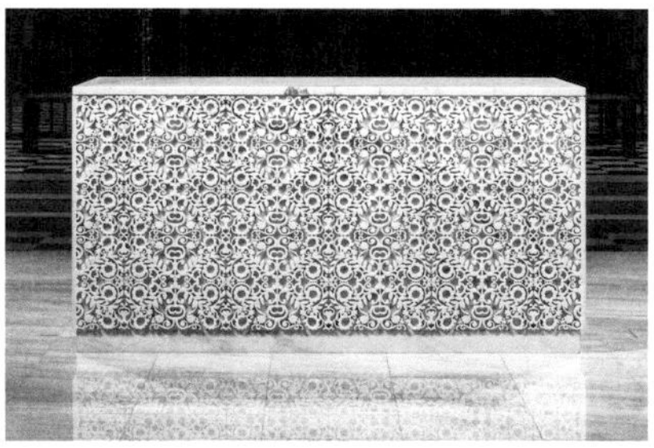

[Fig. 13] Ornament on the new stone altar by 3h architects in the cathedral of Szeged

[Fig. 14] Archabbey of Pannonhalma remodelling

Spaces of Intensity and Light

Claus Käpplinger

This book, *Spaces of Intensity,* is an invitation to journey to places, spaces and perspectives that may still be unfamiliar to many, even three decades after the fall of the Iron Curtain. At that time, the borders that had divided Europe in two since the end of World War II lost their significance in an astonishingly short space of time. The longstanding face-off of two irreconcilable systems was rapidly replaced by exchanges and encounters of all kinds that began to bring together East and West, making developments possible that were previously almost inconceivable. Hungary has a long history of cultural encounters and confrontations between West and East, between Occident and Orient, and the opening of the Hungarian border to Austria on 27 June 1989 heralded the beginning of the end of the Iron Curtain and set in motion new events that were to change Europe.

While many young Eastern European architects, like Katalin Csillag and Zsolt Gunther of 3h architects, went to the West to study or to gain their first professional experience, Western European architecture has shown far less interest in the experiences and potential of the eastern half of Europe. Many architects and intellectuals are still rather surprised to note that Eastern Europe boasts its own singular voices and achievements that stand alongside those of the West and can perhaps even offer us more lucid and distinctive positions. The view from West to East is, unfortunately, still very selective and superficial, focusing on picturesque scenes of old landscapes and cities, and only rarely venturing beyond the familiar to discover a very productive and stimulating contemporary culture.

The philosopher and cultural critic Slavoj Žižek is familiar to many in the West on account of his highly stimulating perspectives and reflections on the globalisation discourse, though few are aware that he is Slovenian. Also familiar to many outside Hungary are the writers and essayists György Konrád and Péter Esterházy, both now sadly deceased before their time, who in their work and passionate standpoints repeatedly scrutinised Europe's ups and downs, past and present. The writer László Krasznahorkai and the director Béla Tarr, on the other hand, are probably less well known to Westerners. Their works explore the essence of people, spaces and perceptions that differ sometimes markedly from Western European perspectives. For this reason, we have taken the liberty of introducing the four photo essays in this book on Hungary's spaces and places with quotations from Krasznahorkai – among others from his monumental work *Sátántangó,* published in 1985, which Béla Tarr, in turn, captured in images of immense intensity immediately after the fall of the Iron Curtain.

Transcending Borders

Although Hungary has produced a great many outstanding architects and striking buildings since the 19th century, very few are known outside Hungary today compared to its writers, philosophers and musicians. Those who did achieve international fame such as Oskar Kaufmann, Tibor Weiner, Ernő Goldfinger, Marcel (Lajos) Breuer or Pierre Vago are all émigrés, either by choice or by force. In the 20th century, emigration or at least a period of apprenticeship abroad seemed to be almost de rigueur for Hungarian architects seeking wider success. Motivated by a similar desire to broaden one's horizons, the young Hungarian architect Zsolt Gunther, who had studied under Zoltán Farkasdy at the Technical University of Budapest, moved to the University of Applied Arts in Vienna in 1986, i.e. before the great upheavals that were to come, to study under Hans Hollein and François Burkhardt. Not long after, together with two other young architects, Péter Balogh and Tibor Stahl, and the then student Katalin Csillag, he even won first prize in the important urban design competition for the "Expo '95 Vienna" [Fig. 1] that was planned for Vienna and Budapest but, unfortunately, never took place after it was voted down in a Viennese referendum.

Driven by a fascination for urban development, he moved between West and East several times in the years that followed, working first under the urbanist Béla Nagy in Budapest before moving to Delft in 1991 to work with Mecanoo, Erick van Egeraat, Chris de Weijer and Francine Houben, who at the time were setting out to conquer the architectural world with avant-garde concepts. The young architect's next steps were no less avant-garde, even constructivist, taking him to Graz, and thus closer to home, to work first with Volker Giencke and then Ernst Giselbrecht. At Giencke's office, he encountered a completely different kind of architecture, whose decidedly non-Euclidean geometries exerted a special fascination, but soon also made him despair that his own architectural path would be another, where space and materials are more defined than in the "Gienckoids", which were ultimately more paths than places. The switch to Ernst Giselbrecht in Graz, whose architecture is hardly less constructivist but mostly orthogonal, was for Gunther a logical step and also gave him the opportunity to become more familiar with administrative and industrial architecture.

Katalin Csillag, a few years Zsolt Gunther's junior, also hails from the region around Győr in Western Hungary. Having completed her studies under Tamás Karácsony at the Technical University of Budapest in 1992, she too found her way to Graz where she worked in various offices before she came to work with the architect Helmut Zieseritsch, where she acquired profound know-how especially in housing and learning to find creative solutions to the restrictions of tight budgets and numerous regulations. And, as with many other young architects, it was smaller housing projects that enabled Csillag and Gunther to venture out on their own, a step that was easier to master in the surroundings of their homeland in Győr, where they had family and living costs were lower than in Austria.

First Steps as Independent Architects

The design for a house in Győr [Fig. 2] and first prize in a Europan 4 competition for an industrial quarter in Graz-Eggenberg [Fig. 3] featuring a hybrid configuration of plants and constructions (unrealised) gave Csillag and Gunther the necessary impetus to found their own architectural office in 1996: 3h architects. Its unusual name is also a clear statement of intent that their architecture should be clear, precisely placed and perhaps even a little tense, like the hard line of the 3h pencil from which the office derives its name. It was an unequivocal rejection of the all too opulent tendencies of Hungarian Postmodernism that had flooded the country after the fall of the Iron Curtain. They were passionate to strive for something new, something more akin to the spirit of the rationalist Hungarian Modernism of the inter-war years and the "long 1960s" [Fig. 4] than the architecture of the moment. Theirs was not the expressive play of forms and colour, nor the brick architecture of the mid-century years, nor even the biomorphic timber architecture of Imre Makovecz and his students. Opportunities for young architects were, surprisingly, much better in the provinces than in the Hungarian capital, where long-established and incoming foreign architects vied for architectural prominence. Győr, which lies some 60 kilometres from Austria and 80 kilometres from Bratislava in Slovakia, began to attract significant Western investment from the mid-1990s onwards, transforming it into a major centre for production and logistics. After numerous competitions and several small private houses, 3h architects gained their first international recognition with the design of a building for the large Audi factory complex in Győr in 2003. Inspired by István Haász's sculptural works of concrete art, Csillag and Gunther placed a bright red, dynamically folded, somewhat enigmatic object into the broad plains of Western Hungary, which is able to hold its own against the huge factory complex. The "Red Poppy" Audi Forum [Fig. 5] is a flexible pavilion for conferences, seminars and cultural events that appears to have a different form when seen from varying distances and directions, much like István Haász's works, which are both sculptures and paintings.

The construction of an administration building for Audi in the immediate vicinity soon followed, but Csillag and Gunther were already turning their attention to other building tasks to counter the dangerous tendencies in the rapid transformation of their homeland, and focusing more on the genius loci and the possibilities of a more gradual, continual development of the provinces. Aspects of identity, context, scale and the structural elements of the Western Hungarian landscape became important for them as characteristics of a region that had developed its own spatial forms over centuries, despite its own evolutionary discontinuities. They began examining characteristic features such as the extremely elongated rural plots, the sharp delineation between street and private space, or transitional elements such as the porches, barns and gates of old rural architecture. Their intention was not simply to replicate but to sensitively transform, and during this time they were able to complete two impressive projects of socially committed architecture in Csorna and Koroncó.

The projects, in Csorna for children [Fig. 6] and in Koroncó for adults with intellectual disabilities, respond sensitively to their respective contexts, implanting spatial configurations that provide highly differentiated sequences of spaces for their respective users. Alongside accommodating different activities, a central concern was to shield the residents, both for the sake of privacy and against the hot Hungarian summers. This had a decisive impact on the form and fit of the parts in both buildings. This has resulted in spaces of varying permeability with views in and out and an exceptional play of light: in Csorna, the entrance space and loggia have an almost monumental quality; in Koroncó, a delicate permeable screen of wooden lamella graces the front of the building.

New Realism and Inverse Tradition

At around the same time, and completely independently of each another, Katalin Csillag and Zsolt Gunther in Hungary and Caruso St John, Tony Fretton and Sergison Bates in Great Britain were developing what came to be called a new architecture of realism, which the architecture theorist and architect Florian Beigel, who died in 2018, described as follows: *"We think architecture is an art of the everyday, and sometimes an art of the special occasion. We are for a more quiet architecture, thoughtful, with a generosity of spirit and mindful of affordability."* For these architects, the aim is neither to radically reinvent architecture nor to produce glittering icons in the vein of Rem Koolhaas or Zaha Hadid. Instead, they strive to work with what the site provides, to transform their structures, materials and spaces sensitively and sensually into a new sense of continuity, to build on and tie them into their context rather than adding new singular sensations to the urban fabric.

Far removed from the copyism of contemporary retro architecture, they are once again seeking a more intensive dialogue with what exists as well as with architectural traditions and models, which they adapt, transform and refine in the respective context to create spaces that are both usable and distinctive, spaces that are rich in meaning and semantically eloquent but whose narrative only reveals itself at the second or even third glance. Rather than propelling forward the rapidly changing fashions of contemporary architecture, their aim is to slow down the pace and provide opportunities to tarry and engage.

[Fig. 1] Urban competition Expo '95 Vienna, 1st prize, 1991

[Fig. 2] Bank and residential building, Győr, 1996–1998

[Fig. 3] EUROPAN 4 competition, Graz-Eggenberg, Austria, 1996

[Fig. 4] Ede Kelemen (ÁÉTV): Former Socialist Party headquarters, Budapest 1970

[Fig. 5] Red Poppy Audi Forum, Győr, 2003

[Fig. 6] Model of the school for children with intellectual disabilities, Csorna, 2004

[Fig. 7] Aerial view of a typical village with extremely long plots in Western Hungary

The rapidly changing face of the Western Hungarian province after the fall of the Iron Curtain, and the replacement of many old buildings with often rather faceless and out-of-scale new constructions, prompted Katalin Csillag and Zsolt Gunther to question their architectural concepts and search for alternatives in the context of their cultural environment. Two essays by Gunther, *"Short reflections on the province"* (2002) and *"Metaprovince: Building in low-tech, thinking in high-tech"* (2004), trace a shift away from the predominance of images in contemporary architecture towards a more holistic architecture that focuses more on the physical place and its sensory qualities, or as Gunther expressed it in 2004, referring to his Western Hungarian homeland: *"In connection with the dominant perspective of sight, we should also mention that, alongside tangibility and spirituality, materiality is still a very evident quality of rural areas. Visual images are not the only means of conveying emotions, joy and desire; the same can be said of the smells, tangible realities, faint sounds but also loud rattling of the provinces."*

He pursues these observations in his text *"Metaprovince: Building in low-tech, thinking in high-tech"*, linking them to other broader considerations: *"Even in the provinces we can find less visible everyday objects or buildings that have their own tradition. The found object offers a counterpoint to the virtual world because it is tangible. It is full of fallible characteristics. Before it was found, it had been drifting. The traditional use of materials and the presence of materials close to nature – thatch, hay, wood, sand, earth plaster – along with their changing textures hint at an environment full of emotions. Parallel to experiencing through seeing, we experience the environment with other senses: the provinces are a space of diverse sensory sensations. And here we come back to the haptic experience, to the complex perception of materiality."* On a broader level, *"the most important aspect for the survival of the built environment is the settlement and land structure characteristic of almost the whole Carpathian basin, in short its morphology. The relationship between the elongated, rectangular sites, the practice of building along its edges, the resulting side gardens and buildings are the product of a mostly uniform spirituality. This kind of positioning of buildings is the dominant but not the exclusive form of appearance. These morphological elements have survived because there have not been significant changes to the ownership patterns of these old structures. However, today they are being overshadowed by the currently popular but bland and rampant development of free-standing buildings and the old structures are now regarded as no longer appropriate to the requirements of our times."*

Troubled by the lack of a connection to context in many contemporary buildings, Gunther proposed a strategy of "inverse tradition", which he views not as a means of conservation but as a dynamic process of both sensorial and typological design decisions made in dialogue with the as-found situation and the cultural context. Conceived as an open design strategy, "inverse tradition" aims to reconnect more strongly to the historical elements and structures of a place [Fig. 7] in order to maintain its distinctiveness, while at the same time finding new, more diverse responses for its development. For Gunther and Csillag it marked a shift away from the Modern credo of autonomously conceived bodies, perfect geometries and surfaces, towards more sensory approaches and layering and materialisation, which, given the often difficult building processes, also leaves more room for the imperfect and the ephemeral and corresponds more closely to the everyday haptic reality of Hungary. For 3h architects, it heralded a new architectural direction characterised by constructive simplicity and rationality, coupled with a detailed consideration of the typological qualities and morphological structures of their homeland. Gunther elaborated his ideas further in his doctoral thesis *"Inverse Tradition – Provincial Architecture of the Future"*, which he completed at the Moholy-Nagy University of Art and Design in 2009, the campus of which they would comprehensively transform some 10 years later.

From the Province to the Metropolis

Three competition wins for two residential buildings and the institute for children with physical disabilities in Budapest motivated Katalin Csillag and Zsolt Gunther to relocate their office from Győr to the capital in 2006. The communicative perspectives of the much larger capital, which dominates almost all areas of the country's cultural life, were simply much greater. Other, more practical considerations such as proximity to the new building sites and a more diverse client base were a further reason, and the vibrant Hungarian capital presented many new challenges and the opportunity to develop their architectural strategies in more diverse contexts and on a larger scale.

Budapest is a city with a long history, which since its conquest by the Ottomans in the 16th century has repeatedly risen anew from the ruins and experienced many dramatic changes of regime. With its rich historical legacy of both fractured and aborted developments, as well as surprising continuities, Budapest is particularly fascinating for its role as a Central European metropolis at the junction between East and West. It has many harsh contrasts, but also remarkable urban spaces and stylistic fusions of elements subsumed from other cultures but nevertheless appropriated and reshaped with great national self-will into something unmistakably Hungarian.

It is a city that is both old and new, rational and also illogical, Baroque and yet industrial. It favours narratives rich in association over grand master plans, regulatory systems or stylistic purity. As such, it is a city in constant dialogue with itself and also often with distant points of reference – the ancient architecture of Central Asia, Italian Baroque or Rationalism [Fig. 8], Scandinavian Neoclassicism or turn-of-the-20th-century Nordic National Romanticism – yet it is seen by many foreign visitors as an impressively homogeneous city. Here, one sees not the sparse landscape of the Hungarian plains or the rural archetypes, but rather an exuberant abundance of spaces, forms and cultural contexts – a challenging new environment in which to put Csillag's and Gunther's strategy of "inverse tradition" to the test.

But, through their sensitivity to the potential of a place and its unique characteristics, the architects were able to find compelling answers to the transformation of old building traditions in the new metropolitan environment. For the apartment blocks on Futó utca in the centre of Pest, the architects drew on the old tradition of intermediate residential courtyards with walkways running around them – the equivalent to the Austrian *Pawlatschen,* which probably found their way to Budapest from Bohemia via Vienna – as a model for the new building blocks. On top of that, figuratively and literally, the architects paraphrased the Budapest tradition of continually extending and raising existing buildings – often by whatever means at hand – to maximise space by adding a demonstratively contrasting upper section to the top of the street-facing block. While the strategy of planning a new building in Futó utca with additional storeys apparently stacked on top may seem strange at first it establishes an unexpected connection to the older neighbouring buildings at a lower height on the other side of the street, mediating between the change in height from the old to the new buildings in the old urban district. The spatial qualities of the apartments in Futó utca are also notable in that they tie in with Budapest's outstanding residential architecture from 1920 to 1960, which cannot be said of many contemporary housing projects in Hungary, due to the prevalence of profit-oriented and cost-conscious property developers and lack of cooperative housing associations.

For the institute for children with physical disabilities, Csillag and Gunther created an extension for new shared apartments and therapy and social rooms, which was completed in 2010. Here, the architects developed a similarly compelling architectural structure: an intermediate sequence of several building sections along a primary circulation axis that opens at recurring intervals into square-like spaces with ramps and plateaus, inviting the children to venture out and discover, encouraging them to be more mobile. The architecture of the new buildings deliberately recedes, their size and cubature picking up the structure of the villas in the vicinity rather than following the model of Béla Lajta's former school for the blind from 1908, a masterpiece of the Hungarian pre-Modern era. With carefully placed glass slits and openings, offering different perspectives on the magnificent old building, as well as a few select instances of colour, the architecture creates a new framework for the old building that takes the form of an elongated village street, whose distinct building volumes and incisions mediate successfully between the school building and its neighbours. The stimulating variety of its interiors provide a sheltered environment for the children, while also creating numerous opportunities for encounters as well as for secluded retreat. The architects' solution, sensitively weighed up, earned them nominations for both the renowned Piranesi Award and the Mies van der Rohe Award in 2011, though unfortunately the project was not awarded a prize.

[Fig. 8] Béla Hofstätter & Ferenc Domány: Tenement house of the Pension Fund of the Manfréd Weiss Companies, Budapest, 1937

[Fig. 9] Competition project for Museum of the Second World War in Gdańsk, Poland, 2010

[Fig. 10] Model of a family house in Paloznak, 2006

[Fig. 11] S House for a family, Budapest, 2012

[Fig. 12] Extension of the medicinal and thermal baths in Pápa, 2011

[Fig. 13] Árkád Shopping Centre, Szeged, 2007–11

[Fig. 14] Model of K4/KPMG headquarters, Budapest, 2011

[Fig. 15] John Pawson: Renovation of the basilica of the Archabbey of Pannonhalma, 2012

New Dimensions

In the years that followed, the architects participated in numerous competitions at home and abroad with some successes [Fig. 9] that unfortunately rarely progressed to actual building commissions. Private commissions for single family houses [Figs. 10–11] and extensions as well as a first thermal bath in Pápa [Fig. 12] and a mall in Szeged secured the survival of the office and allowed them to gain valuable experience with larger projects and difficult clients. The successful project for the Árkád Shopping Centre in Szeged [Fig. 13], built from 2007 to 2011, is one such example that won a Gold Award by the German Sustainable Building Council. Situated on Szeged's inner ring road next to much smaller-scale neighbours, the building is pleasingly spacious and light-filled in its circulation areas and elegantly incorporates parts of the old factory that once stood on the site as *spolia.*

Two further interesting and unusual projects – both office buildings – were completed in 2011, one on each side of the Danube in the centre of Budapest. In Medve utca in the old lower city of Buda, 3h architects developed a building for the geographical IT company Geometria that deliberately resists completely closing a gap in the perimeter of an old urban block. Instead the building makes its central theme the deep incision into the block from street to block interior and plays with our perception of light and space. Using differing degrees of transparency along with staggered arrangements of partially transparent and partially fritted glazed boxes, the Geometria Office Building creates a stimulating interplay of screens, spaces and volumes that breathes new life and astonishing depth into the old Euclidean geometry. In place of the traditional central perspective seen from a fixed point, it invites its users and visitors to appraise the building by actively changing position. Its light-filled interior presents a work environment comprised of various spatial compartments of varying visual and acoustic permeability.

The K4 Office Building [Fig. 14], by contrast, is an urban-scale building at the northern end of Dózsa György út, one of Budapest's main streets that passes by Heroes' Square and the City Park. Situated at the major crossroads with Vaci út and exposed to constant urban traffic, the project stands alongside other office complexes from different periods and provides 23,000 m² of modern office space in a striking building for large companies to use as their representative headquarters. Here, too, 3h architects decided against closing the perimeter of the block and proposed a rather unconventional solution that sits alongside its neighbours at the back and fans out in three finger-like sections to the front, stepping back from the plot perimeter and opening out demonstratively towards the urban junction to create an attractive urban space open to passers-by. In the design of the three "fingers", the architects have drawn on the dominant horizontality of Modernist buildings but also played with it, varying the proportions of the solid bands and fully glazed sections so that each "finger" becomes successively more transparent and less solid. As such, the enormous mass of the building acquires a surprising variety in its appearance. As a fourth and further element of the Modernist canon, the architects raised the building off the ground and added a canopy to the ground floor, except that here the supports are vigorously diagonal, and the canopy formed of a rhomboid grid. Their sculptural quality recalls the post-war Modernism of Oscar Niemeyer or Le Corbusier, while also relating to the dynamic topography of the new urban space.

Church and High Culture

Over the years, Katalin Csillag and Zsolt Gunther have repeatedly turned their attention to sacred spaces and church architecture, taking part in competitions such as that for a new church in Kismegyer. The materiality and intensity of sacred spaces and their dramaturgical orchestration of space and light has over the years drawn them increasingly to the design of churches, which since the fall of the Iron Curtain has experienced a renaissance in Eastern Europe, and in Hungary in particular. It was therefore not by chance that Csillag's and Gunther's expertise and comprehensive knowledge of church architecture should catch the attention of John Pawson, for whom they were able to act as local project architects for his sensitive transformation of the choir at the Benedictine Archabbey of Pannonhalma [Fig. 15], founded in 906. The collaboration with the British master of minimalism and sensory spaces was fruitful in both practical and cultural respects, providing an opportunity to review their architectural position in dialogue with Pawson and the existing building, and to develop the courage to embrace empty space boldly. At the same time, they were able to refine their programmatic approach of diverse simplicity, which differs in many respects to John Pawson's minimalism.

At about the same time, in 2012, 3h architects were commissioned to make extensive alterations to the cathedral at Szeged, whose altar space along with other damaged areas such as the undercroft, terrace and towers needed redesigning to accommodate new uses. The most significant interventions were made in the undercroft, the floor of which was lowered to create a fascinating sequence of new spaces of changing visual permeability which, radiant in bright white, have an almost graphic quality and accommodate various uses, including meeting rooms, exhibition spaces and a new columbarium. The newly created entrance foyer with a restaurant and pilgrims' rooms incorporates the remnants of the earlier Romanesque church that once stood on the site, and radiates a sense of pervasive grace and tranquillity that invites one to stop and contemplate the people, the architecture, the different spatial strata, their connections and the varying intensities of light. Unexpected openings appear at different points creating communicative transitions that establish connections and lend the once overbearing basement a sense of tremendous spaciousness. The use of perforations in different patterns [Fig. 16], the visual dematerialisation of the walls and ceilings and the permeability of inserted objects such as benches or steel paravents contribute to this, as do the carefully measured material contrasts that lead the visitor with seductive elegance from one room to the next. One even has a sense of being in contact with the activities on the square above from within the new foyer, with daylight spilling in from above through open risers in the stairs to the cathedral entrance and from cut-out but inaccessible atria. The architects would return to this device a few years later in their design for Moholy-Nagy University of Art and Design [Fig. 17].

In Szeged, Csillag and Gunther also embarked on a more intensive examination of the theme of ornament, which has always played a significant role in Hungarian culture, defining its respective position in the fluid transition between Occident and Orient. In the case of the cathedral, which, driven by a wave of national Romanticism, was rebuilt from 1913 to 1930 at a new location after a major flood, the building is a comparatively modern construction with elements of Neo-Romanesque, Art Nouveau and rural folk culture. The architects elected to place relatively discreet ornamental insertions at selected points such as the new main altar or the vertical junctions between the undercroft and the basilica. They take the form of a laser-cut block of marble or ceramic tiles with an ornamental pattern from rural folk culture, not reproduced but reinterpreted by contemporary means, for example by changing its scale, to challenge our perception. This dialogical approach to context aims to reveal hidden details or to make visible what was previously only subconsciously perceived. The many new steel elements in and around the old Romanesque tower, as well as in the western twin tower of the cathedral, point to the existence of iron concealed within the walls, the stair railings or sculptural walk-in space-within-a-space installations, establishing an open dialogue with the only superficially monolithic structure of the original building.

Such sensitive insertions into existing buildings, which through their progressive rather than conservational approach attempt to reinterpret the situation as found, have helped 3h architects breathe new life into ever more historical buildings, not just by adding new extensions and functions, but by establishing a dialogical narrative that allows the often very disparate history of these buildings to speak to the visitor. They have since undertaken numerous projects for churches and monasteries, from the Benedictine church at Győr, whose roof structure will house a new bell museum, to the Convent of the Sisters of Mercy of the Holy Cross in Budapest [Fig. 18] or the Abbey Church in Bélapátfalva, [Fig. 19] which in future will serve as a venue for exhibitions and seminars. Alongside the church, public clients have also come to recognise the contextual and sensory qualities of 3h architects' approach, and in 2014 this led them to become involved in the successive revitalisation of one of Hungary's most beautiful and famous 18th-century castles: Esterházy Castle in Fertőd.

The wonderful horseshoe-shaped Baroque complex, whose building fabric has survived, even during Socialism, but whose interior nevertheless underwent some brutal alterations, is being transformed into a cultural site of international significance. The first construction phase saw the renovation of the low side

[Fig. 16] Restaurant area with perforated steel paravent around the old Romanesque tower, Szeged, 2015

[Fig. 17] Cut-out atria below the entrance stairs of the old main MOME building, 2019

[Fig. 18] Renovation and extension of the Convent of the Sisters of Mercy of the Holy Cross, Budapest, 2015

[Fig. 19] Renovation of the Abbey Church in Bélapátfalva, 2018

[Fig. 20] New entrance foyer in the Esterházy Castle, Fertőd, 2019

[Fig. 21] Model of MOME, Budapest, 2016

[Fig. 22] Extension of the Kós Károly vocational school in Érd, Hungary, 1st prize, 2016

[Fig. 23] Invited competition for Pick Museum, Szeged, 2017

wing to the left with the orangery, which after 1945 served as a sports hall for an agricultural school with the loss of much of its original substance, including the historical roof construction. Here, too, the architects have combined different historical traces and reinterpreted elements to create a new richly diverse whole that connects old and new for use for exhibitions and events. Since very little historical documentation of the design of the rooms was available, and on-site investigations turned up only a few remnants of the original colour scheme, the architects have employed abstract white surfaces in the remaining areas along with individual, carefully implanted surfaces of richly contrasting materials. Through the use of a new stone inlay floor with geometric patterns, and a reflective stainless steel counter for the reception, they establish an oscillating interplay of surface and body – as the eye attempts to grasp the three-dimensional patterns of the two-dimensional planes – recalling the optical illusions and deceptive patterns of the Baroque [Fig. 20] . The culmination of these visual spectacles is the former orangery whose new barrel-vaulted steel ceiling shines radiant in white, its panels recalling the coffered painted ceilings of the Baroque, though here in place of paintings of the heavens, a radical, almost futuristic pattern of illuminated panels shines brightly from above. In spaces of expansive breadth, meandering direction and surprising depth, visitors to the new side wing experience stimulating changes of dimensions and spatial impressions, with enfilades that are sometimes polychromic, sometimes monochromic, each interacting differently with the light to create unique and intensely sensory atmospheres.

Three Distinct Individuals in Green Surroundings

In 2015, 3h architects won the competition for the design of a new campus for the Moholy-Nagy University of Art and Design (MOME) in Budapest incorporating the university's existing main building from the 1950s. Csillag and Gunther once again set about examining the site and its history with a view to picking up loose threads and weaving them variously into a new, reinterpreted structural concept. Starting from the existing main building, designed by their former teacher of architecture Zoltán Farkasdy in the style of Socialist Neoclassicism, and the linear axis it intended to form with three buildings, only two of which were ever built, they created a new ensemble with the old building as the centrepiece of a family of three related individuals bound together by a fourth element in the form of a topographically aligned circulation axis.

Three main buildings [Fig. 21] now grace the site – one for undergraduate studies, the former main building for the Master's degree programme and one for innovation and communication studies – each bright white but with very different volumetric forms, room configurations and visual permeability. The new main circulation axis and backbone of the campus runs between them, burrowing into and rising out of the undulating terrain as it links the new main entrance to the library, cafeteria, exhibition foyer and professors' rooms. These spaces have different qualities of natural light and visual connection to the outside world but still retain a definite sense of intimacy. The dynamism of the architecture with its precisely placed incisions and deep progression of spaces characterises the four buildings, but each has its own distinctive spaces and atmospheres and its own places for communicative interaction and concentrated study, some more extroverted or more introverted, some more secluded or more exposed. In the former main building, for example, some of the old ceilings and walls were removed to create spacious, open platforms for creative work that now relate visually to one another, establishing a connection in the third dimension. Combined with the careful orchestration of both natural and artificial light, there are no longer any dark, buried corners, only a range of variously communicative spaces with different intensities of illumination and a fluid connection to the green surroundings of the campus.

Csillag's and Gunther's architecture exhibits an architectonic virtuosity and haptic variance that derives from the different constructional assembly and materialisation of their buildings, which deliberately abstains from creating a homogenous overall appearance in favour of almost demonstratively articulating their heterogenous qualities, giving each a divergent haptic character: delicate steel frames with large, transparent sections of glazing in one building, solidly delineated spaces and exposed rough-concrete punctuated façades in another. Through its combination of atmospheric variety and disciplined Euclidean geometry, the new Moholy-Nagy University of Art and Design pays homage to the spirit of the Bauhaus teacher Moholy-Nagy, presenting itself as a very elegant example of how great complexity can be achieved with a simplicity of means.

Similar qualities in other cultural contexts is also the focus of the 3h architects' project for the modernisation and extension of Király Baths, the oldest remaining thermal baths in Budapest, dating back to Ottoman times. Repeatedly altered and insensitively adapted over the centuries to meet changing needs, and largely neglected in recent decades, the conversion and extension aims, through selected, well-placed interventions and additions, to revitalise the old typology and Ottoman bathing culture and bring it into the 21st century. By stripping back later Baroque additions, the original structure of toplit domes and galleries will be resurrected in a reduced form with restrained ornamentation and extended with rooms and vaults that afford a better, more permeable connection to the outside world, setting up a dialogue between the old bathing culture and new wellness concepts, in which spaces of specific physical and spatial intensity can arise at the intersection of the two.

3h architects' projects do not seek to create sensationalist works of iconic architecture but rather, through diverse contextual strategies, to sensitively respond to the history, place and prevailing conditions of the respective objective. Drawing on the rich culture of their country, they are never afraid to probe deeper to seek answers and strive for an architecture of open dialogue across all ages and geographical places. This architecture does not subscribe to any particular movement or possess a stylistic signature, it seeks to find a specific, appropriate sensory and functional solution [Figs. 22–23] . As such, their work does not possess one single voice, but many voices. For this reason, this book, itself likewise a product of intensive dialogue, comprises three distinct elements – essays, images and project profiles – that reveal and discuss the many facets and aspects of their inspirations, deliberations and design decisions. Renowned architectural theorists and historians as well as the architects themselves elaborate key themes in the work of 3h architects in quite different ways, evoking a variety of associations and discussing them in new contexts. Parallel to this, the young Hungarian photographer Balázs Danyi endeavours to convey the spaces, buildings and moods of the architects' Hungarian homeland, which had a formative influence on them and continues to inform their work on an everyday basis. This book, therefore, offers the reader different ways of engaging with a fascinating cultural space and the work of 3h architects. *Spaces of Intensity* documents the impressive depth and breadth with which the architects consistently strive to examine the respective context and weave it together with the demands of the present into a new narrative.

"The entire end-of-October night was beating with a single pulse, its own strange rhythm sounding through trees and rain and mud in a manner beyond words or vision: a vision present in the low light, in the slow passage of darkness, in the blurred shadows, in the working of tired muscles; in the silence, in its human subjects, in the undulating surface of the metaled road; in the hair moving to a different beat than do the dissolving fibers of the body; growth and decay on their divergent paths; all these thousands of echoing rhythms, this confusing clatter of night noises, all parts of an apparently common stream, that is the attempt to forget despair; though behind things other things appear as if by mischief, and once beyond the power of the eye they no longer hang together. So with the door left open as if forever, with the lock that will never open."

— László Krasznahorkai, *Satantango*

Context

TEHERBIRAS
0.5 TONNA

Finding a New Context

Zsolt Gunther

My partner Katalin Csillag and I have always been enthusiastic visitors to art exhibitions, especially those where lesser-known works of art are presented in a new light. We primarily do it for artistic pleasure, yet we are often struck by works affecting our architectural thinking. They are really inspiring when they create relationships with other art works. We had this experience when we went to see *The Shape of Time,* an exhibition at Vienna's Kunsthistorisches Museum.[1] The basis of the selection was provided by American art historian George Kubler's book of the same title.[2] Historical paintings – mainly from the Renaissance and the Baroque – were displayed alongside modern and contemporary works. At first sight it was more or less a mystery to me what might connect these works of art. However, spending some time in front of the paintings, the concordant layers became obvious: sometimes the atmosphere, often a gesture and sometimes an idea represented the connection.

The paintings by Rembrandt and Mark Rothko hanging side by side made the greatest impression on me. Rothko's geometric painting depicting rectangles with blurred outlines was exhibited next to Rembrandt's self-portrait. Both artists were stimulated by mysterious, intensive light, which became a prominent experience in these works. Yet light appears in different ways in the two paintings. [Fig. 1] While radiance breaks through from darkness with elementary force in Rembrandt's portrait, in Mark Rothko's work, light is silky. Light has transfigured itself; however, the effect is unquestionable. No wonder, since Rothko confirmed that he had studied Rembrandt. It was there that I understood Kubler's theory: art history can be described by a web of artworks and artists influencing one another, as the metamorphosis of original works. At the time this idea turned traditional periodisation in art history upside down by bringing to the fore art as a phenomenon.

Even if Kubler's theory cannot be directly applied to typologies, it nevertheless has helped us to understand the nature and development of typologies better. Typology as a theme appeared consciously in our conversations and research only a few years ago. Prior to that we had used and modified it instinctively. As we attempted to talk about it, I became interested in what the essence of typology was and what caused it to change.

Initially, we attempted to clarify the notion of typology. At first approach, form or shape – whether it originates from volumetry or emerges in the ground-plan – seemed obvious as a compositional gesture. Yet we did not equate typology with style. Typology for us is far more essential and lasting than architectural style. Style is rather a phenomenon, while typology is of a structural nature. Let us illustrate this in connection with a concrete design of ours, which in addition is characteristic of the Hungarian, somewhat confused context. Socialist Realism after World War II was an approach forced on artists by cultural policy in Eastern Europe. Since it did not exist as a style, architects were able to think freely and created a local classicist style. However, it enveloped the spatial structure of Modernism like a shroud. The portico as a row of columns signalling the entrance emerged on several buildings. [Fig. 2] The main entrance to the University of Applied Arts [3] designed by Zoltán Farkasdy is, however, placed on the façade asymmetrically, significantly removed from the central axis, and thus refers to a Modernist design approach. Behind, the ceremonial hall with its foyer is located with a partly Modernist, partly classicist arrangement. The uncertain change in typology in this sense served to create a new style. The style, however, was ephemeral; this peculiar fusion was replaced by the spatial structure of mature Modernism within a few years.

If it is not the form or its phenomenon that provides the core of typology, what could its essence be? It became clear to us only later that there is a latent, internal structure in which we found several intense factors. One is the set of social constraints, expectations and emerging new requirements. Another point is the advance and development of the economy and technology, while a third is represented by cultural canons and their changes. Spatial arrangement is rooted in local culture, while the "type" derives from the fusion of these two. The architectural programme intended for this becomes its cornerstone and, if this is so, typology itself can alter.

In his study "On Typology", [4] Rafael Moneo lists the potential for change in typology: "In this continuous process of transformation, the architect can extrapolate from the type, changing its use; he can distort the type by means of transformation of scale; he can overlap different types to produce new ones. He can use formal quotations of a known type in a different context, as well as create new types by a radical change in the techniques already employed." We can see that transformation can be extremely varied. What kind of directions have we considered important?

Initially, it was difficult for us to resist the *tabula rasa* of Modernism: a clean slate was tempting. After all, it promised a great degree of freedom. What came into being as new was self-expressing, strove for autonomy and was not connected to the old. Thus, as a first opportunity we turned to the means of radical typological invention. The specific programme – within that significantly seeking identity and the desire to create it – resulted in moving towards a vision. The House of Hungarian Music as a paraphrase of transparent pavilion architecture can be included here. [5] It was prefigured by Mies van der Rohe's New National Gallery (Neue Nationalgalerie) in Berlin, whose floating top and system of pillars, *inter alia,* were transformed by us radically. Then we realised how much more magical it was when the new was created in the old, something that already existed, since the connection could be perceived there. Alienation suggested by Modernism is replaced by an entirely different approach: specific relations full of meaning are woven together with the location and the elements found there. So we shaped a new approach to existing buildings – that was the second direction of our seeking a path. The constraints of existing spatial structures are inspiring, especially in historical spaces. The conversion of Szeged Cathedral and the Esterházy Castle illustrate this.

The third area of typological development involved responses to the constraints of location. A site's morphology, its opportunities for construction, often enforce types that differ from the traditional, especially when a new spatial programme has to be realised. At the same time, they always provide our buildings

1 *The Shape of Time,* Kunsthistorisches Museum, Vienna, 6 March – 8 July 2018.
2 George Kubler, *The Shape of Time. Remarks on the History of Things.* New Haven and London, Yale University Press, 1962.
3 Today, the Moholy-Nagy University of Art and Design. Its reconstruction and extension were designed by our office.
4 Rafael Moneo, "On Typology", *Oppositions* 13, 1978, p. 23–45, 27. The MIT Press, 1978.
5 House of Hungarian Music. Design competition, 2014.

with a unique character – in contrast with the universality of Modernism. Our buildings outside the Hungarian capital illustrate this potential well. Perhaps due to our disposition, we have not moved towards the spectacular, but rather to the more sensitive typological developments. For that very reason, typological developments that can be linked to existing spatial structures and morphological constraints are among our favourite designs.

Beginnings in the Provinces on a Small Scale

In our early designs we were much involved with rural architecture. There is a way of construction characteristic of the Carpathian Basin that has become a synonym for poverty these days. It is a building on the edge on a narrow plot. [Fig. 3] A narrow building, opening up in one direction, does not suit today's way of life. Negative features override the positive ones, whereas the compact, sheltered spaces by a house suggest intimacy and the right scale. In the case of this type of construction, the houses were built such that they always faced the sun with their open side, while towards the neighbouring plot – usually to the north – they were closed. Apart from the building's one-sided opening, the other challenge was to break up the monotony of the traditional row of aligned spaces and, at the same time, to improve their usability. How can we align spaces so that they are not simply interconnected, creating instead a vibrant and exciting flow of space?

We provided the answer to this dilemma in Paloznak, a village by Lake Balaton. [Fig. 4] We kept the archetypal, simple exterior form, while the interior was enriched radically. We opened up the ground floor and the loft, and thus the expansion of the former unfolds towards the pitched roof with intermittent planes. From the side we fitted in a covered exterior space accompanying the main body of the building, thus separating the rooms used during the day from those used at night. Within this narrow building we managed to create a varied flow of spaces, which led to the complete negation of poverty in terms of traditional spaces and their use. Narrow plots in more affluent areas or in village centres were often merged. Thus, the way they were built on was also modified: one of the building wings continued to be on the plot perimeter; it was supplemented by two wings perpendicular to that and thus they straddled a U-shaped courtyard. [Fig. 5] Two drive-through passages were inserted between the street and the rear courtyard. We elaborated on the theme of such farmsteads in the school design in Csorna. One of the two drive-throughs was divided into several levels. Here, we reached back to the theme of traditional covered spaces open on one side. The partial enclosure of the sides suggests protection and intimacy, while dividing the space into elementary forms – squares and triangles – makes the space seem somewhat alien. These examples have always reached back to tradition, while rewriting traditional constructional forms. We could also say that we have renewed typology in terms of the nature of space, using tradition as the starting point and without altering the positioning of the building on the site perimeter.

So far we have dealt with the characteristic building opportunities of rural architecture. When we examine the spatial structure of buildings, their ground-plans point to a specific element: the porch, which represents a particular form of transitional space. It is closely connected to the building and can be interpreted as an organic part of the enclosed space. It can be put to superb use during the changing seasons. It protects people from rain and excessive sun, while it is a pleasant open-air space closely linked to the building. In the case of the residential unit in Koroncó, it is broader and higher than usual; the upstairs of the building also joins in the life of the porch. [Fig. 6] The alignment of spaces situated within the rectangular prism satisfies the requirements for use. The porch as a covered foreground – extending the roof generously over this space – is provided along the entire length of the building. The cost of its construction was very reasonable, yet its use value is high. The corridor in front of the rooms and as a supplement to the widening promotes encounters as a communal space. The rural archetypal forms have apparently remained; however, their interior space and adjoining parts such as the porch have been transformed radically. As a result, the relationship between the exterior and the interior has changed.

Meanwhile, our office has moved to Budapest, but it has not forgotten its roots. Buildings characteristic of the countryside and with its typical spatial system are still on the table. Several smaller-scale designs have been made by using and developing our initial experiences.

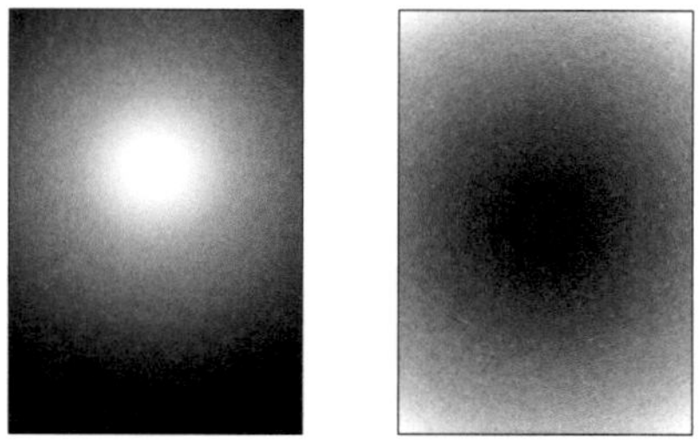

[Fig. 1] Different treatment of light
Rembrandt and Mark Rothko

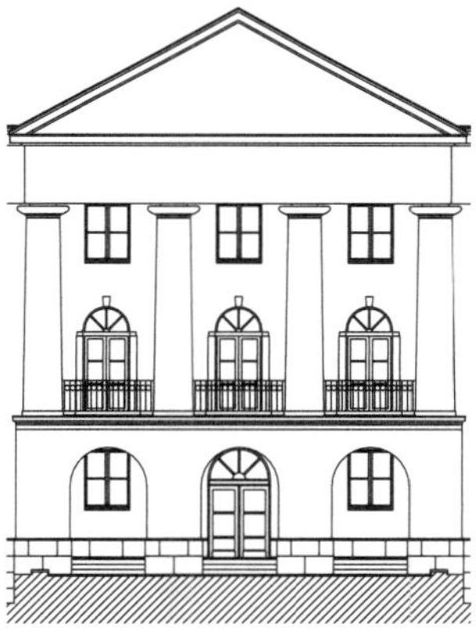

[Fig. 2] The portico signalling the former main entrance
Moholy-Nagy University of Art and Design

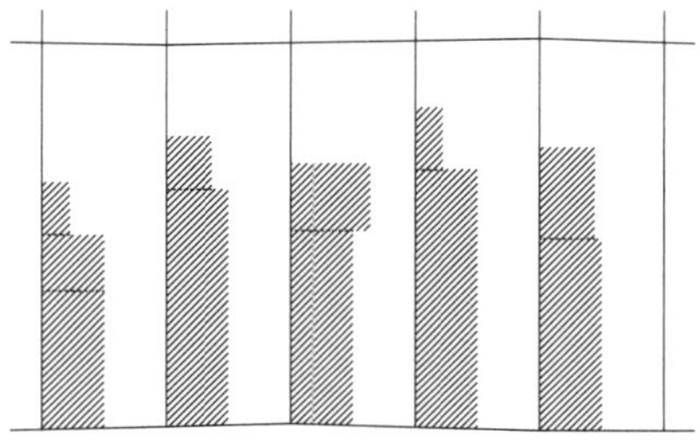

[Fig. 3] Building on the side perimeter of the plot
Traditional rural landscape

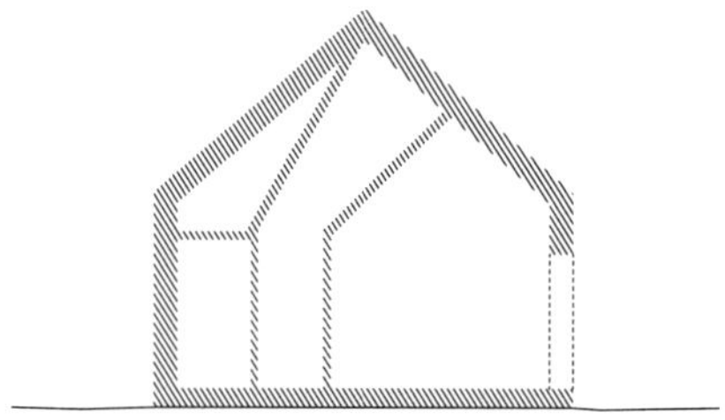

[Fig. 4] House archetype, contemporary flow of indoor spaces
Traditional shape, varied sequence of spaces
Detached house, Paloznak

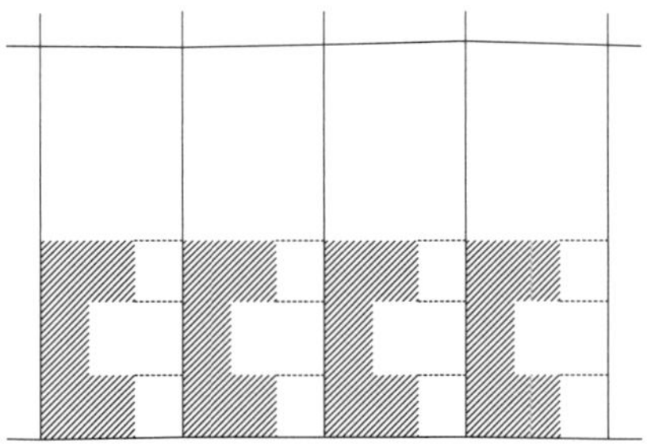

[Fig. 5] Merger of narrow plots
Renewed array of exterior with traditional buildings
School, Csorna

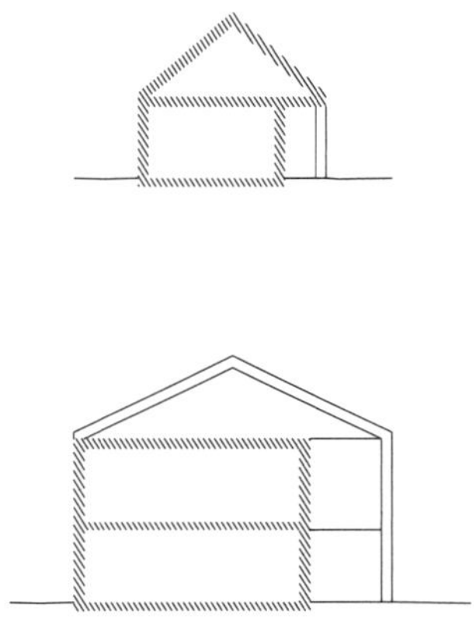

[Fig. 6] Traditional porch
Wider and taller porch
Porch typology
Accommodation building, Koroncó

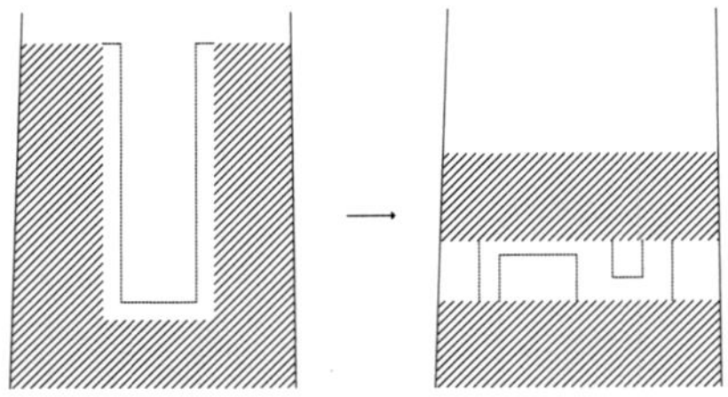

[Fig. 7] Block of flats with access deck walkways
New type of access deck walkways
Urban transitional space
Block of flats, Futó street

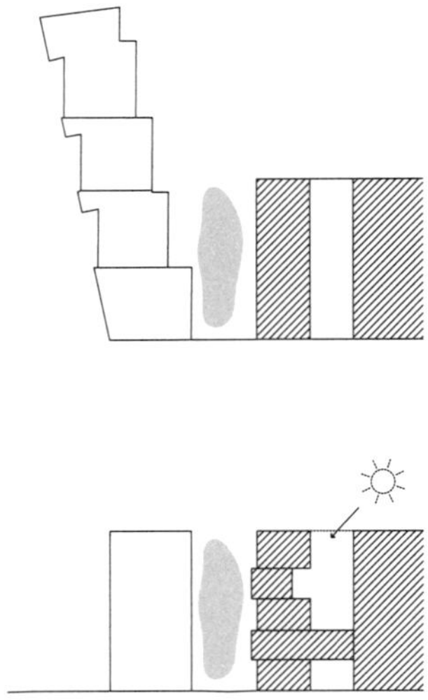

[Fig. 8] Floor plan and section
Dense office typology
Geometria office building, Medve street

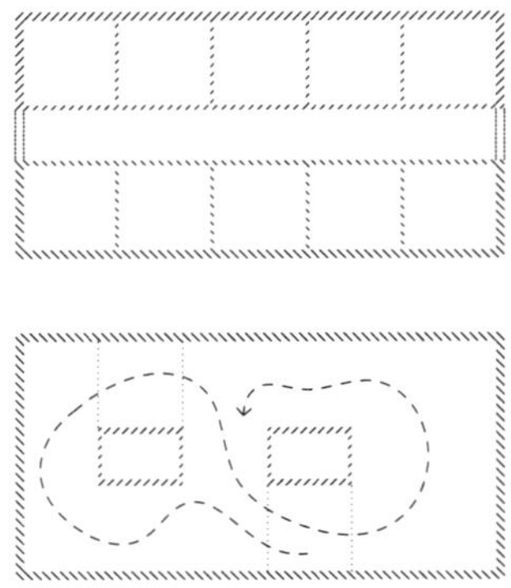

[Fig. 9] Classrooms distributed along a central corridor
Classrooms dispersed and surrounded by communal area
New structure of education
Moholy-Nagy University of Art and Design, former main building

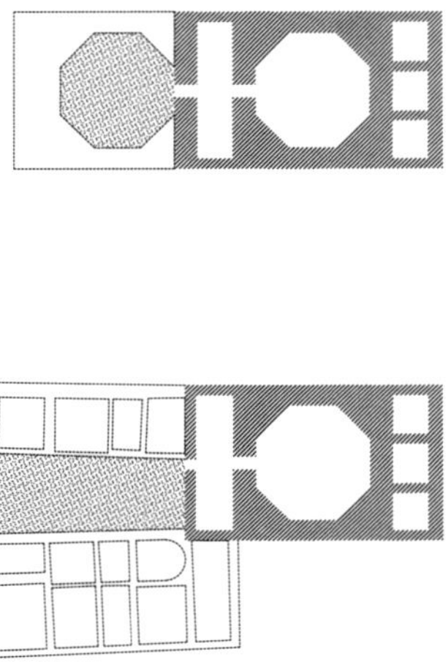

[Fig. 10] Missing (hypothetical) and existing
Hypothetical and reconstructed frigidarium
Reconstructed typology,
Király Baths

Continuing in the Large City

We have seen that transitional spaces in the form of a porch are very popular outside the capital. We met similar transitional spaces – albeit on a different scale – in the dense urban fabric of Pest. The apartments of tenement blocks were accessed by means of a gallery, which was open on the side and covered. The entrances to the flats and the windows of the rooms opened from this commonly used passage, the so-called access deck walkway. [Fig. 7] Despite the fact that residents often found the closeness disturbing, the walkways supported social cohesion and resulted in a sustainable, dense urban fabric. A scene of personal encounters was established in the form of a specific public space within the building, at the same time serving as a filter between the street and the flat. In our design we attempted to realise the advantage of apartments opening from a walkway, at the same time ensuring that the flat-dwellers would not be disturbed by too much intimacy. We designed the main rooms so as not to open onto this passageway. Thus, we divided the apartments into two zones: one for utilities and another for rooms for living in. The former zones including the entrance halls were turned around and the walkway was fitted into this transitional space. The spaces work surprisingly well. On the one hand, the wide walkways are light and, on the other, they provide sufficient space for residents not only to hurry by, but also to spend some time there.

With reference to density, which is characteristic of Budapest, the extremely difficult character of a particular site compelled us to rethink office typology. The Geometria office building had to be inserted into the dense fabric of central Buda. A peculiar architectural feature catches one's eye in this part of the city: the blocks open up in some places. It is as if an imaginary little street or alley led inside the blocks – giving us a glance into the labyrinth of a disorderly courtyard. At first sight, the narrow building plot has been given its façade lengthwise. [Fig. 8] The other side of the building clings resolutely to the neighbouring building, and there is no hope of smuggling in light from that side. This constraint of the surroundings produced the office building's layout. We grouped the offices to face inwards towards the alley that runs through the building lengthwise and removed the useless spaces looking towards the firewall: a large atrium is sited next to the dense suite of offices. Communal facilities such as kitchens, conference rooms and areas for relaxation appear as boxes in the atrium. Space capsules float at different heights. Their rhythm has been composed to follow a precise dramaturgy in such a way that visitors are tempted to move about, passing between narrow and spacious areas. Light is abundant, despite the closeness of the firewall. The atrium is covered by a glass roof, meaning that an unusual segment of nature is revealed in the centre of the city: the sky with moving clouds.

The building typology described above primarily produced innovations in the interior, on account of the constraints of the building's environment. The next office building, however, presents an unusual approach on a larger urban scale also due to the constraints of its surroundings. The building is located at the intersection of two busy main roads. One road curves and joins the other, and thus the building recedes here compared to others at the junction. On one side it lies close to its immediate neighbour, on the other it stands free. If we view this situation as the fingers of a hand spread apart, we arrive at an open form; this served as the starting point for our design of the building complex. Two rectangular prisms, which follow the rationality of office typology, open as a fan in the direction where there is more space. The third is inserted between the two right-angled elements. Besides the dynamic and sculptural design of the building, the public space formed between and beneath them deserves a special mention: this can flow now in vigorous continuity and mutate from a noisy road junction to the calmer street behind the building. As a result, a funnel-like space is formed, drawing in passers-by, so to say. For those who can resist this attraction, an urban oasis will make them linger next to the pyramid-shaped green garden mounds just a few metres from the bustle of the street.

Time Travel: Reprogramming What Exists

Listed buildings, or at least buildings with a time perspective, represent for us the most comprehensive and at the same time the most disputed field of interpreting context. The starting point is the historical substance, yet it has never been our aim to restore it to its original form. So that we, as designers, can see our scope for action clearly, it is absolutely necessary to review a few issues. Besides the traditional research on listed buildings, it is important to know the original users' customs and values and how they used the space. Bringing this knowledge together with the new requirements enables us to create a sound plan, as the new use of space produces a change in typology. It is especially interesting to compare customs and the utilisation of space when involved with architecture of the recent past, since these were still palpable yesterday, as it were.

The conversion of the central building of MOME [6] is a good example. Education has changed to such an extent that the spatial structure of the building required a radical transformation. MOME's central building was constructed as a People's College in 1953. It is a building of good proportions and a prominent document of the age. Hence we did not want to change its exterior. Traditional teaching methods were manifest in its spaces – classrooms on both sides of the central corridor. Yet the university's new concept of education necessitated spaces to be opened up. [Fig. 9] We transformed the interior radically: corridors were removed, the elements of the central load-bearing wall structure were minimised and the partition walls in the two side tracts were done away with. In order to make these spatial connections visible between the floors, a few areas of ceiling were also removed. As a result an artful labyrinth of spaces has emerged, which has radically overwritten the original, simpler concept of space. Several levels of the façade are visible at a number of places inside. Spatial conditions have emerged which clearly signal that something new has moved into the old. The isolated, mostly closed off educational units have literally provided scope for an unbroken system of home spaces, [7] which is far closer to the present open educational structure.

When studying historical buildings, we have observed that ancient types are vividly alive in our memory. We revive these typological memories consciously in contemporary spaces. We strive for solutions in which the faint memories of a certain type are integrated with new spatial arrangements. This process can be observed in the design for the reconstruction of the Király Baths. We had to seek the origins of the traditional Turkish bath in Roman baths. The trio of frigidarium – tepidarium – caldarium represents a kind of initiation ceremony as part of the bathing ritual. In our case, the original cold zone, the frigidarium, had disappeared in an earlier phase and had been replaced by a Baroque courtyard. [Fig. 10] According to our design this courtyard was covered in such a way that the filtered light from above is retained and the light that arrives through the truncated pyramidal domes and is broken on the colourful Isnik tiles trickles in mysteriously to the entrance area. The acts of arriving and changing take place in their original location again, but instead of "Turkish-like" forms, contemporary elements welcome visitors. Nevertheless, activities are the same as in a traditional Turkish bath. In addition, the locker rooms are placed among the remnants of the Turkish walls. The natural light, which traditionally comes from above, and the splashing of the central fountain all evoke ancient memories and can be connected to the experience of arrival. The warm and hot rooms called for a simple reconstruction, as they had more or less retained their original form and use, so they were to be conserved. As a result of the reconstruction, the suite of spaces lies on the ancient foundations; however, in its appearance there is a caesura between the Turkish parts and the connecting contemporary space. Perhaps this gesture makes the travelling through time more palpable, as it leads you through the different areas of the baths from the present through the Baroque to as far back as the Turkish times.

Rewriting Typology

Our design typology is closely connected with context and as a rule reacts to it. Context to us is nothing other than a reference, let it be to the environment, history or the atmosphere of a place. It presupposes what already exists as well as relating to it. This attitude aims to involve understanding and complement it far more than opposing the given situation.

We are working much on developing a typology connected to the designs. We believe that this work reinforces the relationship between our buildings and their surroundings as well as making one aware of a place's character. In every case we have started off from the existing building or the constraints of the location. The dialogue between the two as a receptive medium and typology creates stimulating tensions, which emerge from the transformation of spaces. This metamorphosis apparently produces a new unity, yet it avoids the sensation of a false homogeneity. We explore the layers of a building: we show the origin of spaces, their essential features and their integral transformations.

What concerns us is the interdependence of site, building and space, where not only the existing building or the location determine the new, but where the space and its programming – i.e. its typology – also react to the context. We often develop a new programme – one which transforms an existing building by generating a modified type or, as a new building, produces a surprising change in its surroundings. In this way the context is always recreated, reinterpreted and interlinked. Thus, the context is not only fed from the past, it also has a future.

An earlier pattern can be discovered in our new typologies, similarly to works of art. In the paintings displayed at *The Shape of Time* exhibition in Vienna we were able to detect essential, rather than superficial associations. Mark Rothko studied Rembrandt's paintings thoroughly and enthusiastically in New York's Metropolitan Museum, so that he could instil their essence into himself. We also dig down to the roots of traditional typologies and reinterpret their fundamental patterns. In the process we reach new solutions. This correlates with George Kubler's theory that earlier works of art have inspired later ones, and it is more important in the process of creativity than the fact that they were created in different periods.

6 The Moholy-Nagy University of Art and Design, which was preceded by the School of Applied Arts and then the University of Applied Arts.

7 A home space is actually a studio where students work on their designs.

Out of Nowhere

Accommodation for
22 People with Intellectual
Disabilities,
Koroncó
2001–2003

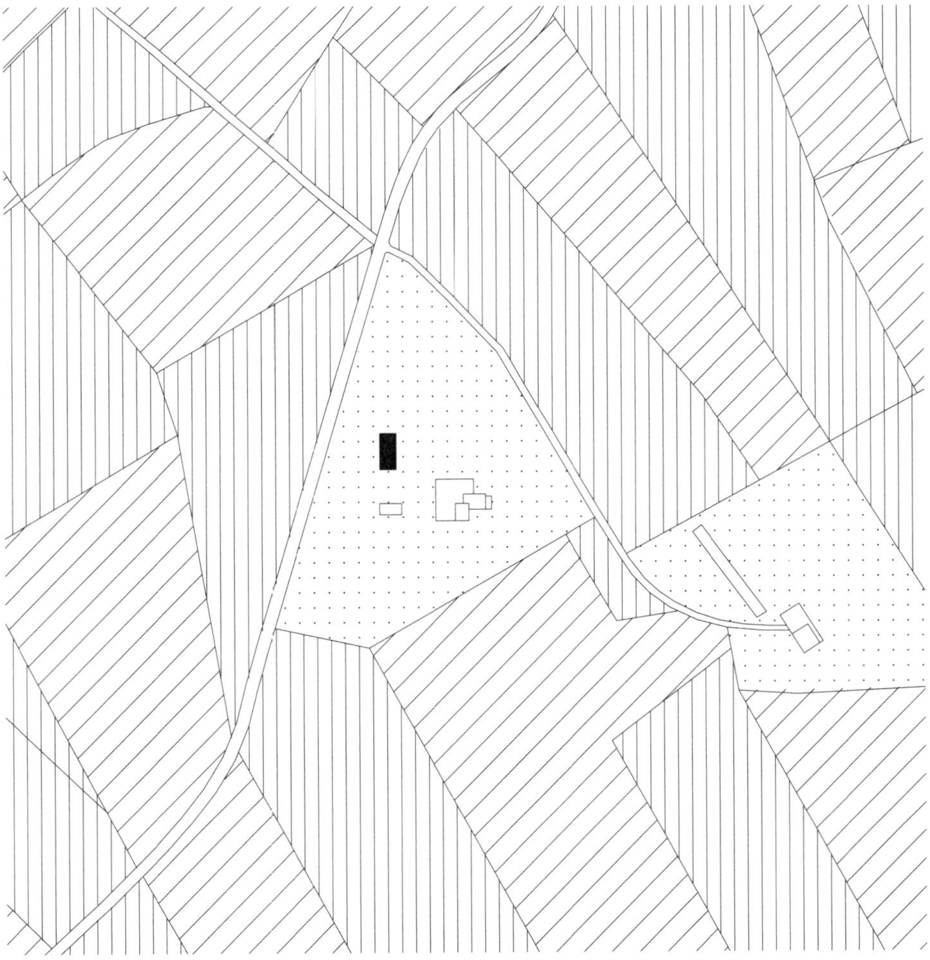

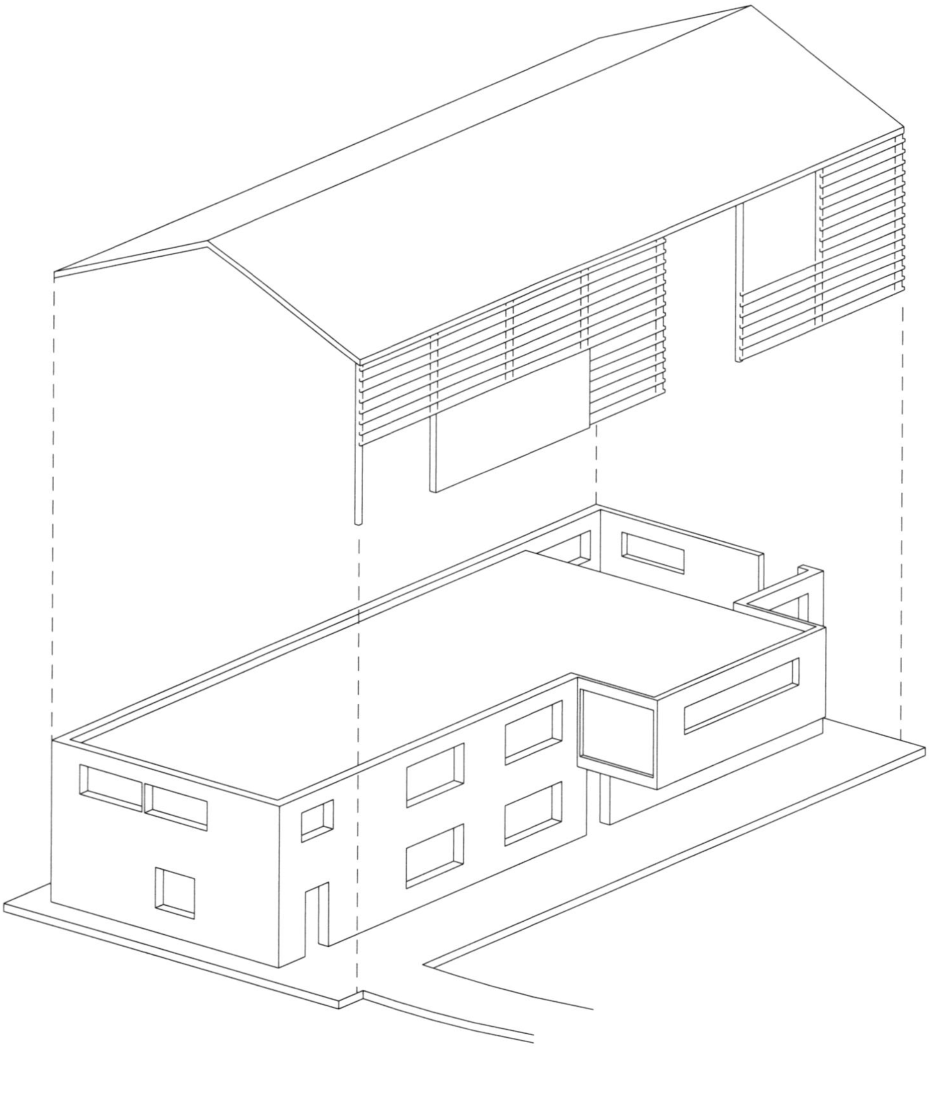

As young architects we fought a lot against pitched roofs until we were obliged to consider what benefits they had besides the presumed disadvantages. In the case of the Koroncó residential unit, use of the simple gable roof was compulsory. Koroncó-Zöldmajor is situated in the middle of a grove of slim pine trees. People with intellectual disabilities live and work in a last-century, run-down mansion. The surroundings radiate calm. An accommodation unit was added to the mansion in the context of a further development project.

As regards pitched roofs we began to look into what rural architecture and the traditional construction methods involved. The most important lesson was that simplicity and extreme economy characterised rural architecture, by means of which our predecessors achieved maximum effect using minimal means. We sorted through the elements of rural architecture methodically.

An empty loft not only worked as a junk room, but efficiently protected the rooms below against the summer heat. Sunshine reaches the roof directly, beneath which the air warms up, but does not radiate down to the premises below. A porch occupies the foreground of the building, where pleasant spring and autumn days can be enjoyed while being protected against rain and wind. It shields the rooms behind from the midday sunshine, yet it lets in the winter sun. It is a transitional space that can be used splendidly in the local climate. However, the traditional alignment of rooms, the provincial *enfilade,* no longer suits the requirements of our time. The inclusion of a corridor probes into the mass proportions of the original peasant house.

We developed the loft and the porch as traditional elements in the case of the Koroncó residential unit. The empty loft was opened at both ends, in order that the hot air inside can leave and the rooms underneath are less affected by the heat. The two ends of the porch were also opened up. The transitional space connects visually to its surroundings in a more organic way and beneficial airing is effective here, too. The living room opening from the corridor was designed on the second storey of the porch, thus the enclosed and open communal spaces became visible for each other. The loft and the two-storey porch grew into one and that already presented an experience of space, even on this scale. It can be seen that instead of the traditional aligned suite of repeated spaces, the modification of relatively simple elements resulted in complex spatial situations.

The transformation of the loft and the porch fundamentally influenced the appearance of the building. The extremely simple structure with a rectangular ground-plan, created with a fine lamellar structure on one long side and extended with a porch-like foreground, was designed as if the roof could be neglected. Nevertheless, the tiled, intentionally rural wooden structure is not attached to the building as an inorganic appendix; instead, an entirely free relationship between the two units has been created with tiny gestures. The roof seems to be floating above the upstairs terrace, it is supported by the steel structure of the porch and separate from the walls on one of the long sides and is not closed off at the gables on both ends. The building with its modern character and the ancient form of the roof with its associative nature open up towards each other in an aesthetic sense. The values of their coexistence are manifold – on the one hand, they rely on one another, while on the other, they lead a free, independent life.

The simplicity of the building responds to the homogeneity of the surroundings. In addition to the visual experience, the scent of the pine trees, the softness of the fallen needles and the rustle of the trees – in short, the natural environment – determine the impression. The untraditional use of the porch material blends with this atmosphere. Wooden laths on the metal pillars with rhythmic gaps and the permeable surfaces filter the wind. It does not recall the image of a traditional porch, but in essence it remains the same. It is a sheltering, inviting living space during a cooling summer shower and sweltering heat alike.

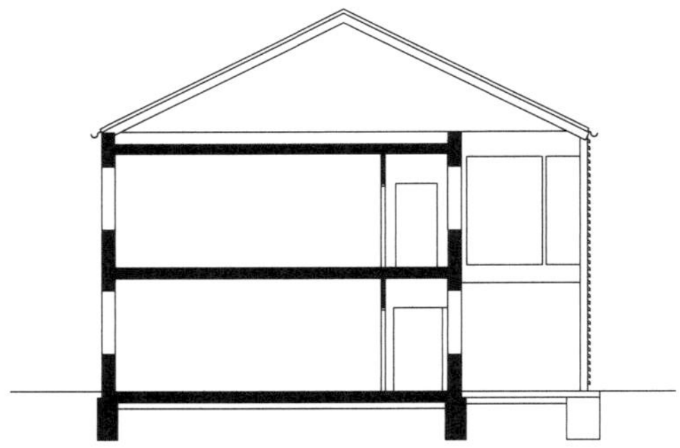

Cross section

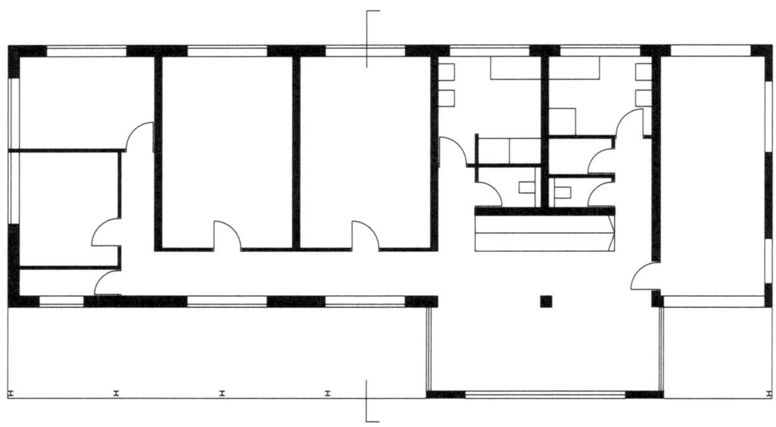

First floor plan

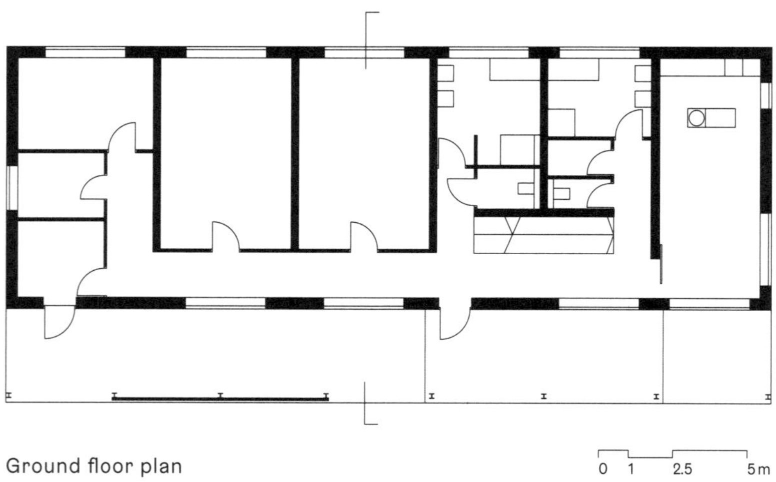

Ground floor plan

The concept of a porch is alien to a flat-roof building. Yet the reinterpreted two-storey open foreground enriches the otherwise simple volume with opportunities that it would not be able to provide on its own.

The pitched roof and the porch embrace the flat-roof core building protectively.

The covered, open "porch" functions as an interface between the sheltered living space and nature.

The natural materials with different grades of permeability entwine the building in harmony with the surrounding pine tree forest.

Transcripts

Special School for Children with Intellectual Disabilities, Csorna 2002–2003

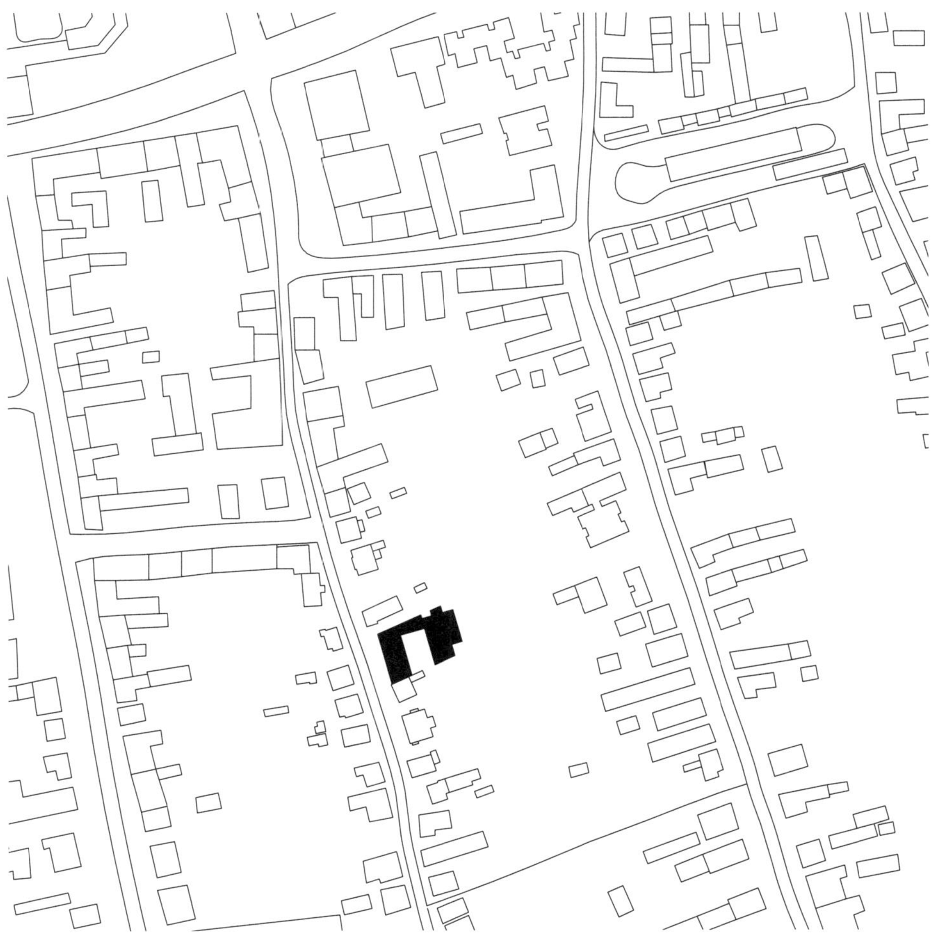

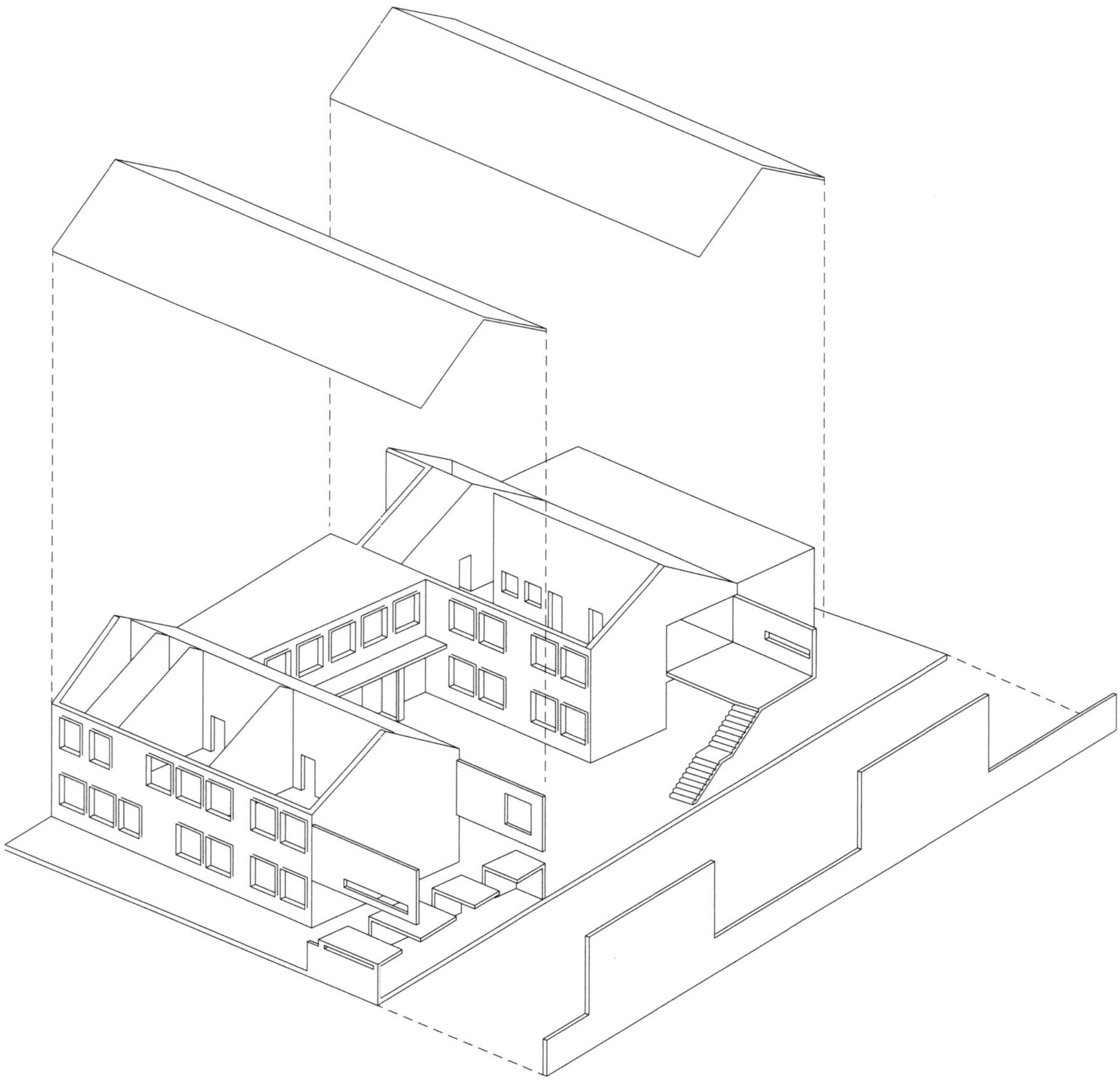

Csorna is a market town with a history of more than 700 years. The establishment of the early medieval clustered settlement was followed by the late medieval "planned" settlement areas, which took on a market town character. The uniform appearance of the streets was lent by the gabled façades of detached houses, with solid fences and large gates between them. In the inner, wealthier parts of the settlement the plots were widened and more expensive buildings were constructed. As a result the gable ends disappeared in the street, giving way to a continuous series of buildings running parallel with the street. The history of our street and plot is similar. From the historic substance only an extension-like part remained to the rear of the plot, which had to be preserved

As indicated by morphological research, the dwelling was supplemented by a prosperous farmstead with a drive-through courtyard. We resolved the task by deliberately abstracting the traditional elements found here. The result is a coherent modern building that works according to its own, hidden rules, while recognising its roots. Recalling tradition can be detected particularly in the way the new intervening spaces are shaped.

The unbroken row of buildings on the street is bordered by a gateway at the edge of the plot, which continues with a drive-through or covered passage for vehicles. The gateway itself is open to the height of one level but inside it opens up to a further level. The upper space is enclosed by reinforced concrete slabs, although there are openings in the wall. So the traditional barn with a drive-through space reappears in an abstract manner. The space continues into an inner courtyard surrounded by walls providing shelter and security. This courtyard is a place for relaxation between lessons and is suitable for holding celebrations. Proceeding in the direction of the courtyard, the next drive-through space is divided into two levels. The top level is directly connected to the assembly area inside, while the bottom level leads to the courtyard.

So far we have noted the characteristic elements of peasant houses in a market town. However, our building has features that point beyond this. The stairs established along the axis of the drive-through spaces are suggestive of arriving at a mansion. Proceeding through the two-level drive-through, followed by ascending the steps prepares one for the act of arrival reminiscent of the architecture of nobility. The double level of the first drive-through gateway is apparently unnecessary. Does space as a luxury allude to aristocratic expectations? Or does the building simply take a deep breath here? Yes and no; our transformations allows a growing complexity of areas of space, thereby connecting them to one another, in certain places unexpectedly. Unanticipated views unfold before ceaselessly wandering eyes, which help map the structure of the building, as if rural and thrilled professional architecture are fused instinctively while walking around. Untangling these features is a truly intellectual adventure.

The interior space constructs itself by simple means. The entrance zone links the two masses parallel with the street. The position of openings and the deliberate treatment of light counteract the sparsity of space. Light comes through the windows and is filtered by the sandblasted glass wall bordering the stairs. The light from the skylight above the stairs cuts into this diffuse light. The alternation of sloping and flat roof surfaces upstairs becomes a kind of dialectic. The experience of the sloping roof is dramatised in the assembly area and classrooms.

Traditions – and tensions due to their alienation – are manifested in the use of the façade materials. The brown plaster is reminiscent of the wooden planks used for barns and the colour of arable soil. The raw concrete surfaces appear as the partially enclosing elements of covered spaces, which are open from the side. Contrary to our expectations, the wooden gate of a barn is absent and instead a void, an opening dominates.

As with every transcript, this building's initial constraints only relate to its embryonic form. The building does not react to the real, constructed substance, but rather to memories, feelings and bygone urban scapes. It weighs up what hidden values are to be highlighted. It picks out, alienates, discards parts and includes new ones, fusing the whole together.

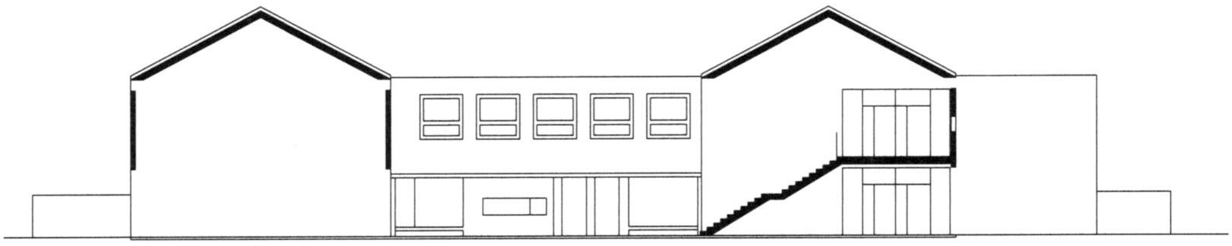

Cross section

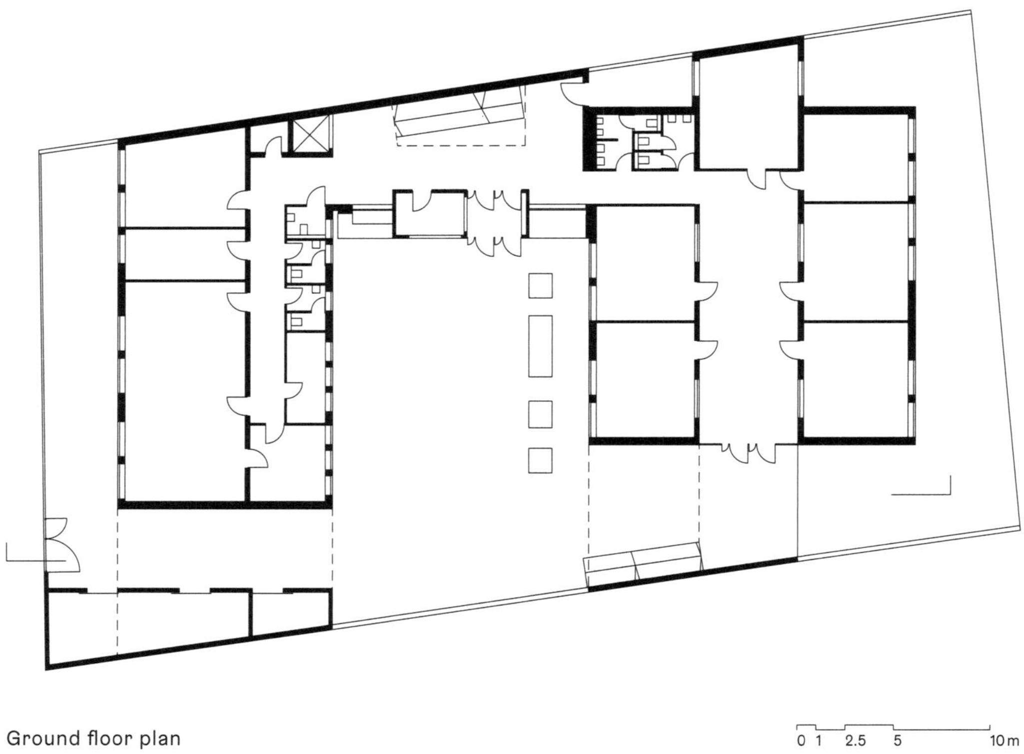

Ground floor plan

An inner courtyard providing security has been formed by using a U-shaped construction. The drive-through is repeated in the rear wing and leads on towards the garden courtyard.

The dialectic arising from the composition of pitched and flat roofs unfolds mainly from the direction of the garden courtyard. Metal frames in uniform sizes constitute a defining element of the façades.

The interior space continues seamlessly into a covered terrace, open at the sides, from which the stairs offer a stimulating view of and access to the courtyard.

The upstairs rooms utilise the spatial opportunities provided by the pitched roof. Thanks to the roof windows, the spacious interior corridor is also well lit.

Solutions for Accessibility

Institute for Children with Physical Disabilities, Budapest 2004–2010

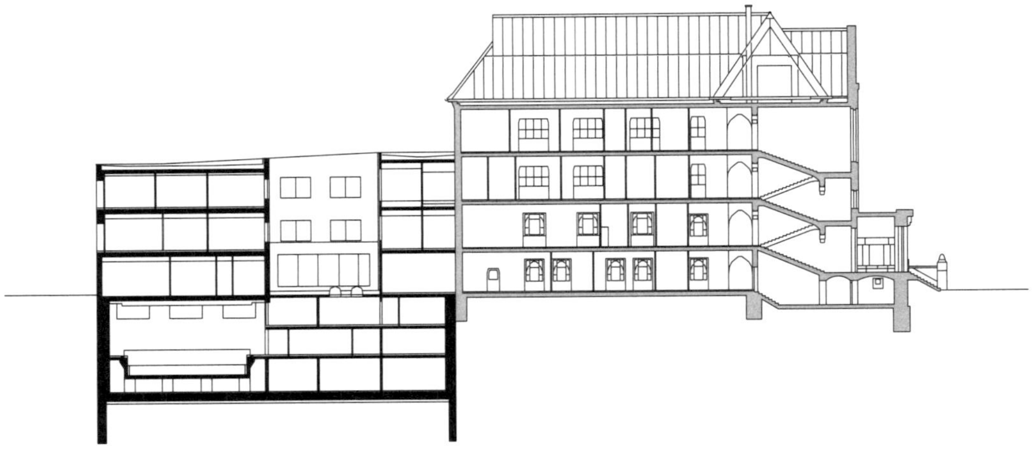

Section through the old school and its new annex

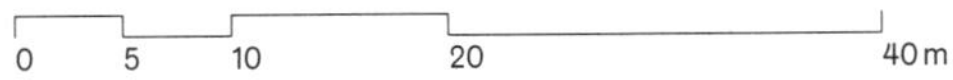

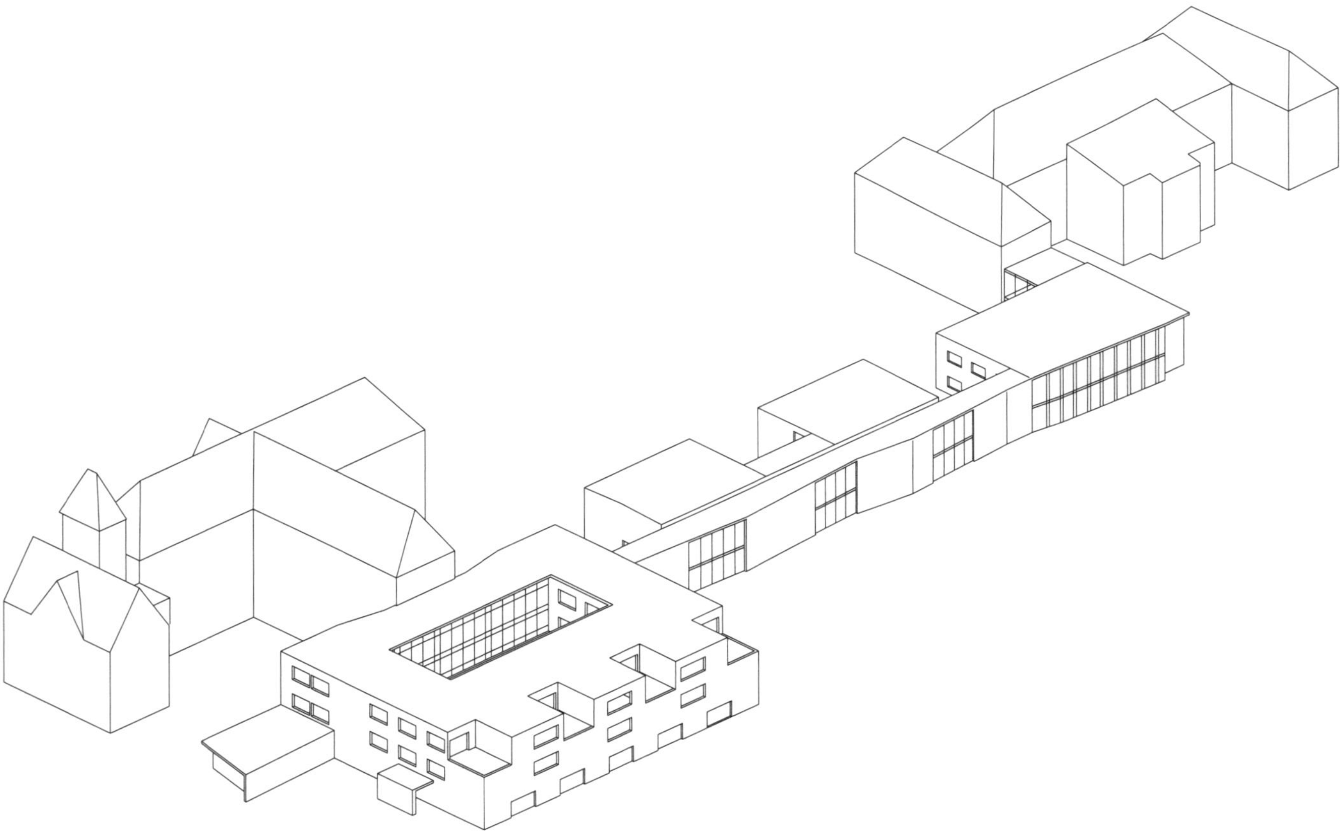

The institute for the blind in Budapest, designed by Béla Lajta in 1908, is an iconic work of pre-Modern architecture in Hungary. What makes this brief historical period special? The era represents the transition from Historicism to Modernism. At that time things could be undertaken that were prohibited according to the canon established later. This period was primarily characterised by exploring ways of escaping from the schematic programme of Historicism in two directions. On the one hand, it sophisticatedly kept its distance from ornamentation and, on the other, it was busy working out new ornaments that were true to the age. It simplified what was unnecessarily over-complicated, while in addition a few attributes of new Modernism appeared such as asymmetrical construction. No wonder Lajta's pre-Modern building, with its somewhat ponderous curvy ornaments and sometimes irresolute proportions, inspired us to a great extent during the design process.

That was precisely why designing the new school for children with physical disabilities (Mozgásjavító Institute) represented a challenging story for us. Perhaps we were not yet mature enough to lay hands on an old building. In the process, we realised that a lot of experience was needed to convert a listed building in an expert way. Initially, we carefully skirted round the building. The institute for children with physical disabilities – next door to the institute for the blind – originally began working in 1913, in the building designed by Alajos Medgyes. Then it moved to Lajta's building after World War II, while continuing to use the original building. A comprehensive project for the two buildings to be used for physically disabled children only became possible at the beginning of the 21st century.

At first sight, the task of design raised architectural and organisational problems, in that we faced the dilemma of connecting several existing buildings. Creating a new axis behind the historical buildings to connect the two presented the key to the solution. Thus, we transferred the grandiose main entrance of the institute for the blind to behind the building, practically to the rear courtyard. This gesture enabled us to align the old and new elements along this axis, the old on one side, the new on the other. At the same time, barrier-free access for people with physical disabilities was resolved successfully. The accentuated entrance canopy situated in the centre of the courtyard protrudes as the extension of the axis from the two-storey block rising behind it. This axis has become the institute's high street, so to speak. The spacious assembly hall with a glass wall on one side joins the side wing of the old building at right angles and continues through the new main building, which accommodates the classrooms, gyms, function spaces, a cafeteria, and a swimming pool in the basement. It then extends into a long, street-like corridor. Since a line of villas had been built along the road between the two historical buildings – a type of construction characteristic of the neighbourhood – we placed residential blocks along the connecting axis on the scale of the neighbouring buildings.

Let us return to the new main entrance. Beyond the reception area wheelchairs used outside can be parked and directly exchanged for interior ones. This spacious area connects with the theatre and through that with the cafeteria. It is not a flow of spaces that is formed in a modern sense, but rather the alignment of spaces preferred by historical and pre-Modern architecture. This method of construction probes the boundaries of historical architecture in its logic in a certain pre-Modern way. Volumes are still emphatically present, yet the axes become permeable and views from one space to another open up unexpectedly in a diagonal direction.

We considered the way of incorporating the listed building to be important. We did not want to compete with it, but rather create the counterpart of a building that was modern in its own time. We designed a white modern companion with simple volumes next to the basically brick building, which appears as a static mass and which is connected to the new block. Thus, the courtyard begun by Lajta's building has largely been enclosed. At the same time, by leaving the corner free, the ensemble lets you see into the partially enclosed courtyard. This gesture was characteristic of Béla Lajta's time. The new glass façades linked to Lajta's wing are slightly diagonal, thus turning to the old block with a kind of embracing gesture. In this detail a gentle yet strict and definite design emerges, characterising the whole building. There is no brutal conflict between the modern glass wall system and the old brick façade with its craftsman-like character; in contrast the new building has its own identity.

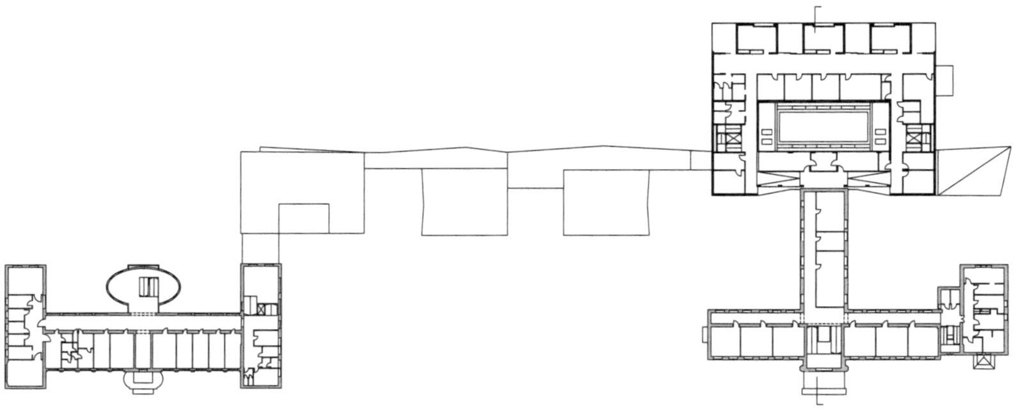

Second floor plan

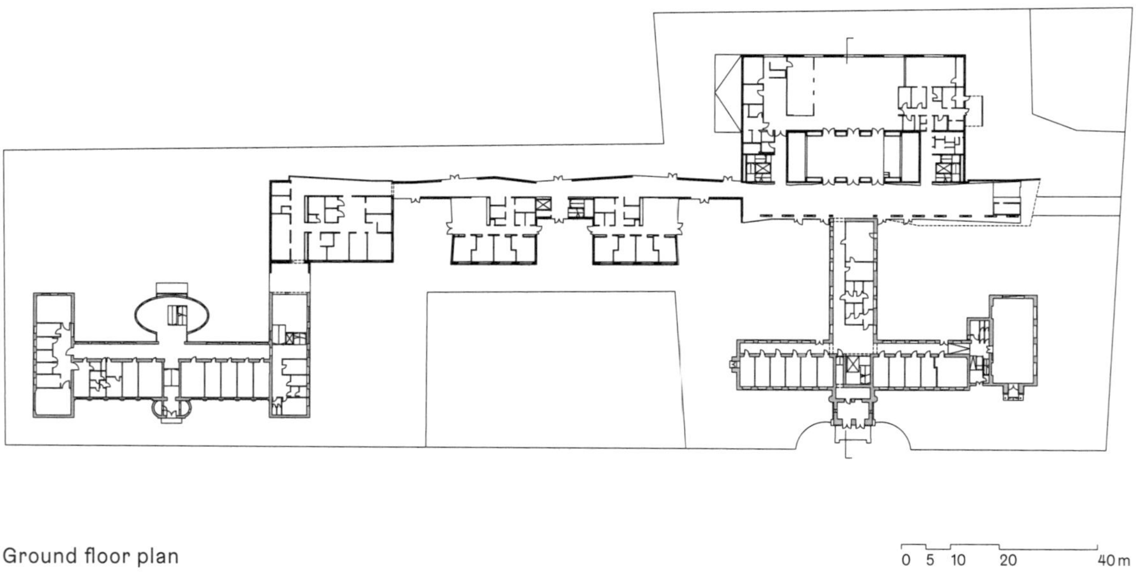

Ground floor plan

With its inviting gesture, the new main entrance became a significant opening element of the internal “high street”. It provides unhindered access when children arrive.

The massive volume of the new building is a counterpoise to the existing solid brick-built school. The larger cut-away spaces in the top floor serve as roof terraces for open-air classes.

The first courtyard is the scene of ceremonies, besides being a recreational area used during breaks between lessons. The space intertwines the old wings with the new school and is protected on three sides. The V-shaped columns are striking elements of the internal high street that pick up the shape of the trees.

The new and the old appear together in different situations. Their subordinate and co-ordinating roles keep changing.

The high street, which also acts as the aula, runs through the entire institute. It is the "spine" of the small new settlement, which has narrower and wider, quieter and busier spatial sections like an urban fabric.

The spine as the connecting axis becomes two-storied in the residential units. The side wall of the corridor is colourful to aid orientation and the glass walls opens up to the living rooms.

The cafeteria is where lunch is eaten collectively. Children in the same group eat at round tables, which are complemented by the ceiling design. Pictograms are significant elements in this space.

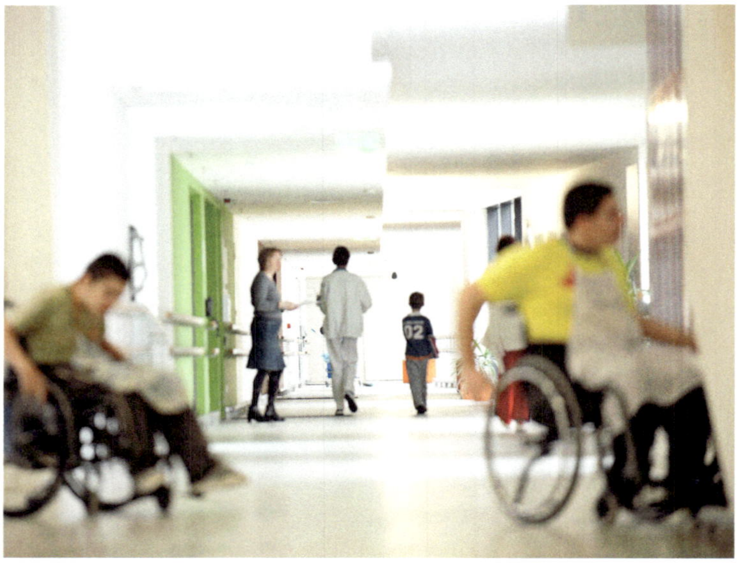

The high street is an important living and communication space. It is the location for activities and encounters, collective games and celebrations.

The swimming pool is the most popular place in the new school. Water enables the children to move freely. In addition to the 25 metre pool, there is one for learners, where children take their first strokes, as well as some therapy rooms.

We faced two challenges regarding the positioning and the volumetric development of the newly designed buildings: one was their connection to the historical building, the other was their integration into the fine fabric of the surrounding villas.

The large-scale volume of the new building responds to the solid, quite compact appearance of the old school. The use of colour and material is deliberately different.

Earth and Light

Church in Kismegyer,
Győr,
2004

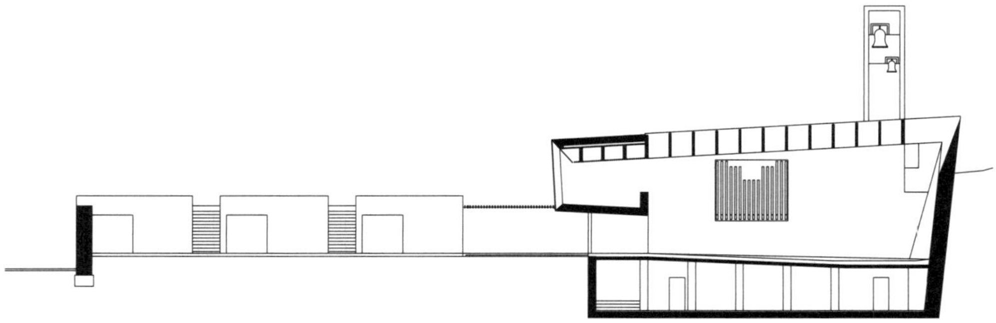

Longitudinal section

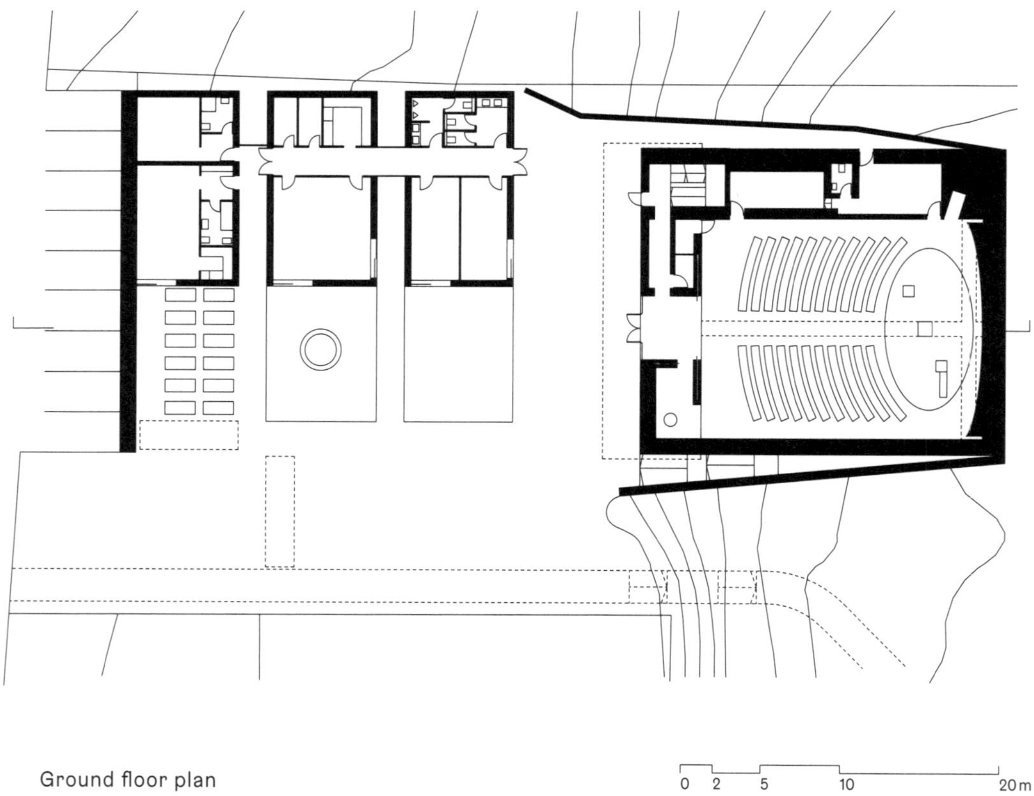

Ground floor plan

Transcendence seems to disappear from liturgy and the sacred space that accommodates it. As architects, we can only make an attempt to re-establish the mystery of spaces with our own means. An invited design competition announced by the Benedictine order presented an opportunity for that, namely to design a parish church near Győr. Despite its apparent simplicity, the site turned the design process in a direction that involves ancient architectural topoi such as massive walls, concentrated light and intensive materiality. These themes inevitably recalled the use of early Christian chthonic space and materials, and thus we reached back to the roots of Christian mysticism.

In order to understand how to position the church dug into the earth and its use of earth-like material, we had to analyse the location thoroughly. The site allocated to the church is at the foot of a small hill in a suburb of Győr with detached houses. As if to crown the hill, a Baroque pilgrimage chapel stands at its summit, surrounded by a graveyard. Our predecessors had selected the site of the building well, since height played a significant role everywhere on the Little Hungarian Plain. Proportionately, the chapel matches the size of the hill. We designed the church so that it would not disturb the sensitive symbiosis of chapel, graveyard and hill.

We inserted the new building smoothly into the side of the hill, shaping its top as an extension of the slope. This gesture entirely contradicts the centuries-old communication practice of the Catholic Church, whereby it places its sign proudly, so to say, in the surroundings, flaunting itself in the role of *ecclesia triumphans.* Our church, a little set back, can be approached via a garden. The presbytery and the garden create a new, unique compositional unit. The cloisters encircling the garden recall the memory of those who lived in monasteries, while at the same time they do not disclaim their metamorphosis. The cloisters attune you to the church subconsciously: reaching the garden makes you feel you are stepping over the threshold into another, quieter world.

On entering the church, you find yourself in a puristic space. The slightly sloping church space finishes at the chancel in an elliptically shaped horizontal semicircle. Above the membrane-like false ceiling, beams running across reveal themselves and are made sculptural by the light filtering through from above. Since a large part of the church was designed to be below ground level, it seemed obvious to use the excavated material, the earth, for a topographical transformation. Earth is closely connected to Christian traditions emotionally – just think of sacred early Christian catacombs.

Earth appears on the "altarpiece" with overwhelming force: the eastern wall of the chancel, which is partly dug into the ground, presents the image of an adobe wall in its full width. Instead of an image depicting saints, the cross-section of the earth presents itself and a wooden crucifix appears on its surface. Light coming from above sometimes skims the wall, sometimes fully illuminating it. The embracing form that starts at the bottom straightens up at the top and becomes breezier.

Light evoking a mystical atmosphere plays a leading role in this liturgical space. Pure, sharp light penetrates the church through the glass cross on the ceiling. The quantity of light is deliberately reduced in order not to make the church too light. The coloured glass panes of the western window are placed horizontally and with the changes in their thickness they facilitate the entry of light into the church, ranging from in-depth, deeper and translucent light to more mottled light.

The haptic experience of materiality and the massive walls make the inner world of the church very powerful and recall the innocent beauty of early Christian spaces. The varied and sometimes dramatic appearance of its light is also reminiscent of the chapels full of mysticism designed by the greatest masters of the Baroque, Borromini and Bernini. This phenomenon also relates the church to the baroque spirituality inherited from the small chapel on the hilltop.

Light is the central theme in this church. The adobe wall "altarpiece" fills the entire wall as a distorted surface of the chancel and joins the skylight cross in the roof. The organ is located in a recess in the thick wall.

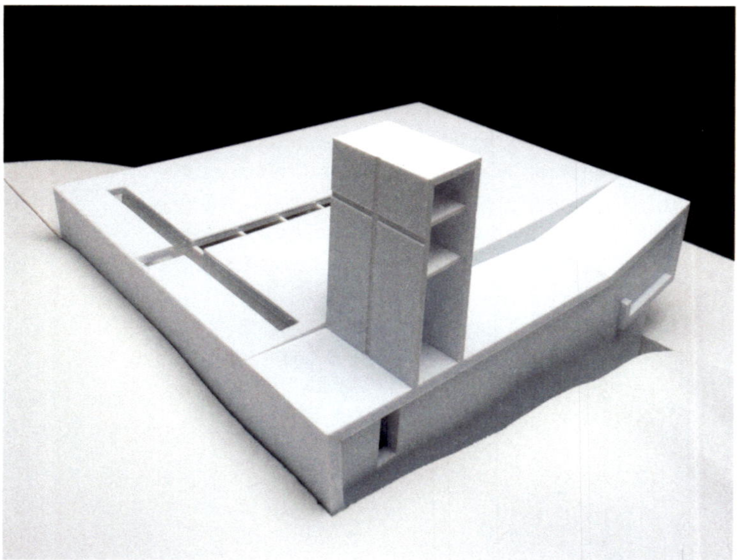

The church, integrated into the hillside, emerges only slightly from its surroundings of detached houses. Only the bell tower with its cross stands out from the building as a widely visible sign.

The coloured glass panes of the western window play the role of a rose window. The light coming through provides the church with a special atmosphere.

"[...] he was certain that he wouldn't be able to go any farther, but no, inside, past the wide-open door a longish corridor opened up, in the corridor, there was only an empty table and an empty chair standing orphaned on the side there, he stepped into the corridor, and he noticed that to the left of the table there was a similarly opened, narrower door, then he saw eight steps leading upward, and still beyond that, looking from down here, another space opened up, or a room – he stood on his tiptoes, the better to see, very cautiously, what was up inside there, but up inside, in that raised room, only a dim obscurity appeared to him, from which further dimly obscure rooms opened up ..."

— László Krasznahorkai, *Seibo There Below,* A murder is born

Intermediate Spaces

YAMUNKÁS · BERGARBEITER
1913
100
2013
ÉVES A
RÁNYÁSZSZAKSZERVEZET
BDSZ

Three Hungarian Scenes

Holger Kleine

Scene I: The Uninhabitable Shelter

For many centuries, barns and stables were the largest man-made indoor spaces in a village. They surpassed the village churches not only in their dimensions, but also in terms of the mystical quality of the light that pierced the glassless meshes, constructed with bricks or wooden slats, or that suddenly flooded the interiors when the huge barn doors were opened. Although all but the most insensitive of souls would have been struck by their atmospheric beauty, barns and stables were not a subject of theoretical study in architecture. They were simply not noble enough. In fact, most utilitarian buildings for human use and habitation are rarely mentioned in classical architectural theory, despite the fact that one of the most frequently cited definitions of architecture – by Le Corbusier – merely accords mankind the role of the beholder and perceiver and not of the inhabitant: "Architecture is the masterly, correct and magnificent play of volumes brought together in light." [1]

Can one still preserve some of these spatial qualities and experiences in the present day without descending into kitsch and nostalgia?

Villages, when they have not been abandoned altogether, are now inhabited by commuters who have bought up and lovingly converted the barns and houses into fortresses of narcissistic mediocrity. In the small town of Csorna in the border triangle between Hungary, Slovakia and Austria, however, one suddenly chances upon a slab of raw concrete hovering in the air between its neighbours. With its visor-like slit, it creates the somewhat surreal impression of a slice of a bunker suspended in mid-air. [Fig. 1]

The bunker-like segment facing the street is the first indication of the scene of a conflict that is being played out behind it in two locations, one behind the other: the first is the drive-through or passageway to the schoolyard, the second a recreational area. Both are covered by a similar roof and are delimited – but not fully enclosed – by similar walls. [Fig. 2] Accordingly, they both function as a passageway and a recreational space. In this scene, the protagonists of the conflict are the roofs, and the antagonists the walls. They speak different languages and present their case in different tones of voice: the roofs are pitched, tiled roofs, intact and traditional. They make no great show of things and appear as one would expect. The walls, on the other hand, are bare slabs of concrete floating in space, they are pierced by openings and bear the scars of formwork joints. They are jarring and unsettling. Like their language and tone of voice, the actions of the two are also opposing: the roof aims to shelter, closing off the space to the sky, while the walls expose the interior by keeping the space open.

Despite their opposing thrusts, these actions contribute together to two opposing impulses: by forming two covered spaces, the two passages hinder one from rushing through and invite one to linger. At the same time, their position and relationship to one another suggests moving forward: by lying one behind the other they form a sequence of passageways, but by lying at the edge of the site they do not lead directly to the yard and school entrance, instead leading past them to a fence, which in turn halts the impulse of movement.

Thus, the contrasting poles of gateway and hall (or: barn), natural and foreign, intact and scarred, opening and closing and moving and remaining are placed in irreconcilable opposition to each other. And this is a good thing, because drama – and architecture is nothing but drama – should render a conflict visible, not repress it. Ideally, however, it should create a new quality, a quality that only becomes apparent by refraining from resolving the conflicts at this initial level. In Csorna, it is the quality of the light in its form and corporeality.

Because the roof blocks out the light, it darkens the space, and because the walls are perforated, they shape the light passing in front of the dark background. The play of light within the space invites us to remain within it, while the passageway opening affords a view out into another similarly shaped passageway (i.e. not towards an endpoint), causing the eye to wander back and forth. It compares, appraises the spaces from inside and outside and understands the spectacle of light as a *self-referential* interplay. But because this interplay takes place at two points, through which one passes daily when entering and leaving the school, we not only observe this interplay from outside, but find ourselves inside it over and over again, suddenly, unexpectedly, as it were still "lost in thought". In addition to these opposing forces, in the context of the school as a whole there is a friction between how the space is used in its function and how the space presents itself. Walter Benjamin's much-cited observation [2] that architecture, unlike the other arts, is perceived primarily casually, in a state of distraction, should not be mistaken as implying that architecture does not present itself, but rather that the charm of its self-referential nature lies in how it becomes apparent unexpectedly. Who does not appreciate that, or would even have it otherwise?

Architecture comes into its own by means of the presence of light. For Arthur Schopenhauer, the ability of architecture "to unfold and reveal the nature of *light* [...]", in the way its "variously formed masses catch, impede and reflect the light [...] to the great enjoyment of the beholder", was the second purpose of beautiful architecture (the first being to reveal the struggle between gravity and rigidity). [3] At the same time this "finding oneself" awakens in us the desire not only to contemplate the play of light, but also to take possession of it, to inhabit it. Who would not wish to dwell in a space into which light can flow truly unhindered? In which one can appreciate both the beam of light and the wall, the patch of light and the floor, unhampered by glass and textiles, window frames and fittings? In which there is, first and foremost, only light, and then ourselves, partaking of the spectacle with pleasure and humility? It is the trivial demands of human habitation, the necessary subdivisions and extensions, and the glazing of openings (not to mention smoke extraction mechanisms) that breaks up the light into many parts and robs it of its atmospheric power. And that is precisely why we only experience this quality of light in shells or encasements and not in houses – it is the realm of barns, ruins, building sites and transitional spaces.

Architecture, however, can only meet the needs of habitation when it rigorously divides space into indoors and outdoors, into public and private. And that is something that ruins and transitional spaces, however beautiful or sublime, cannot provide. Put another way: transitional spaces, as spaces able to shift the emphasis towards the uninhibited play of light, are predestined for revealing the irreconcilable conflict between the opposing but equally justifiable demands –

1 Le Corbusier, *Towards a New Architecture.* New York, Dover, 1986 (1931), p. 37.
2 See Walter Benjamin, "The Work of Art in the Age of Mechanical Reproduction." In: *Illuminations.* New York, Scocken, 2008, p. 239.
3 Arthur Schopenhauer, *The World as Will and Idea. Volume 1.* London, Trübner & Co., 1907, p. 279–280.

for inhabitable shelters on the one hand and a powerful play of light on the other. The covered spaces in Csorna achieve this with bravura, as seen in the "masterly, correct and magnificent" play of dappled light beneath their roofs. It is through this that they remind us of the beauty of the barns that have disappeared, without resorting to kitsch or nostalgia, even as the inhabitants have endeavoured to soften the hardness of the concrete with vines that now envelop their surfaces.

As mentioned before, the redeeming role of light in this scene is made possible here by the unresolved conflicts in the preceding instance. Now, at the next level, new irreconcilable conflicts appear. Formed light, as we have seen, can only fully reveal its qualities in transitional spaces, in what one might call semi-architectural spaces. In enclosed spaces, it loses much of its intensity. In interiors, therefore, light needs to be transformed and to be given new properties if it does not wish to exit the scene as the loser. What kind of properties might these be?

Didactic Interlude I: The Dialectical Image

Mini-dramas – such as Samuel Beckett's short plays – often deal with a single image. The entrance scenario at Csorna is one such example. The image of the scene becomes apparent less through one's movement in space than in a single glance, i.e. less through the passage of time than through a momentary flash of recognition. It is, however, of a thoroughly inconsistent, dialectical nature, as it does not reconstruct, but rather constructs something new from past and present. According to Walter Benjamin, there are not only dialectical movements, but also dialectical images.
He characterised this as follows: "It's not that what is past casts its light on what is present, or what is present its light on what is past; rather, image is that wherein what has been comes together in a flash with the now to form a constellation. In other words, image is dialectics at a standstill. For while the relation of the present to the past is a purely temporal, continuous one, the relation of what-has-been to the now is dialectical: is not progression but image, suddenly emergent. – Only dialectical images are genuine images (that is, not archaic); and the place where one encounters them is language." [4] This language, one might add, can also be that of concrete and the sun's rays. Could it also be that of Barrisol films and LEDs?

Scene II: The Gallery of Absent Images

Up until the Renaissance, pictorial representations were mostly tied to a location: frescoes and murals adorned ceilings and walls, mosaics the floors, and even the altarpiece had its predetermined place. Only with the rise of early Florentine capitalism did artworks start to become a commodity, and for this the work of art had to become mobile. Canvases were lightweight, robust and could be rolled up to save space. Their ease of transport paved the way for the widespread rise of canvas painting in the modern era. Increasing mobility in general also gave wall paintings an advantage over ceiling paintings, which could only be produced for specific locations.

The so-called "salon style" of covering a wall with paintings, which became popular in the late Renaissance and is familiar from the Hermitage in St Petersburg, is often maligned for having been chosen solely to display the wealth of the collector. For this reason it has fallen into disrepute among modernists, despite the fact that it facilitates a much broader range of thematic curatorial arrangements through the possibility of relationships in horizontal, vertical and diagonal directions. Complex group formations offered an opportunity to present not just personal preferences and tastes, but also world views and movements of thought within a limited space.

By the end of the 19th century, all that was still deemed worthy of this cosmos of relationships was the horizontal series of pictures. There were several possible reasons for this: on the one hand, the rise of an evolutionary historical conception, as the dominant perspective of that time found its principle echoed in the linear progression of pictures; on the other, the rise of empathy as an aesthetic experience entailed that each artwork should optimally be viewed individually. The greatest disinterested pleasure, the most concentrated study, the strongest auratic effect of a work of art could only be achieved, so it was supposed, when the work of art was hung at eye level, with the neighbouring paintings at best only vaguely visible in the perimeter of one's vision. To these *comme-il-faut* ideas came, with the advent of rationalist Modernism, the white wall as a suitably neutral and mute background. The context of a work of art was no longer provided by its

[Fig. 1] View from the street, special school for children with intellectual disabilities in Csorna

[Fig. 2] Passageway to the schoolyard

[Fig. 3] Picture gallery of Esterházy Castle

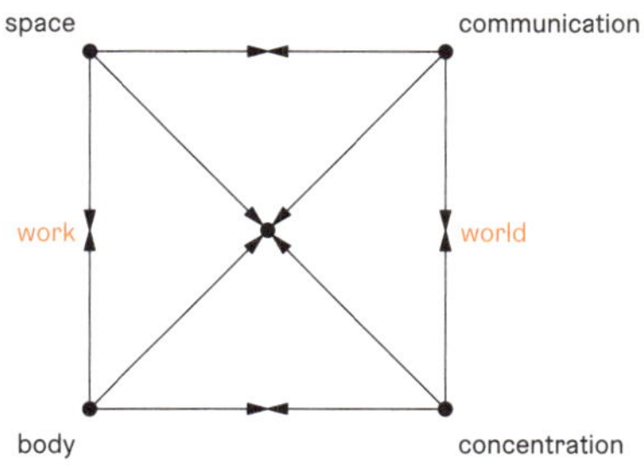

[Fig. 4] Scheme of spatial-dramatic situation from Holger Kleine

[Fig. 6] The void in the interior of the BASE building of MOME

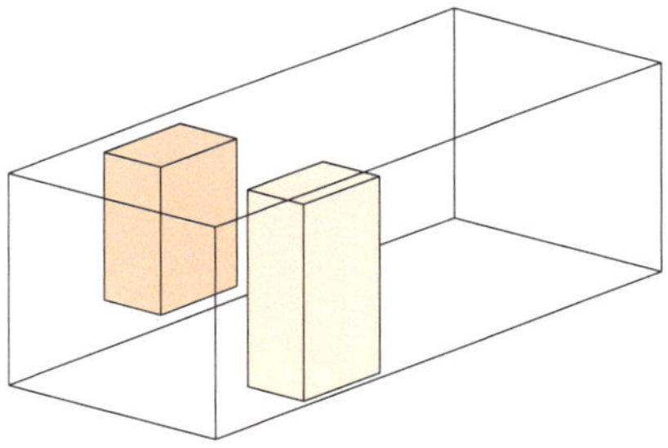

[Fig. 7] Vertical spaces in the BASE building

[Fig. 5] MOME, body-separating space

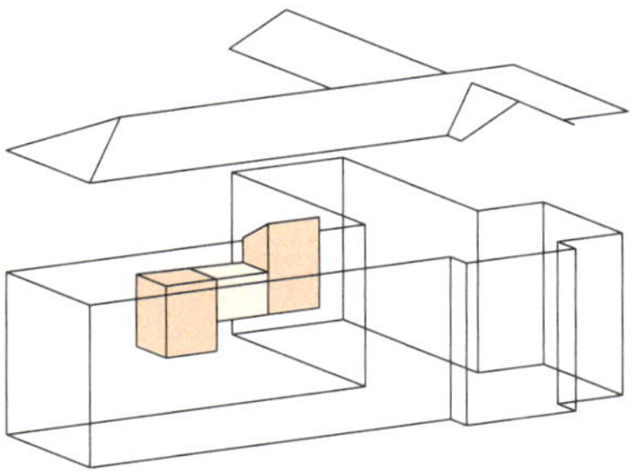

[Fig. 8] Cascade configuration of spaces in the transformed old main building of MOME

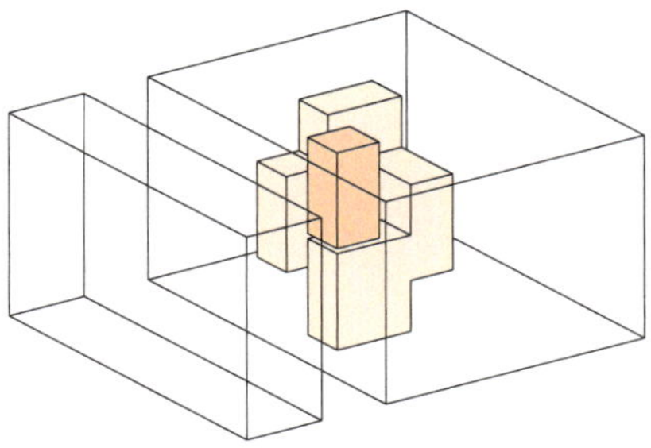

[Fig. 9] Spiral configuration of spaces in the UP building of MOME

surroundings – the hanging surface, room, furniture and decorations – but by the observer, who was expected to construct the context by means of their own powers of association.

On the face of it, the new gallery extension at Esterházy Castle subscribes to this curatorial standpoint – were it not for its disconcertingly beautiful ceiling! Its coffered barrel vault revives the device of ceiling paintings, reintroducing precisely the genre of painting that had fallen victim to the mobilisation of art. Here, though, emptiness shines out of its pictures: oil has been turned to light, the narrative motifs to abstract panels. The canvases of light glow silently, but in their totality and in the context of the palace, their silence is eloquent. [Fig. 3] Here, they are Conceptual Art, not Minimalism, more Dan Flavin than Donald Judd; they form a gallery of absent images. One can read them as illuminated traces of those paintings that once hung in this palace and have since been "secured" or "relocated" – or have "disappeared" without trace in the confusion of political events.

Behind paintings, walls do not darken. If – with good or bad intentions – one removes pictures that have hung from their hooks for decades, a lighter patch remains as a trace of the presence of the pictures' absence on the wall. By employing the cunning trick of transferring these patches of light from the former salon-style hanging to the ceiling as illuminated portraits, they have, as in Csorna, made the walls and ceilings the actors in a scene of play and counterplay. The ghostly counterplay of the ceiling contradicts the will of the walls to simply be their sublime selves irrespective of history.

Both the traces of light in Esterházy and the floating slice of a bunker in Csorna – whether or not it was the architects' intention – represent a break with a collectively adopted repression. They are constructed dialectical images. At the table of today's post-socialism, both would probably be uninvited guests. But it is to the ghostly appearance of such guests that great dramas such as *Macbeth* or *Don Giovanni* owe their eeriest moments. Why? Because the uninvited guest is invariably the voice of conscience.

Didactic Interlude II: The Spatial Dramatic Situation

If architecture really is about drama, as we claimed earlier, then it *necessarily* involves rendering conflicts visible and articulating them. In our two ase studies, we have identified a number of conflicts. If we attempt to identify the commonalities and differences of these conflicts, then these have, so I argue, one of two frames of reference. The first is the references to the work itself. By this I mean that the elements of architecture are varied and can conflict with one another. We have seen this in conflicts such as roof vs. wall, opening vs. closure, intact vs. scarred, oil vs. light. In essence, these are conflicts between physical elements of architecture and/or between them and spatial components of architecture, as architecture is ultimately either space and/or body. Because of this, body and space are always related to each other dialectically: remodelling one entails remodelling the other.

In addition, we have seen in the buildings above that they trigger different impulses simultaneously and by the same means: to move or to remain, inward focus or outward focus, active engagement or contemplative enjoyment. The architecture engenders these impulses in us, establishing a relationship between the work of architecture and the world at large. Here, the world is the reference.

The predominant impulses here – again reduced to the most general common denominator – are either the invitation to, and enabling of, the user to concentrate inwardly on themselves or to communicate outwardly with others. [Fig. 4]

To create a work of architecture that can be used and interpreted in a variety of ways, space and body and communication and concentration are dependent on one another. Their common interest is the work of architecture, while their competing interests lie in the desire of each to realise their own goals as best as possible. Sometimes they may act together to achieve these goals, but more frequently they obstruct one another – which is why the conflicting situation is not so much resolved as made apparent and played out anew! Drawing on and extending G. W. F. Hegel's drama theory, we call this play and counterplay of the four protagonists the spatial dramatic situation.[5] In the conceptual framework of the spatial dramatic situation, direct opposites or causalities, such as form follows function, are set aside in favour of a dialectical interplay in which the respective interdependent conflicts can play out. To trigger such a dramatic situation, a university campus would seem to offer plenty of opportunities ...

Scene III: An Open Field

... because it contains studios, workshops and workplaces that are typically designed as spacious, communicative and connected areas, but are then subsequently partially compartmentalised by various means: mobile or flexible, permanent or temporary, planned or improvised, sound-absorbing or visually screening. 3h architects' extension to Moholy-Nagy University of Art and Design in Budapest (MOME) acknowledges this conflict between the needs for communication and for concentration from the outset by proposing, through its design, a broad range of spatial situations with varying degrees of openness.

The MOME also employs a similarly unorthodox and relaxed approach to dealing with the conflict between body and space. The existing Neoclassical building already provided the architects with an obvious means of resolving the conflict between body and space: its longitudinal wing is little more than an arm enclosing the auditorium. Here, the space forms the body and the body indicates the space. However, the relationship is so tame and lacking in mystery that it was crying out for an injection of dynamism. In response, the architects came up with not one but three dynamism-inducing variants that could hardly be more different. Two of them are located at either end of a newly established circulation axis. At its end facing the city, this manifests itself as a *body-separating space,* a 5 metre wide axis that slices the volume of the building in two with razor-sharp precision. [Fig. 5] Through the bright, porous volume of the building, an imposing chasm has been cut, the glazed inner surfaces of which are smooth, dark and reflective. Its clear and precise contours are pierced only by the glass bridges that cross it.

At the other end, by contrast, the axis appears to bounce off the volume of the building without having any effect. Neither the cubature nor the distinctive rhythmic pattern of pillars and windows registers any response. This apparent indifference is, however, only a posture, for on entering the building, one is surprised to find that the line of the axis continues on within the volume of the building, hollowing out a 14 metre wide void in the interior over its entire height and length that runs right up to the end wall. [Fig. 6] The pattern of flanking small window openings suggests rooms and floors that do not exist here in the line of the axis. One is involuntarily reminded of the imposing vertiginous spaces seen in the ruins of Scottish castles, where the absence of the wooden floors leaves windows and niches in the enclosing walls hanging in mid-air, no longer reachable. The third and final variant is the axis itself, as it traverses the hilly terrain, variously buried in or half dug into the terrain, passing beneath buildings or continuing as a garden path. It has no distinctly delineated form and consists only of a casual sequence of *bodiless spaces.*

These three forms – the *body-separating space,* the *body-hollowing space* and the *bodiless space* – together with the pre-existing *body-forming space* do not together form a closed square, but are just four possibilities among many. But it does not end here: at the next smaller scale, that of the buildings' inner circulation, ever new variants reveal themselves. Sometimes one sees a body within a body – buildings' cores enclosed by winding, hollow vertical spaces [Fig. 7] – and sometimes the spaces between them are crossed by bridges or descend in tiered levels. New ravines, cascades, [Fig. 8] spirals and serpentines appear, [Fig. 9] sometimes as spatial constellations, sometimes as pathway configurations. What they have in common is that they subvert the conventional open atrium type by introducing bodies that continually obscure one another as one moves through the space, encouraging one to explore – a Baroque idea that 3h had already successfully transferred to the modern age in their Geometria office building.

The simple causal relationship between body and space in the pre-existing building is contrasted with the interplay of reciprocally varying and relativising situations in the new MOME buildings. This play of situations is important because it resists total use of the space by introducing obstructions, while at the same time encouraging new, unplanned forms of appropriation. It provides an open field – or in other words: the spatial dramatic situation is constantly perpetuated anew. This corresponds to the *zeitgeist* and is a quality that MOME shares with many contemporary stage dramas. This understanding of *zeitgeist* derives from an ethical standpoint that Karl Friedrich Schinkel had already formulated in his day: "The work of art should enrich life, just as it is given life through the ideas it embodies." [6]

4 Walter Benjamin, *The Arcades Project.* Cambridge, MA, Harvard Univ. Press, 1999, p. 462.

5 For more background on the "dramatic situation" in Hegel's work and on the origin of the term "spatial dramatic situation" and an explanation of its mechanisms in contemporary museum architecture, see: Holger Kleine, *The Drama of Space.* Basel, Birkhäuser, 2018, p. 79 and 270ff.

6 Karl Friedrich Schinkel, *Das architektonische Lehrbuch.* Cited in: Fritz Neumeyer, *Quellentexte zur Architekturtheorie.* Munich, Prestel, 2002, p. 213.

Intimate Neighbourhoods

Block of Apartments
in Futó Street,
Budapest
2001–2005

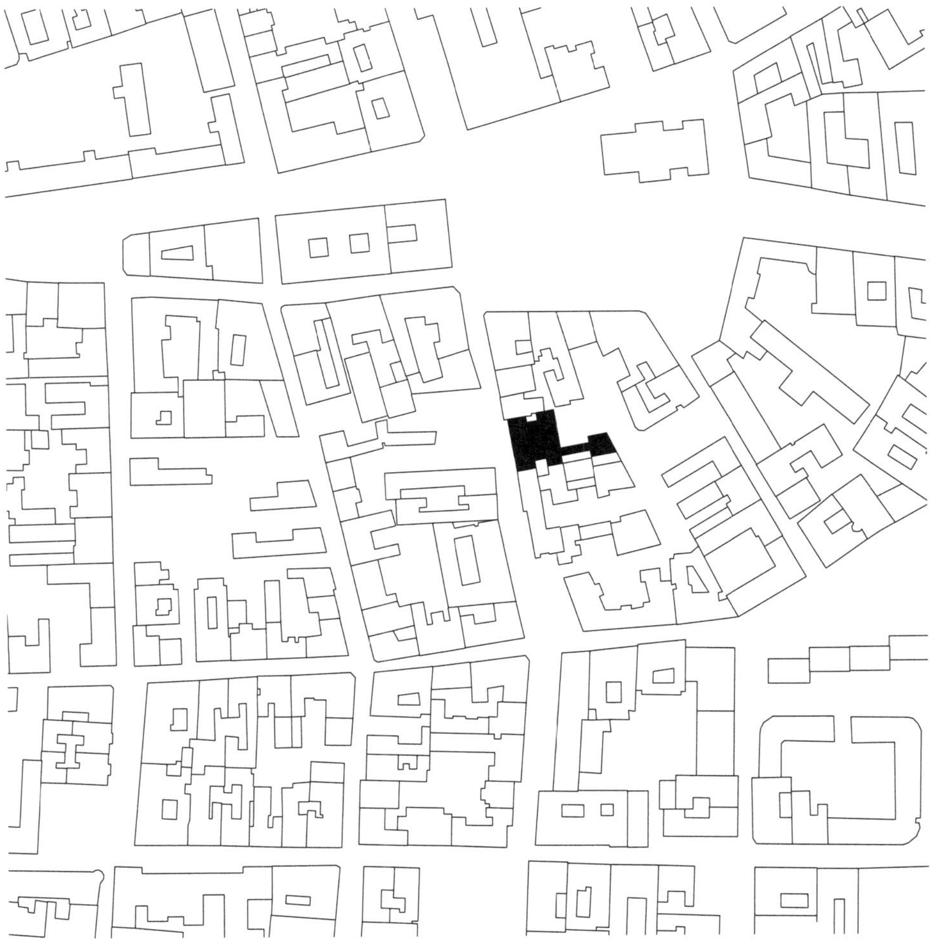

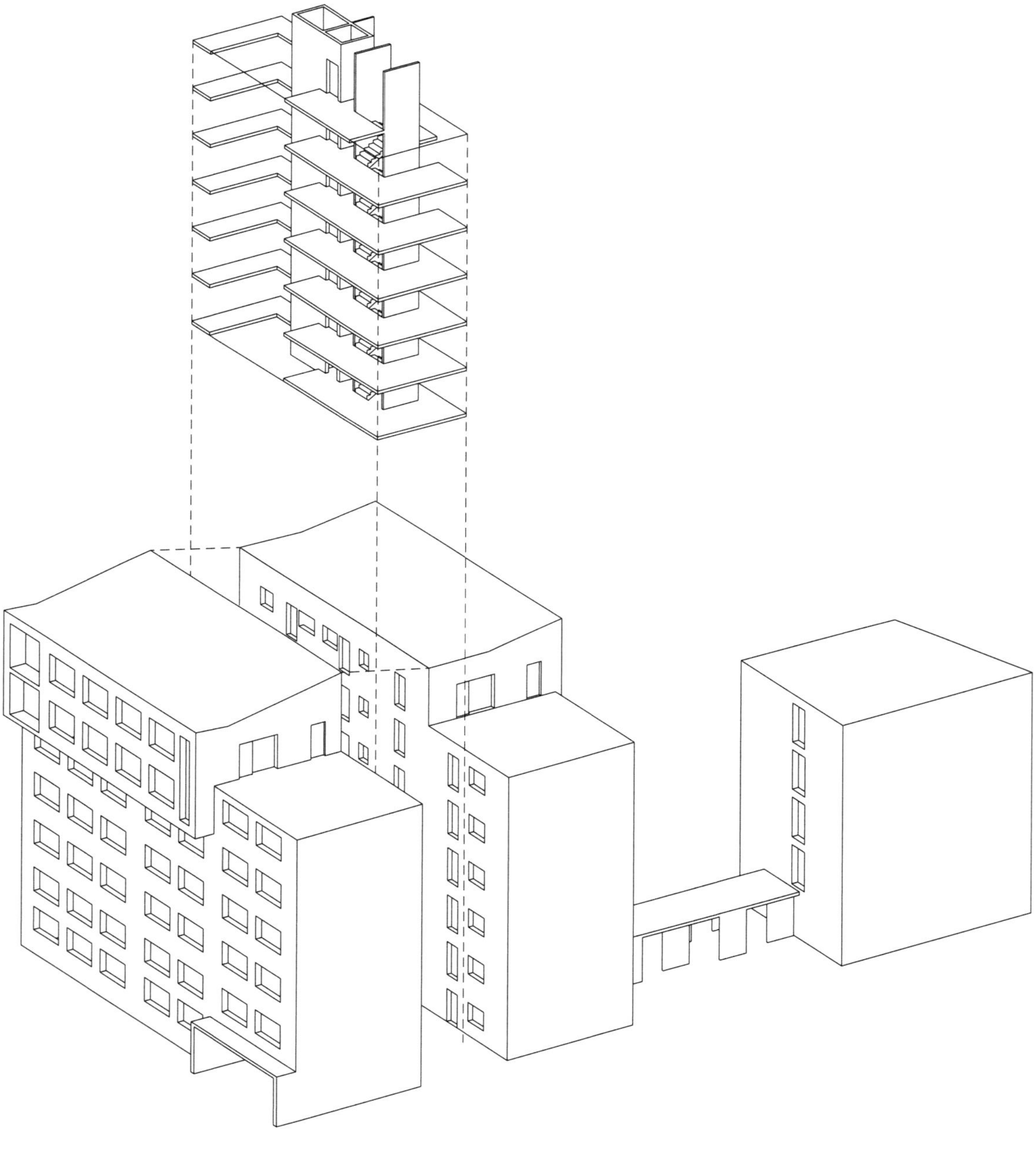

Budapest is divided into two by the Danube. Morphology describes Buda, while density is characteristic of Pest. Eaves of different heights and firewalls randomly appearing in the courtyards break up the monotony of density. Here and there the firewalls are dirty and plaster is peeling off. A window may be slightly open. Behind it a spoon clinks in a bowl. There are shared toilets at the end of the balcony access galleries, the blaring loudness of quarrelling residents and the stifling heat in the depth of often gloomy courtyards. Is this degree of familiarity disturbing in today's individual world? Or are they the scents, colours and textures of a bygone age, which the city still emanates?

This type of residential environment has by now lost much of its value and has primarily become a synonym for poverty. Yet let us not forget that walkways, whether at ground level or for access galleries, has also worked as a space of personal encounters – one that is slowly disappearing from our present residential patterns.

This is the environment in which we designed our residential building. Revitalisation of the notorious area of the 8th district began at the beginning of the 21st century. The proximity of the Great Boulevard accounts for the area's increasing value or gentrification. The construction of the new buildings took place in parallel with rehabilitating the neighbouring public spaces. The residential building concerned was constructed as a first stage of the process. Since it represented one of the initial phases of rehabilitation, we could not design grandiose middle-class apartments. There are 53 one- and two-bedroom flats in a block, mainly housing families.

The building had to be dense and react to the theme of the access galleries. How could the negative connotation of density be turned into something positive? How could it work in the dense urban fabric of Pest's inner city? How could the existing systems be turned upside down? The outcome may seem banal, yet it has resulted in something entirely new in terms of its structure. The dense part of the plot was created by rotating the two wings with access galleries towards each other. Only the kitchens and bathrooms look out onto the narrow inner courtyard straddled by the two wings. This design provides the spice of the concept: the rooms look onto either the street or the courtyard, which has a dense array of plants, while the stretched intervening space with its relatively wide corridors serves for the movement of people and communication.

In its use of materials the exterior fits in with the neighbouring buildings. The composition of the plastered façade is based on the contrasts of smooth and sculptural, dark and light, reserved and intensive as well as point and counterpoint. The asymmetrical approach of the building is emphasised by a dark box, which is followed by a colourful and decorative pergola leading to the inner courtyard.

The inward-looking access galleries of buildings, characteristic of the beginning of the 20th century, represented a focus of social life for residents. The access galleries in our design recreate the atmosphere of neighbourhood relations in the old city centre. In this form the building returns to the roots of the culture of access galleries in Pest's central area.

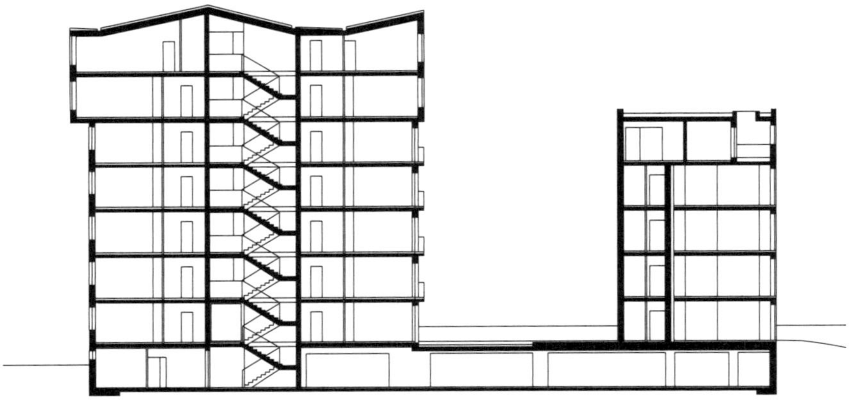

Section

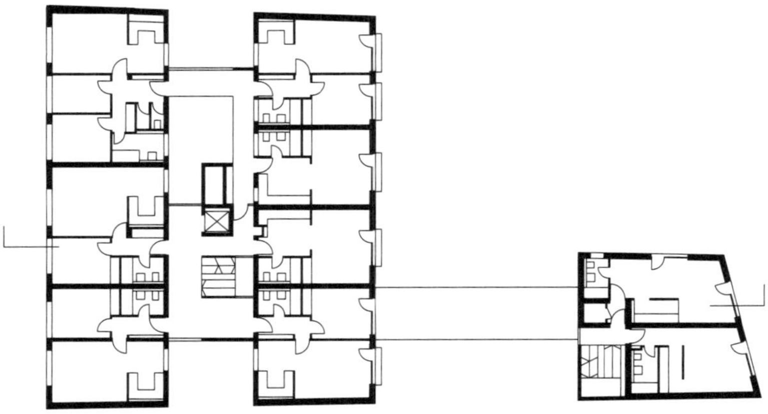

General floor plan

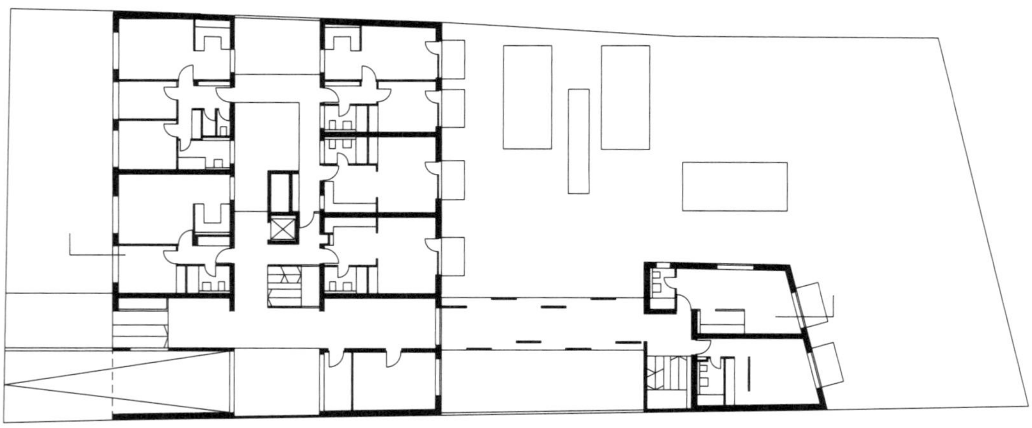

Ground floor plan

The unbroken row of buildings in this section was constructed around 2000. Two emphatic elements mark the difference between our design and its contemporary neighbours: the entrance gate and the darker colour of the volume uniting the top floors to an attic.

The density of Pest's buildings can be recognised well from the apartment's terrace on the top floor.

A smaller building was implanted in the inner courtyard, which corresponds more to its scale and responds to the typical arrangement of the buildings not fronting the street.

The photograph shows well the high density and characteristics of the central urban district. The firewalls seen in the inner courtyards of the buildings evoke the specific atmosphere of Pest.

KPMG

Different Shades of Modernism

K4 Office Building,
Budapest
2011–2014

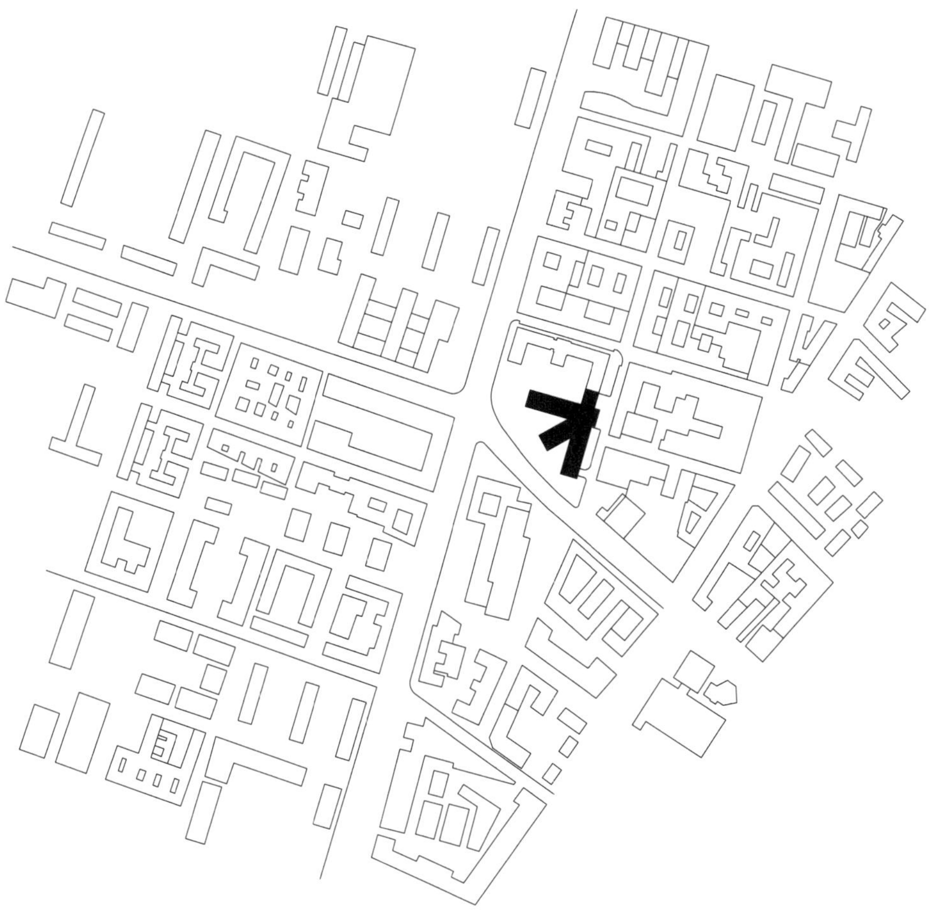

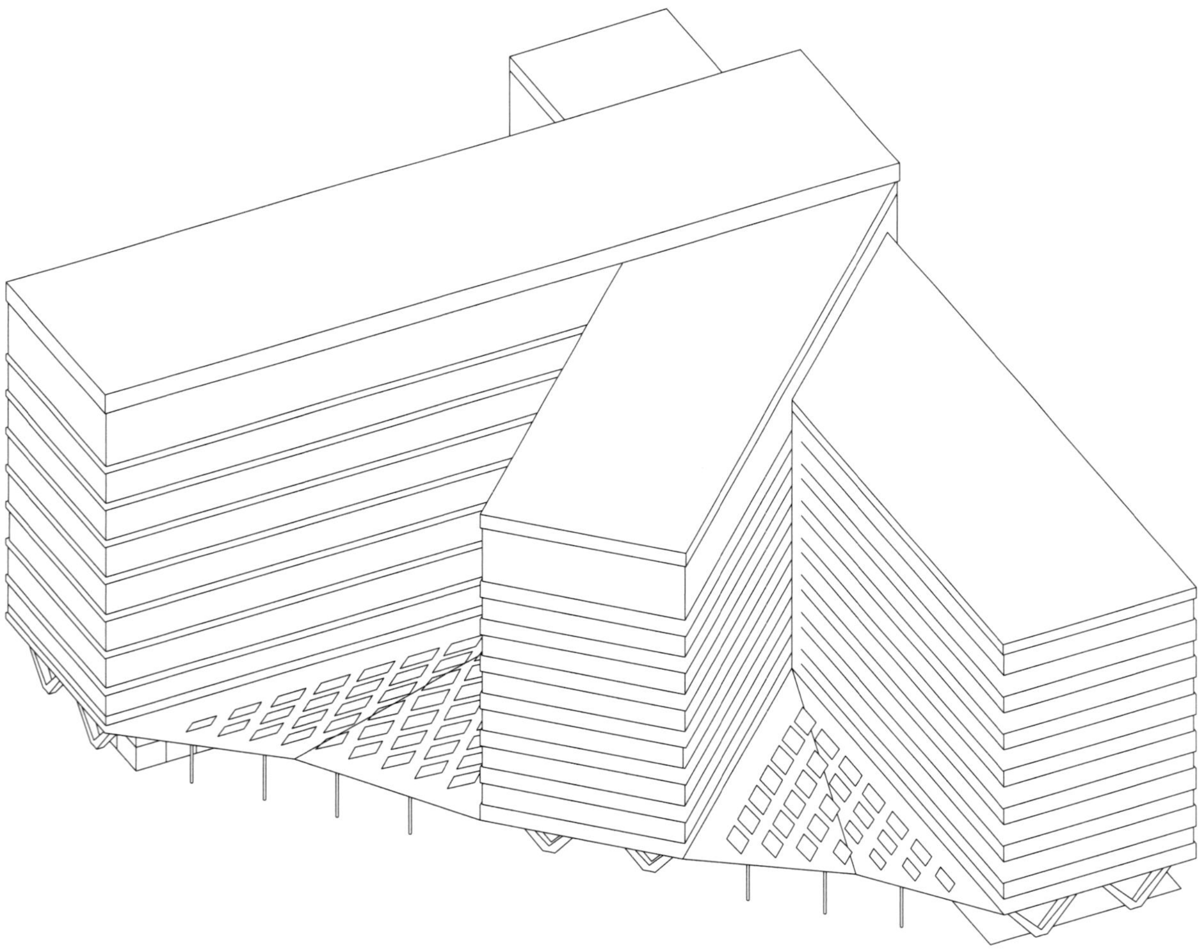

The synthesis of different eras of Modernism has always excited us – in other words, putting usual elements together in such a way that a unified collage may come about with clearly separable reference points. This attitude was not at all conscious at the initial stage of planning the K4 office building. However, as we progressed with the design we increasingly enjoyed putting together elements that can be separated by different eras. When we reach back to the beginning of Modernism, the ribbon window as one of its major attributes comes to mind. In the 1950s, special supports, for example V-shaped columns, became prominent for the purpose of more expressive design, especially in South America, while the space blob created by the parametric method is the product of our time and can be seen in the canopy.

In order that they all appear in unison, the building has been dressed in sparkling white. However, let us move away from this experimental stream of thought and examine the building from the aspect of its urban fabric.

A special point can be found in Budapest's north-eastern business district: a crossroads with a large span cuts into the orthogonal urban fabric. The designed volumetry recedes compared to other buildings at the junction. It can be interpreted as a construction in a backyard, which gains its central position from the angle of the intersection. Given the irregularity of the urban fabric at this location, the focal point switched to a freely designed building.

The rectangular prisms, which follow the rationality of office typology, open up like a fan in the direction of the extending space. Two elements form a right angle and thereby endorse the orthogonality of the urban fabric. A third is wedged in between the two and overwrites their seemingly simple relationship.

The office blocks follow the line of the Dózsa György Road, and the volumes gradually descend towards the neighbouring residential areas. Dynamic design is an important principle, which becomes obvious during the movement of the observer: the rectangular prisms constructed in a strictly geometrical order sometimes conceal and sometimes reveal one another. The alternation of positive and negative spaces, rotating the descending blocks around one central point, are parts of a design method that becomes a comprehensible whole when walking round the building. The canopies stretching between the blocks with rhombus-shaped openings become increasingly spacious towards the inner side of the building. The shapes of the lower and upper planes are modified in space so that their intersection changes evenly and also shepherds the light to the inner, darker corners. This geometrical trick makes for airiness and lightness, since in this way the plastic surface does not seem heavy.

The idea of progressive transition is also echoed in the façade. The glazed surfaces flow like ribbons across the blocks, although the proportion of glazed and solid surfaces differs in each block. The northern block is glazed from floor to ceiling, the windows of the next block are of the usual parapet height, while there are significant solid ribbons on the southern block.

The garden square, constructed from prism-shaped mounds following the curve of the road, has an abundance of plants. This is not only aesthetically appealing but also environmentally friendly, since the garden functions as a soundproofing wall due to its inward sloping structure as well as a dust filter thanks to the vegetation. A dynamic, funnel-shaped public space has been formed behind the garden square in the immediate vicinity of the building. It not only leads across to the school and residential buildings on the other side, but also tempts passers-by to spend time under the shelter of the canopy. An attractive urban space has been created under the "fan".

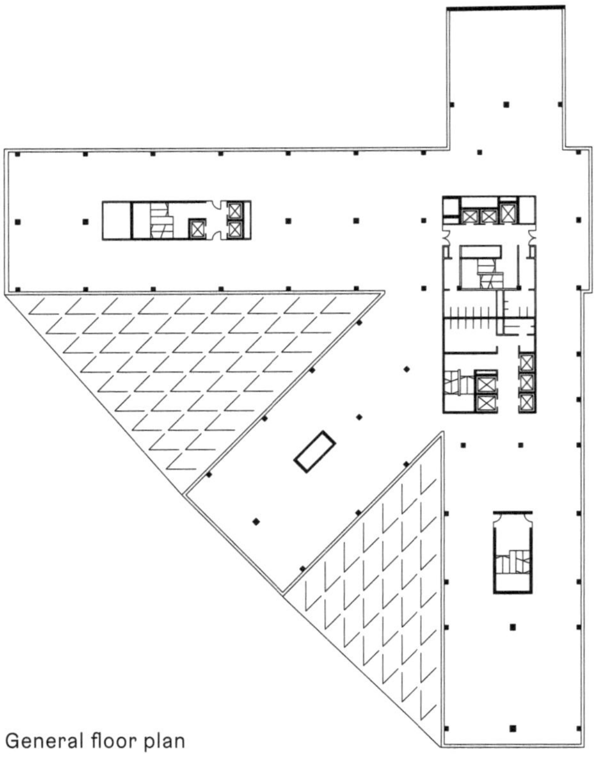

General floor plan

Ground floor plan

The canopy's openings become increasingly spacious from the square towards the inner side of the building, thus letting more light through and intensifying the perception of changing urban densities.

There is an unimpeded passage between and underneath the wings of the building. The airy canopy, which is connected with a new, raised green square, is especially spectacular, when it is illuminated at night.

The entrances to the new office building have been designed to be cheerful and airy to enhance the change from public to private spaces.

KPMG

The architectural elements of Modernism that appear emphatically on the building invite you to a kind of time travel: ribbon windows, V-shaped columns and the parametric design all engage in a dialogue.

K4's three rectangular prisms offer the city dwellers new dynamic perspectives of the existing urban fabric at an important intersection in the city.

Transforming Identities

MOME – Moholy-Nagy
University of Art
and Design,
Budapest
2015 – 2019

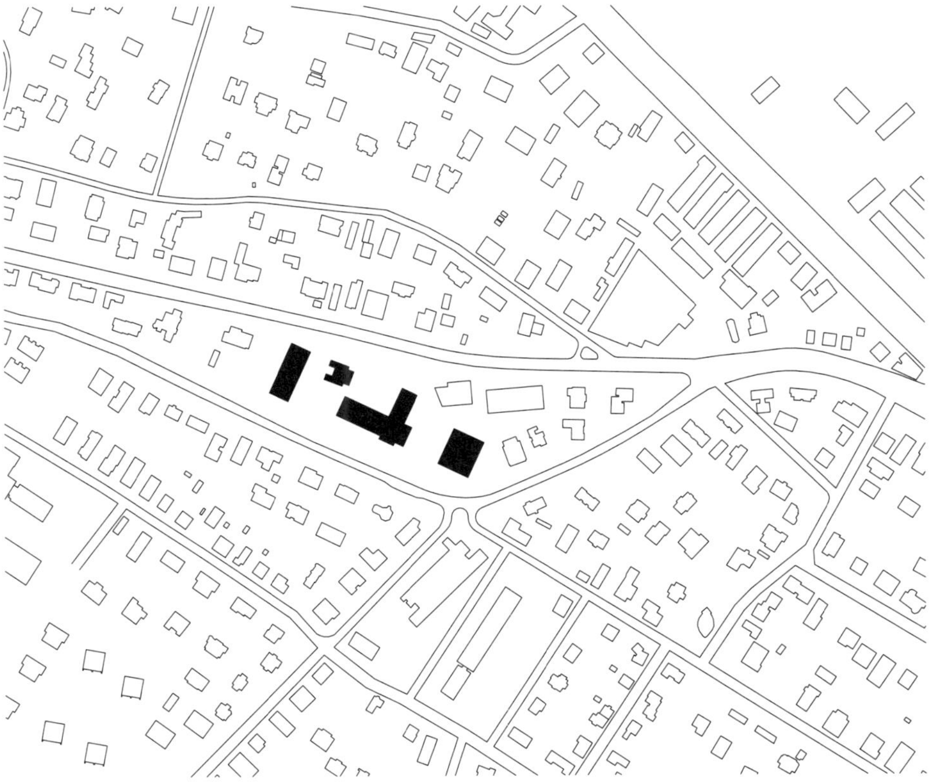

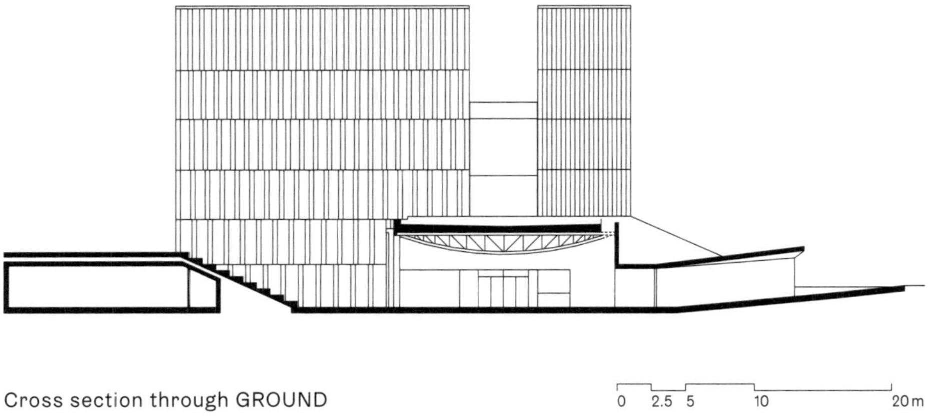

Cross section through GROUND

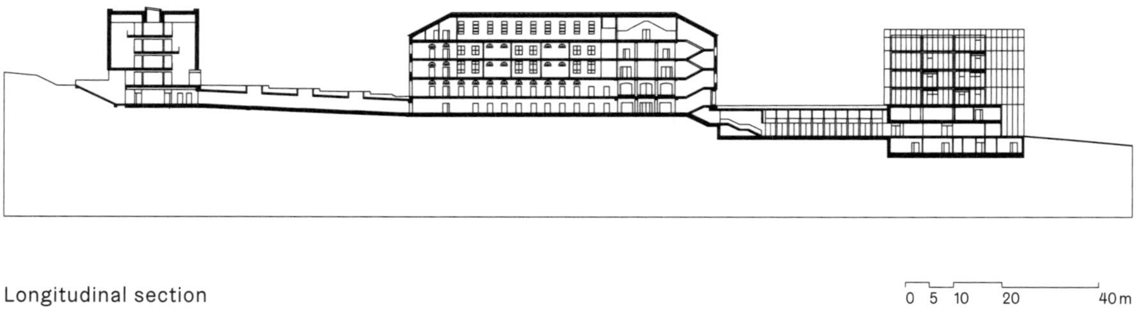

Longitudinal section

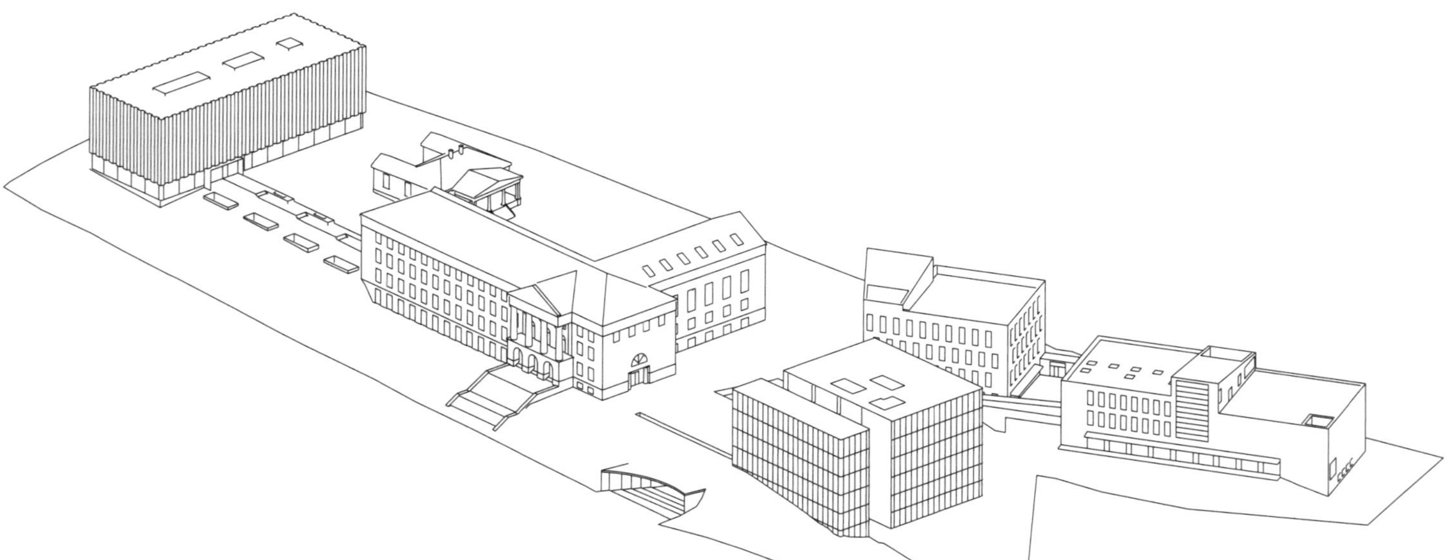

When designing the extension of the MOME Campus we analysed the question of identity. The issues concerned how to connect with László Moholy-Nagy, whose name the university bears and whose creative work focused on innovation and probed both artistic and technical boundaries. In addition, we wanted to see how we could link with the pioneering design style of the last century's Bauhaus movement in which Moholy-Nagy was involved. Furthermore, we considered how we could relay the transformation of university education to the outside world, since as well as professional attentive craftsmanship the need to reinforce skills of conceptualisation and to recognise real problems was also increasingly important.

The topos of the site is closely connected to the issue of self-identity. The university's slightly sloping, park-like surroundings create a specific atmosphere, an island of calm and quiet within the metropolis. The People's College, designed by Zoltán Farkasdy in the style of Socialist Realism, opened here in 1954. The central building, which has since become iconic, preserves many memories of the history of the university. For example, the inventor of the Rubik's Cube sketched his first drafts in a room behind the portico. Comprehensive answers were required, too, by the campus' park together with the dominant building.

How could the new buildings be linked to the topographical features and their strong intellectual heritage? We sought answers in the original designs. According to Farkasdy's intention, the concept aligned three buildings named B – A – C along an axis. Of the three, the simple teaching block B with its central corridor was in a rather bad condition by the time of the design competition and therefore the project earmarked it for demolition. The exterior of the central building A was declared protected. However, its out-of-date spatial structure did not meet the present educational expectations, while the third building C had never been constructed. In line with our ideas, we reinstituted the triple design of the original concept: the volume of the BASE building for undergraduates replaces the old building B. The central building A accommodates MA courses and administration. Its interior was transformed to a large extent, but its exterior was mostly left unchanged. The third building, which is nearest to the city and in a prominent place, is the university's centre for innovation as well as representing its new image. It has been named UP.

The new buildings are deliberately heterogeneous in their appearance, yet the applied façades are conceptually interconnected. The starting point was provided by the portico columns of building A and the banded façade of the BASE building. Thus, the transparent membrane of the innovation centre UP responds to this vertical rhythm. The façade system of upright cast-glass elements enclosing UP evokes Moholy-Nagy's experiments with light, due to the play with the depth of focus. It does this in such a way that the shifting of the glass ribbons on each level, based on mathematical formulae, lends the building a contemporary digital ornamentation. The academic buildings and UP are of a bright, crystalline appearance, in sharp contrast with the dark-coloured buildings of the technological park situated on the campus.

All three buildings are situated along a nearly east-west axis. A "topographical" volume called GROUND was created in the centre of these buildings to transmute the separate elements into a flowing campus landscape. The underground spaces of GROUND were designed as a pulsating centre of interactions, where communication routes come together and which can function as the campus' largest indoor communal space, interconnected with an amphitheatre outside the main entrance hall.

How could the campus' apparently rigid axis be shaped so that the accompanying spaces stimulate the students' creativity? Spaces have been opened up and joined together in each building, thus providing a specific communicative world for each educational unit. The central space of the BASE building is situated at one end of our axis. On its two sides a funnel-like atrium forms a connection between the floors. The experience of space gained during movement is provided by some meandering stairs opening ultimately into the vertical. The central corridors and the accompanying classrooms in building A were dispensed with. As a result, large open spaces were created with model-making studios located as islands in the middle. In order to make the effect more dramatic, parts of the ceilings between the floors disappeared, connecting the three floors of the building in a space continuum. Meanwhile, the inspirational world of the UP building, the system of turning spirals, ascending openings, is based on constant movement. In this sense the new spaces of MOME are scenes of new adventures, which continuously compel you to abandon your cognitive comfort zone. The result is the elementary experience and childlike discovery of the environment and, last but not least, the liberation of creativity.

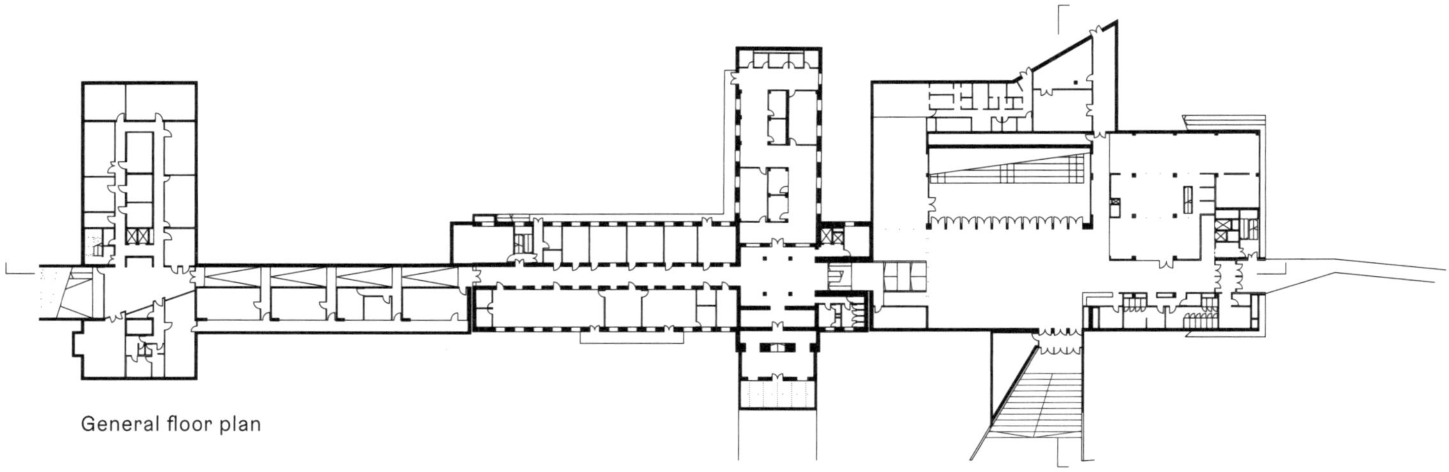

General floor plan

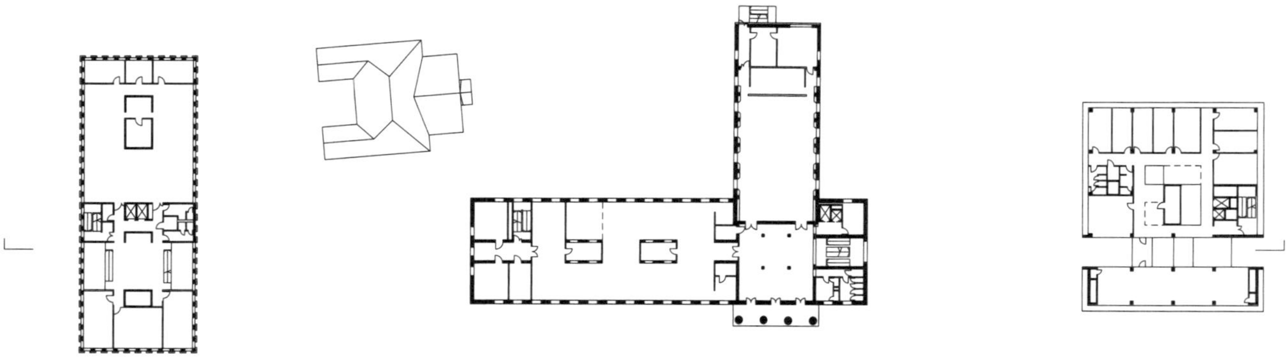

Ground floor plan

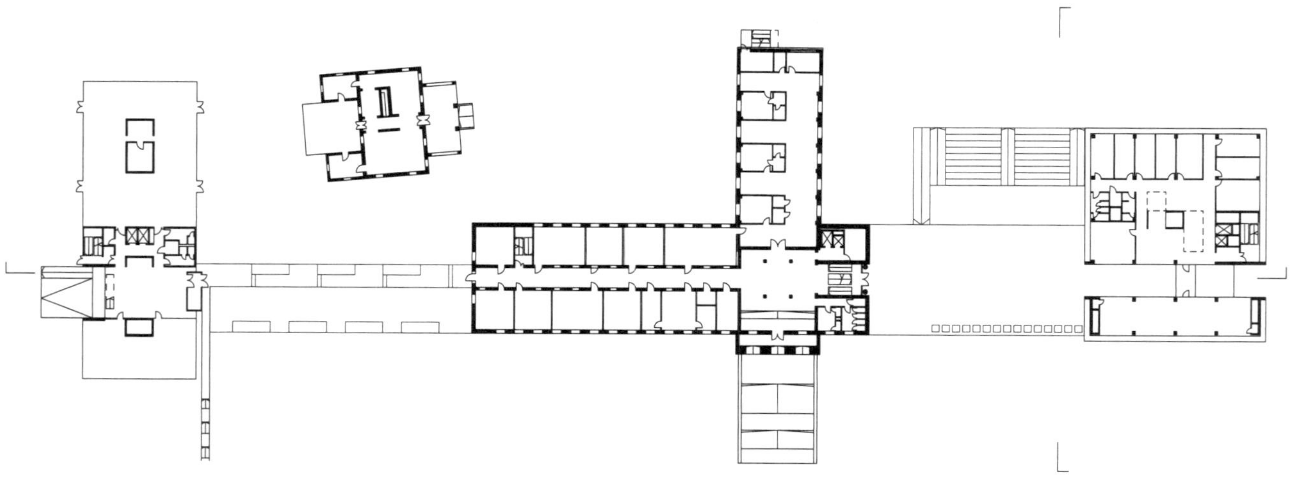

Street level floor plan

0 5 10 20 40 m

The university grounds are situated far from the bustle of the city in a quiet suburban part of the Buda Hills.

When renovating the old main building we strove to prioritise the attraction of Socialist Realism. The redesigned floor covering, indirect lighting and existing ornamentation are elements that reinforce one another.

We turned the original building inside out and the previously enclosed spaces were reconfigured as an open spatial structure, which connects the three levels of the building in a vertical as well as a horizontal sense.

Socialist Realist architecture, which appears in the portico of the former main entrance, reintroduced the use of classical architectural elements.

The elementary presence of the beams used for suspension defines the character of the top level in BASE.

The vertical emphasis in the BASE façade echoes the columns of the old building's portico as well as the smaller-scale glass bands of the Innovation Centre (UP).

The auditorium has been restored with its original ornaments and renovated with state-of-the-art lighting and acoustics.

The suspended structure of the BASE building allows its ground floor to open up visually to its surroundings without any barriers.

The aula is supplemented with a red kitchenette on each level in the undergraduate building. It is a location for informal encounters and conversation.

The studios are in a large open-plan unit, yet the acoustic curtains and movable walls make separation possible.

In the aula the different levels can be accessed via stairs in the open spaces. The floor areas of the aula function as large landings.

The campus operates as a public institution, enabling the city's residents to use its park and visit exhibitions in the communal spaces.

The volume of the UP Innovation Centre has been split into two along the main axis. These two parts are interconnected by bridges on each level, the gap between them marking the entrance to the centre. The cast glass skin lends the building an airy feel.

The potential of the sloping site has been utilised when positioning the buildings. The central space of the campus was modelled underground between the Innovation Centre (UP) and the building for MA courses. It connects to an amphitheatre-like open-air space.

The library, designed by aligning one and two-storey spaces, is situated on the ground and first floors of the Innovation Centre (UP).

The spiral rotation of the voids permits both horizontal and vertical views.

The canteen and the distinctive stairway are connected to the central aula. Three spaces of differing character meet here.

The stairs leading to the former main building constitute an emphatic element. The lighting design is repeated in the aula of each building.

The aula in GROUND is the largest event space in the campus. The curved ceiling stretches from the main entrance towards the campus park.

The canteen's interior is characterized by vertical rhythms, including suspended acoustic elements and wooden laths on the wall. The space is flexible, the built-in box of the café and the stairs for sitting on being the only stationary elements.

ONE

The entire front of the central aula opens up towards the park. The terraced space functions as an open-air venue.

The main entrance of the campus draws in visitors with its funnel-like design. The downward movement contrasts with the grandiose entrance of the Socialist Realist building.

"[…] yet few are those who have entered, proceeded through all of the rooms, towers, and courtyards of the Alhambra in whom the realization arose that these decorations aren't even decorations but the infinities of a language; few, but there are some, and they all wander between the rooms, the towers, and the courtyards, and they have absolutely no idea of where they are and why they are exactly there and not somewhere else, there are those for whom, after a while, their attention begins to turn to these enchanting surfaces, they stand still ever more frequently to examine the patterns …"

— László Krasznahorkai, *Seibo There Below,* "Distant Mandate"

Ornamental Perception

TOLNA
TORDA-ARANYOS
TORONTAL

On the Eloquence of Building

Olaf Bartels

Mute Modernism?

Compared with the variety of decorative forms on house façades and interior walls, ceilings and floors from past centuries, the surfaces of contemporary buildings in Europe appear sober – indeed almost mute. In the streets of Budapest, whose building fabric has survived World War II and subsequent waves of renewal relatively well, this is particularly apparent, even to the foreign observer. Here and there, one is reminded of the period in which Austria and Hungary shared a common heritage and one sees the reciprocal influence of the reform architects active in Vienna and Budapest at the beginning of the 20th century. One can even discern remnants of the Ottoman building culture from the 16th or 17th century and, if one looks carefully, also the attempts at forging a national identity in the years immediately after World War II.

If we know how to read their signs and decipher their formal codes, these buildings reveal as much about the culture of building as they do about the culture of life from which they emerged. One could, therefore, argue that Adolf Loos's pamphlet "Ornament and Crime", published in 1908, was responsible for robbing us of this means of cultural perception. One might even say that Modernism in architecture and its many protagonists, of which Adolf Loos was one of the first, left us not just mute but also blind. Having lost the means of understanding the signs, we now find ourselves in the laborious process of reassembling the requisite vocabulary. But while Loos was without doubt a trendsetting architectural thinker, we would be crediting him here with too much influence. His call to renounce excessive ornamental forms and to exercise efficient objectivity in the disposition of the floor plan, building size, building form and appearance may indeed have helped to elevate expressive restraint in the design of buildings to a tenet of modern architecture. It certainly caused a shift of focus towards the inner values of buildings: to their usability and construction. But it was the fact that, in the value system of the Modern Movement, ornamentation failed to stand the test of efficiency that caused it to become superfluous. In its place, modernists such as Adolf Loos and Mies van der Rohe promoted an aestheticisation of the material itself, carefully selecting and combining building elements of different materials to heighten their effect. Put simply, the aesthetics of the material became the only decoration of their buildings, whether it was the rough texture of exposed concrete, the fine striations of a marble slab or the delicate grain of a wooden surface. Their work expanded the vocabulary and architectural repertoire of decorative means. Without going into further detail, one could therefore also argue that far from silencing architecture, Modernism added a new facet to the language of architecture. [Fig. 1]

A Return to Ornament

Robert Venturi's, Denise Scott Brown's and Steven Izenour's treatise "Learning from Las Vegas", published in 1972, brought the topic of decoration back into the architectural limelight and rapidly gained popularity. Today, the works of Herzog & de Meuron, Jean Nouvel, Nicholas Grimshaw, Neutelings Riedijk Architects and Alen Jasarevic, Sauerbruch Hutton, Hild und K, and Caruso St John testify to the renewed significance of decoration and ornament in contemporary architecture. As such, we are not entering new territory when we consider the aspect of ornamentation in the work of 3h architects.

But what is an ornament in architecture? Is it really the superfluous formal decoration that Adolf Loos so disparaged in his day that he likened it to the tattoos, in his eyes equally superfluous, that he thought to see among savages, criminals and the lower social classes? The floral adaptations, the patterns that arise from rows or variations of geometric forms have the capacity to communicate codes that denote affiliation to certain social groups or reveal complex cultural contexts. Venturi, Scott Brown and Izenour made this patently clear: ornaments are part of an architectural aesthetic that encompasses not just their symbolic nature but also their capacity to influence the atmospheric quality of architecture and how we perceive it.

New photomechanical reproduction techniques as well as digital design and CNC laser cutting and milling techniques have made the production of ornamentation efficient and cost-effective. But while ornaments are no longer expensive, they have yet to become a natural element of architecture. The perception persists that they are a costly extra and therefore inessential. Where budget constraints require every expenditure to be justified, there has to be a good reason for the use of ornamentation. One example is in the continuation or extension of historical buildings to mediate between the harsh confrontation of old and new. David Chipperfield employed this principle in the reconstruction of the Neues Museum in Berlin [Fig. 2], drawing on ornamentation in the old building to create new ornamental patterns for use in the transition between old and new. Another application is as a sunscreen, such as Herzog & de Meuron's fritted façade on the Elbphilharmonie in Hamburg, although here the ornamental effect of the clouds of small light- and heat-absorbing dots is stronger than envisaged. The original plan was for a mainly monochrome façade.

How, then, do 3h architects employ ornamentation in their architecture? The inspiration for their designs derives frequently from the context within which their building will stand. Integrating their buildings into the built context and contributing to the neighbourhood is thus a key concern. Ornamentation can play an important role in this. In many cases, the existing context is diverse and varied, with many stimulating aspects and the building task frequently involves supplementing, extending or re-using existing building substance.

Respect and Distance

In 2009, Katalin Csillag and Zsolt Gunther, together with their then office partner Anthony Gall, exercised respectful restraint in their design for the institute for children with physical disabilities, a boarding school for kinesiotherapy within the grounds of an existing school complex in the 14th district of Budapest. The old buildings, designed for blind Jewish children in the style of the Hungarian Secession by the Budapest architect Béla Lajta in 1908, dated back almost exactly 100 years. Their impressive decorations were a statement in themselves by the architect at the time, anchoring the building with its vernacular references in the Hungarian culture and with its religious symbolism in the Jewish culture. Its brick architecture similarly made reference to Nordic and Scandinavian models of national

Romanticism and placed the school complex in a wider international architectural context. At that time many nations, among them the Finns, Estonians, Latvians and also the Hungarians, were searching for an architectural language of their own, which gave rise to a variety of cross-references in their architecture. [Fig. 3]

The same means also signified its emancipation from Viennese influence, which was then dominant. For the blind children, most of this was of little consequence except for the haptic decorations Lajta provided in Braille on the site's outer fence, which featured quotations from classical works of Hungarian literature.

The new buildings by 3h architects assume a lower profile than their pre-existing neighbours, and there are only a few direct connections between the old and new buildings, the latter being glazed to mitigate any jarring confrontation between the two. The new, plain white rendered walls recede, allowing the richly ornamented surfaces of the old buildings to take centre stage. Overall, the new additions are respectful, with façades that are predominantly sober and discreet. Here, the architects have refrained from any ornamentation of their own. But the architects did not completely renounce all decoration: within the buildings there are carefully placed colourful accents, and the design of the ceilings in the swimming pool and canteen introduces an ornamental structure of its own. Circular recesses in the pool's ceiling, together with the luminous spots of light reflected on the water's surface, create an ornamental pattern through their sequential repetition, at the same time inducing an atmosphere of warmth and safety.

Béla Lajta and Ödön Lechner were both proponents of a new, emancipated Hungarian architecture at the beginning of the 20th century and were both known for their use of ornamentation. Béla Lajta's trade school on Vas utca [Fig. 4] in the 8th district of Budapest from 1912 showcases the narrative use of decorative elements by this architect even more demonstratively than the institute for the blind. Here, Lajta distilled his formal programme into a pictorial narrative about the contents taught within the school building.

Geometria

Another example of 3h architects' increasing preoccupation with incorporating ornamentation into their architecture is the Geometria office building in the Buda district of the city. Due to its narrow street frontage, the building extends deep into the urban block and was given extensive glazing to optimally illuminate the offices within. The tight confines of the block interior, however, also resulted in partially intrusive views. The architects applied a screen of dots to the glass surfaces, obstructing views in from outside, but still allowing the people within a view of their surroundings. The grid of printed matt dots serves as a simple ornamental device on the façade and creates a play of shifting shadows inside that is at once functional and decorative. The principle recalls that of the mashrabiya screens in Ottoman or Arabic architecture, that allow light and air to pass through and the residents to see out, but screen the inhabitants from prying eyes. [Fig. 5]

Both these examples, are, however, little more than warming-up exercises in decoration and ornamentation. One has the impression that the architects carefully identified opportunities to incorporate decorative elements that augment the building's functional design. All the elements serve a purpose and their design codes are very simple. In the case of the school and its magnificent old building, the general tenor of the architects' insertion is of a restrained aesthetic that steps out of character momentarily with a demonstrative statement. Their approach is in effect that of the Modernists with a few slight deviations.

A Festival of Ornaments

The architects have greater scope for action when it comes to extending or augmenting historical building fabric and they make the most of it. The first challenge that the formal disposition of the pre-existing building presents is whether modern additions should augment or contrast with the historical building substance. For a long time, the dominant modern attitude was the principle of confrontation. Carlo Scarpa in Italy, and to a certain extent also Eduardo Souto de Moura in Portugal, allowed the authenticity of the old traditional elements to come to the fore by placing them against a deliberately simple, often contrasting foil. In terms of materiality, these could be exposed concrete or a Corten steel panel.

[Fig. 1] Adolf Loos, House Michaelerplatz, Vienna

[Fig. 2] David Chipperfield, Neues Museum, Berlin

[Fig. 3] Béla Lajta, school for the blind, Budapest

[Fig. 4] Béla Lajta, trade school, Budapest

[Fig. 5] 3h, Dotted windows of the Geometria office building, Budapest

[Fig. 6] Giuseppe Pagnano, Museo d'Arte Sacra San Nicola, Militello in Val di Catania, 1985

[Fig. 8] Nevzat Sayın, residences and studio, Yahşibey

[Fig. 7] Han Tümertekin, SALT Beyoglu, Istanbul

[Fig. 9] 3h, gallery hall in Esterházy Castle, Fertőd

[Fig. 10] 3h, undercroft of Szeged Cathedral

[Fig. 11] 3h, altar, Szeged Cathedral

[Fig. 12] Wall painting of the Madonna, Szeged Cathedral

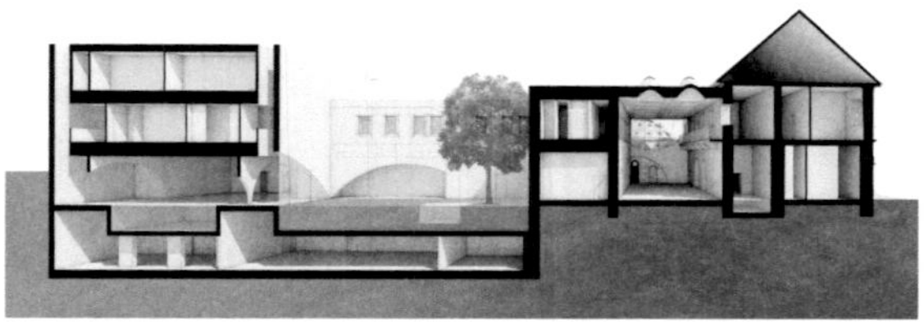

[Fig. 13] 3h, Turkish Király Baths, Budapest

His pupil Giuseppe Pagnano, who has worked in Sicily since the 1980s, took this principle of the frank encounter of old and new to a new level, differentiating between them by means of their formal elaboration and materiality to achieve a high degree of harmony between old and new. [Fig. 6]

The Scarpa principle has also influenced a generation of Turkish architects: Han Tümertekin's architectural handling of 19th-century buildings in Istanbul is forthright and unapologetic in its handling of the confrontation between old and new. He has no reservations about leaving the jagged edges of demolished substance exposed, as can be seen in his SALT cultural centre in Istiklal Street in the Beyoglu district of Istanbul, completed in 2010. [Fig. 7] His colleague Nevzat Sayın took a similar approach with his additions to the village of Yahşibey in southwestern Turkey. Aside from the sensitive insertion of his new buildings into the existing structure of the village, he incorporates traditional natural masonry elements, so that they appear like quotations within his otherwise modern architecture. [Fig. 8]

David Chipperfield, in contrast, took a completely different direction in his design for the Neues Museum. In response to the debate in Berlin on the uncompromising reconstruction of lost buildings and the uncritical reconstruction of the old façades of the Berliner Schloss, he explored a different, interpretative transition between the authentic, preserved historical substance and the new building fabric that augments it.

Esterházy Castle in Fertőd

As part of their contextual approach, 3h architects draw on the traces that they find in the pre-existing situation – and thus also on any surviving ornamentation. These traces serve as a basis from which they develop an architectural concept for their project. The renovation and restoration of the Baroque Esterházy Castle in Fertőd, which the 3h architects have been working on since 2014, presented an opportunity to explore ornamentation on a grand scale. [Fig. 9]

In the interiors of the west wing, very little of the original Baroque substance remained intact except for a few wall murals. This was especially unfortunate in that the Baroque and Rococo periods in Hungary were particularly rich in ornamentation and decorative forms. Resisting the temptation to draw on the historical canon of forms for their reconstruction of the new interior, and in particular of the gallery hall, the architects instead sought to revive the spirit of the late Baroque and early Rococo period in a contemporary form. They have succeeded in doing this most dramatically!

On entering the exhibition wing, the visitor is welcomed by a foyer that immediately recalls the splendour of the Baroque. The floor of white and dark green marble, inlaid in a diagonal grid of precise squares, employs a three-dimensional illusion, tricking the eye into oscillating between two and three dimensions. The floor's distinctive patterning reflects in the brushed stainless steel of the curved oval reception desk, causing its gently curving shape to come alive with the ornamental pattern of the surroundings. The walls, by contrast, act as a soothing counterpart and lend the room the necessary stability, their calm grey wallpaper patterned with subtle golden floral shapes. What a prelude!

From here the visitor passes through quite narrow doors into the gallery hall. Here the geometric pattern of the inlaid marble floor can be seen to full effect and the white walls and white metal coffered ceiling divided into illuminated rectangles, squares and long lines create a fitting frame for the whole. The room is a modern interpretation of the Baroque that consciously plays on one's memory of this stylistic period. Less abstract but nevertheless discreet, the architects employ a similar formal interpretation for the newly installed doors leading from the foyer into the enfilade along one side. Here too, newly devised ornaments on the painted walls, so natural as to be almost imperceptible, complement the reconstructed historical building.

Only in a small cabinet-like gallery, reached via a recessed door in the middle of the rear wall of the large gallery hall, do the architects switch back to more conventional material aesthetics. Here, wood panelling, with carefully aligned wood grain and parquet flooring, determine the atmosphere of the room, where music scores used by Joseph Haydn are on display that bear witness to his time here at the Castle in Fertőd.

In the Esterházy Castle, the dialogue between old and new is not one of confrontation. Here, sober restraint has not been used to bring out the opulent expressiveness of historical forms. Instead, a new architectural creation carries forward the narrative of the Baroque in new materials and with dramatic new devices.

Cathedral of Szeged

Like the palace in Fertőd, the reorganisation of Szeged Cathedral presented 3h architects with a similar opportunity to work with an existing building. Like many such buildings, the cathedral has a long history and predecessor buildings that stood on the same site, of which many traces still exist. Most of the cathedral, however, was built in the 1920s and 1930s in a neo-Romanesque style following a design by the architects Frigyes Schulek and Ernő Foerk, who gave the nave in particular a distinctly national romantic character.

The renovation from 2012 to 2015 gave 3h architects the opportunity to add new layers of their own to the palimpsest. The cathedral's tower and undercroft [Fig. 10] were to be dedicated to new purposes. A café for pilgrims, a reception and exhibition area, a parish hall and a *columbarium* were added, along with new entrances to the underground areas. The newly designed areas adopt a basic palette of bright white walls and a grey concrete floor, with certain places highlighted by accents – oil-fired steel panels, sections of historical street paving, the foundations of the former church or the wood grain of new furniture set between the massive stone piers. For the most part, these serve a specific purpose or employ the aesthetics of the material as an accent. The colourful floral tiling of the counter area in the café, on the other hand, serves no specific purpose other than to draw attention to itself. It recalls old Hungarian folk art, while also being reminiscent of the colours and ceramic art of the Ottoman period, both of which make reference to Hungary's history. The paravent-like wall of oil-fired steel panels that surround the remnants of the walls of the old Romanesque church can be interpreted similarly. Illuminated from behind, light shines through the grid of successively narrowing square holes, recalling the lattice-like screens of the Ottoman *mashrabiya,* that conceal what lies behind, elevating it to something secret and precious.

Like the insertions below ground, the architects' additions to the exterior of the cathedral are similarly restrained. The stone plateau in front of the main portal has been raised slightly and paved with a light-coloured stone, extending out far enough to clasp the free standing Romanesque tower. The only demonstratively new elements are the dark railings and balustrades. In the evening, light emits from the entrances to the undercroft and filters through openings in the cathedral steps, pointing discreetly to the new functions below.

The architects adopt a different approach for their interventions in the nave. The most obvious of these is the simple clarity of the new wooden pews. A highlight is the new main altar made of white marble, which takes the form of a simple block into which an ornamental pattern has been CNC-milled so delicately as to resemble a textile covering. [Fig. 11] It blends harmoniously into the formal language of its surroundings, while making its own clearly perceptible contribution to the ornamental diversity of the altar and choir space. An important source of inspiration here was the distinctly Hungarian painting of the Madonna in the cathedral ceiling's vault. [Fig. 12]

Ornament and Orient

All four works by 3h architects are a promising indication of the future work of the office. This is especially true of their plans for the reorganisation of the old Király Thermal Baths in Budapest's 1st district. The original thermal baths date back to the Ottoman period in Hungary. Over time various Baroque and classicist additions were made, and the baths were also later rebuilt and extended several times. Once again, the architects have been faced with various layers and mixtures of historical architectural forms, surfaces and structures, which are to be placed in a new architectural context. The reference to Ottoman building culture here is appropriate given the respectable legacy that remained in Hungary after the Ottomans departed from Hungary in the 17th century. In Budapest, this is most evident in the city's historical spas. The Ottoman contribution to ornamentation is also noteworthy: the strict prohibition of imagery in Islamic culture led over the centuries not only to the calligraphic refinement of writing but also to a highly developed culture of abstract ornamentation.

The treatment of Ottoman tradition in Hungary represents a particular challenge for the architects in the context of renovating and converting one of Budapest's oldest thermal baths. The design must respect and reflect the many different layers of history that the building has acquired over the centuries, so that these are experienced by the visitor.

3h architects' design is promising. It shows a series of carefully inserted new buildings that add a new layer to the complex of baths. [Fig. 13] For the first time, the original building takes centre stage. A new long hall affords a view of the Ottoman thermal baths' impressive cupola before one enters through the reopened original doorways. The new hall is a modern reference to the *hamamlar,* the Ottoman steam baths, whose history in Hungary does not reach as far back as the thermal baths in Turkey. A centrally heated octagonal stone and a fountain are the dominant elements of this space, which is lit from above by a multitude of small domes that will be lined with Iznik tiles imported directly from Turkey. If realised as planned, the spatial design and ornamentation of the new baths has the potential to convey through its architecture the meeting of Hungarian and Ottoman-Turkish cultures.

3h architects have been fortunate to work in the context of a wide range of buildings rich in ornamentation that can still be found in all temporal and spatial layers of architectural history across Budapest and indeed throughout Hungary. Their approach, which involves elevating ornament to a key element of their architecture, makes an important contribution to a new culture of architecture – one that respects local and historical origins. With each new project, the architects reveal their ongoing process of careful research and questioning, whether in the respectful gestures of the extension to Béla Lajta's school for the blind, the simple dotted ornaments on the façade of the Geometria office building or the resplendent array of shapes and ornaments in Esterházy Castle and Szeged Cathedral. 3h architects employ ornament not just as a decorative form, but also as an atmospheric device with which to establish new dialogues and correspondences between the old and the new.

Inspiration from the Empty and the Full

Refurbishment
of Szeged Cathedral,
Szeged
2012 – 2015

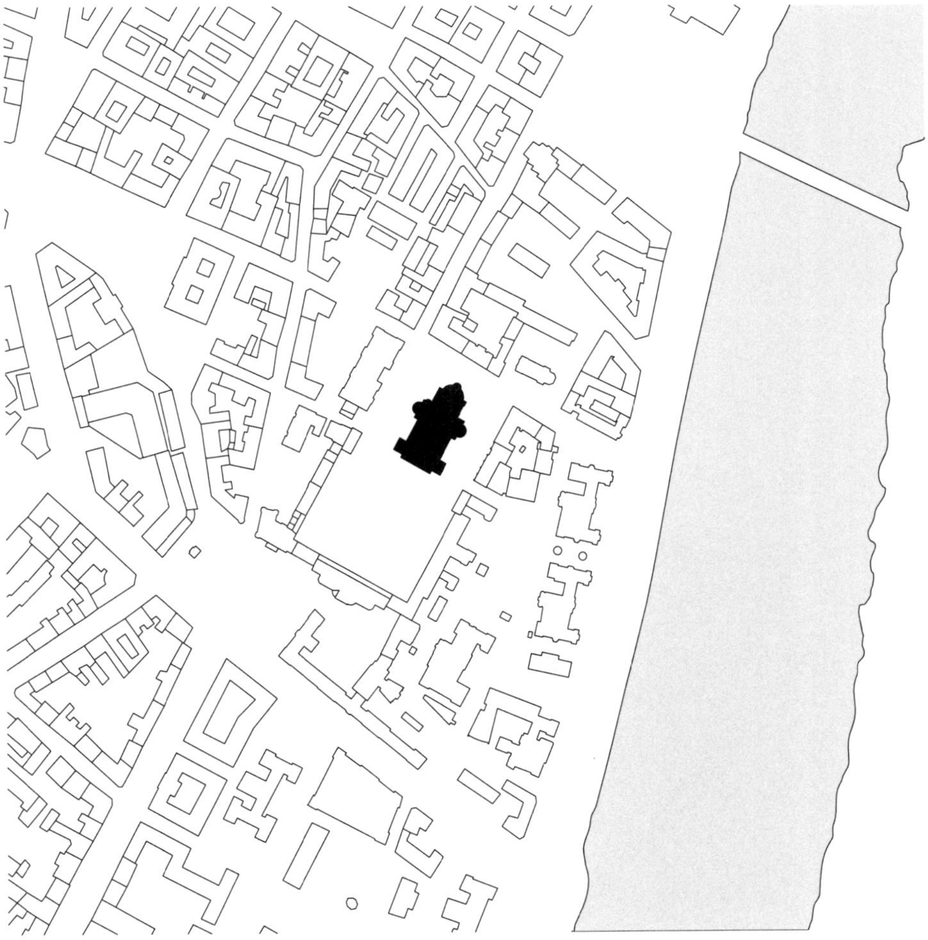

Longitudinal section through the cathedral

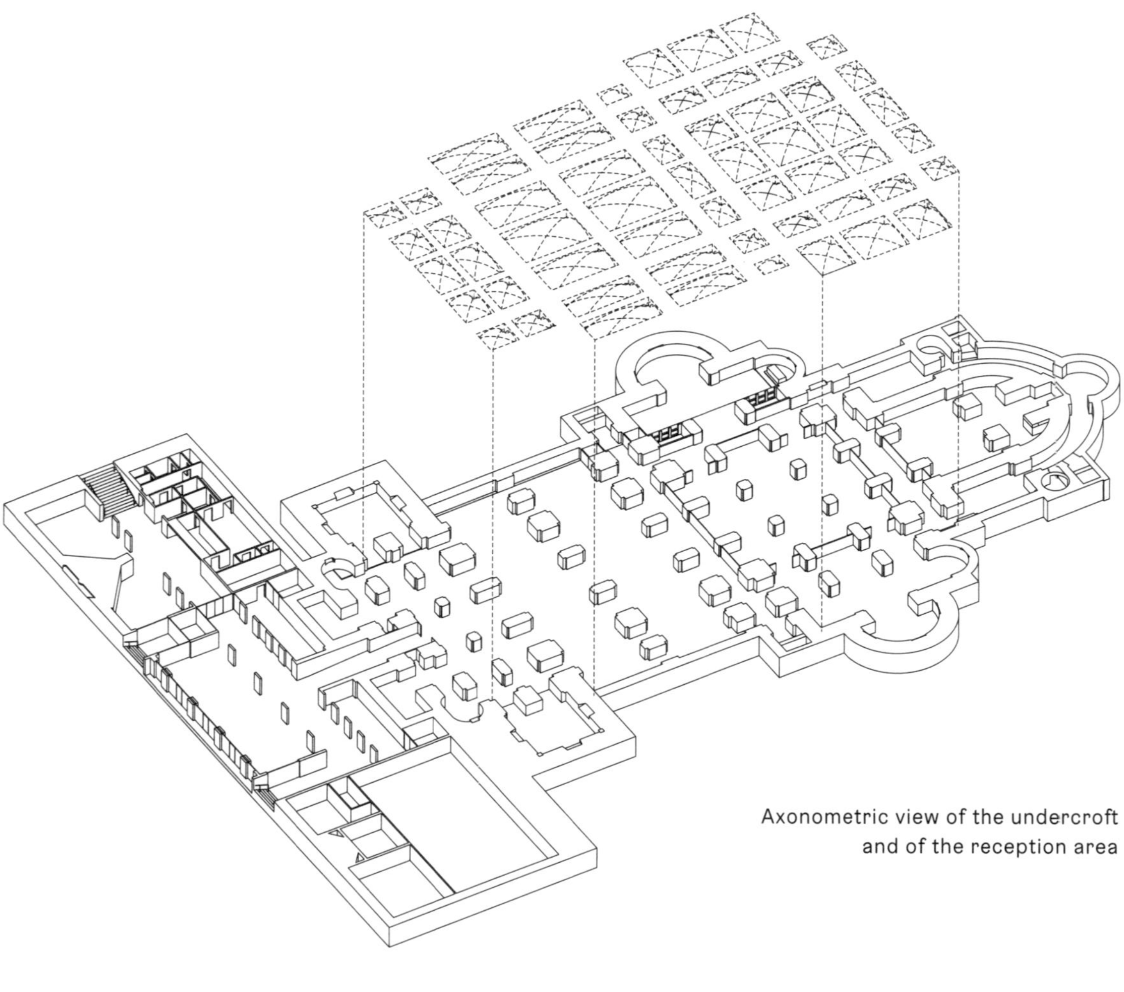

Axonometric view of the undercroft
and of the reception area

While working with historical buildings it became clear to us that the architectural dialogue with previous ages interests us greatly. We have always examined the relationship to historical buildings, which aptly characterises our connection with the past. Modern architecture has opened up many doors, yet it has also closed several. Some of the new possibilities have proved schematic. In fact, what Modernism rejected is beginning to be interesting again. Let us consider what such themes are. Manifold historical spaces are one such theme, while another is the issue of ornamentation. With the renovation of Szeged Cathedral we consciously faced these issues.

One of the key questions concerning the reorganisation of the cathedral was how to use the unutilised spaces and to improve the circulation of visitors and pilgrims. The central space within the cathedral had to be modified for liturgical considerations, while further space was required to open up the building for the purposes of tourism. We found these spaces in the undercroft.

The undercroft's construction is massive with very limited spaces in between. The repetition of vaulted areas results in a soldierly sequence of intervening spaces. The arched surfaces display the softness and spatial variety which often characterise historical architecture. This is where we placed space for exhibitions and new functions as well as the *columbarium.* The reception area underneath the cathedral's foreground is an extension of the undercroft. The entrance was designed by reversing the direction of part of the main steps on two sides, such that the reception area, the shop for ecclesiastical items and the Pilgrims' Cafeteria can be accessed by them. In this suite of in-between spaces the repetition of elongated pillars brings back the undercroft's pulsating rhythm, yet the view of the system of ribs providing space for light prevails rather than the vaults.

What does one do at the boundary of historical and contemporary alignment of spaces? The transition provides an opportunity for dialogue between past and future, a chance for finding connections between the two approaches. This point represents the eye of the needle, the most intensive adventure of space where one spatial quality turns into another. The sensitive transition between flat and curved parts is ensured by an irregular surface – this is unusual, as it is not connected to the site but rather to a specific spatial experience. The spaciousness of the reception area narrows and gives way to the repetitive sequences of heavy pillars and vaults.

The use of ornamentation was another main theme. Historicism is characterised by a stereotypical excess of decoration. The dull repetition of elements always made us feel some kind of surfeit. However, there are moments when in the cathedral the monotony of the canon is broken and unusual elements appear on the surfaces. The sources of inspiration for us included the Szeged Madonna's embroidery patterns, which now appear as a ceiling fresco. The high altar beneath the Madonna adopted embroidery motifs used in the town's vicinity and developed them into a repeating pattern, which was cut into a marble slab using jets of water. Thus, the side of the high altar can be perceived as a decorative altar cloth carved in stone.

From then on the method was quite clear. The characteristic feature of the newly applied ornaments is meaningful simplification accompanied by a change of scale. In addition, we emphasised materiality throughout, often embracing low-value materials. We also applied cutting-edge technologies, including digital techniques. That was how the system of grilles using the pattern that imitates flower beds on Dóm Square and the steel inlays of the railings closing off the space in front of the cathedral were formed. The panelling in the Pilgrims' Cafeteria on the bottom floor of the 13th-century Dömötör Tower was made from perforated and oil-blackened steel sheets. The gradual enlargement of the holes makes the texture of the damaged brick surface behind it increasingly palpable. The enigmatic effect is reinforced by the light dimly cast on the brick surface. In the same space *terrazzo* sheets appearing on the vertical walls of the counter echo the mosaic-like pattern and materiality of the liturgical space.

The examples show that it was essential to connect the new parts to the existing ones, either abstractly or concretely. We added fresh surfaces and objects interpreted in a contemporary way to the atmosphere of Historicism in such a manner that, in line with our intentions, each element reinforces the unity of space and detail in the reorganised cathedral.

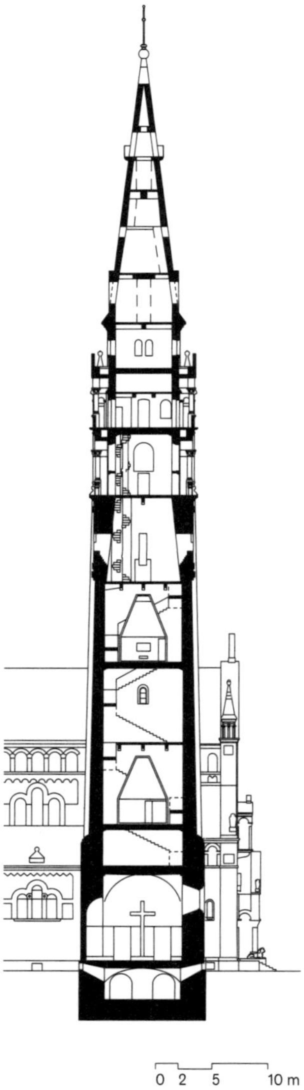

Cross section of the cathedral tower with new volumes

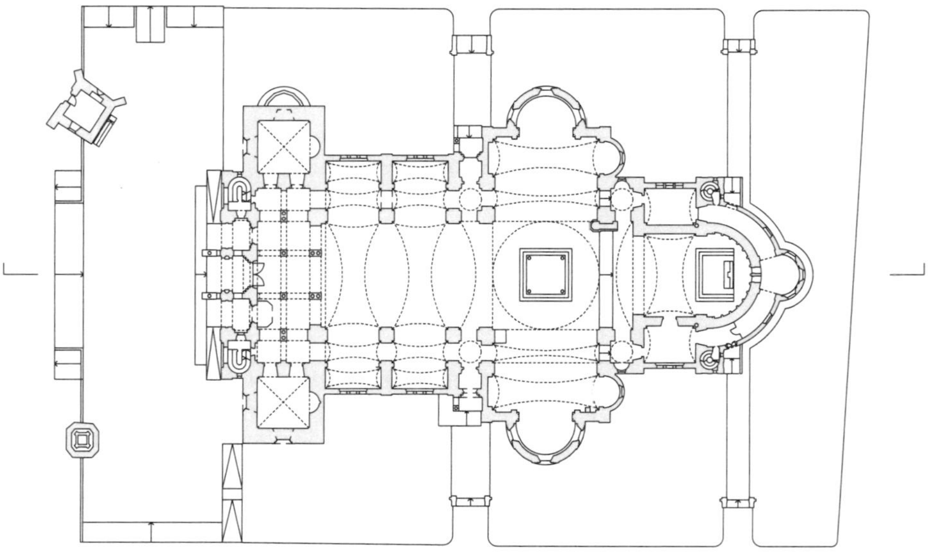

Plan of the liturgical floor level

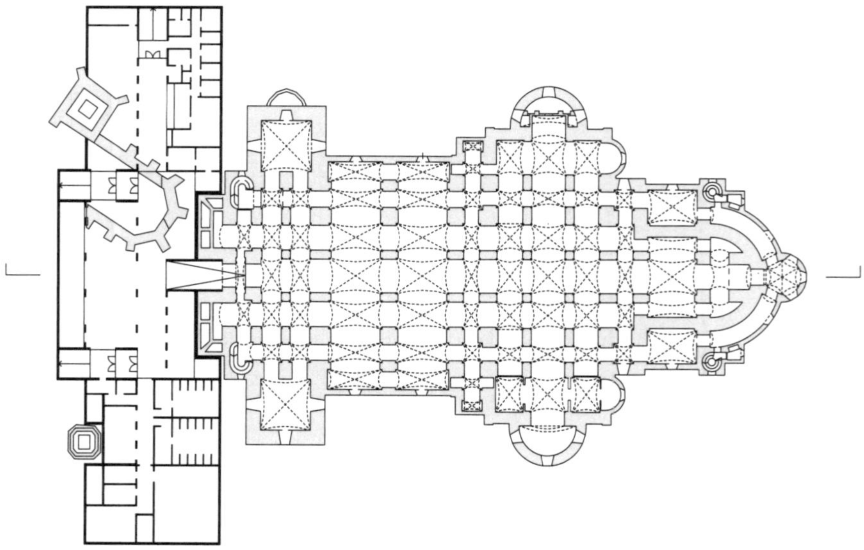

Plan of the undercroft

The group of architectural elements in the square is of restrained character. The steel staircase of the Dömötör Tower appears almost as a shadow. The stairs leading to the elevated open space in front of the cathedral and to the visitor centre can be perceived as a continuation of the parapet material.

After the great flood of Szeged, Béla Rerrich designed Dóm Square and the surrounding buildings between 1928 and 1930, so that the buildings would represent a united ensemble with the cathedral.

The patterns of the new altar were produced by simplifying local folk motifs and were created in marble using waterjet cutting.

Paths written in white unify the undercroft's space. The brass-clad gate of the *columbarium* appears at the end of one of the vaulted passageways.

During renovation the canopy was taken from the chancel to below the crossing by being cut above the pillars and transported in one piece. A new altar had to be erected in the central space.

The construction of towers took place in the 1920s with reinforced concrete structures that corresponded to the style of the times. From today's perspective, incredibly thin structures were made, into which we have installed communal spaces as volumes within volumes on every other level.

The perforated steel sheet conceals the underground brick wall of the Dömötör Tower. The bricks were in bad condition due to the floods and thus had to be covered. The perforation and the lighting make the tower's formerly hidden presence palpable.

The oil-blackened steel sheets of the Dömötör Tower and the terrazzo tiles displayed on the vertical walls of the kitchen area appear as accented highlights in the cafeteria's neutral interior.

The *columbarium* underneath the chancel follows the geometry of the undercroft. The spaces emanate an intimate atmosphere.

The reconstruction of the side chapels under both towers was one of our tasks. The refurnishing of the Baptismal Chapel has created a worthy place for ceremonies.

The structural system of the undercroft still exhibits 19th-century features. The system of heavy pillars and arches constructed of bricks was minimally supplemented in order that the space could be perceived as a whole.

The chancel wall of the much older Saint Demetrius Church, discovered at the time of the construction, is now displayed in the visitors' centre. It explains the strange position of the Dömötör Tower in the square from where visitors can walk now to the undercroft with its ecclesiastical collection.

A new reception area with elongated pillars and ceiling girders has been implanted to intertwine visually the inside and the outside, the Dóm Square and the undercroft.

The elevated open space in front of the cathedral has been covered with limestone. It was logical to use this material for the new stairs and entrance flooring to emphasise its continuity with the existing building.

Baroque Minimum

Picture Gallery
and Exhibition Space,
Esterházy Castle,
Fertőd
2014 – 2019

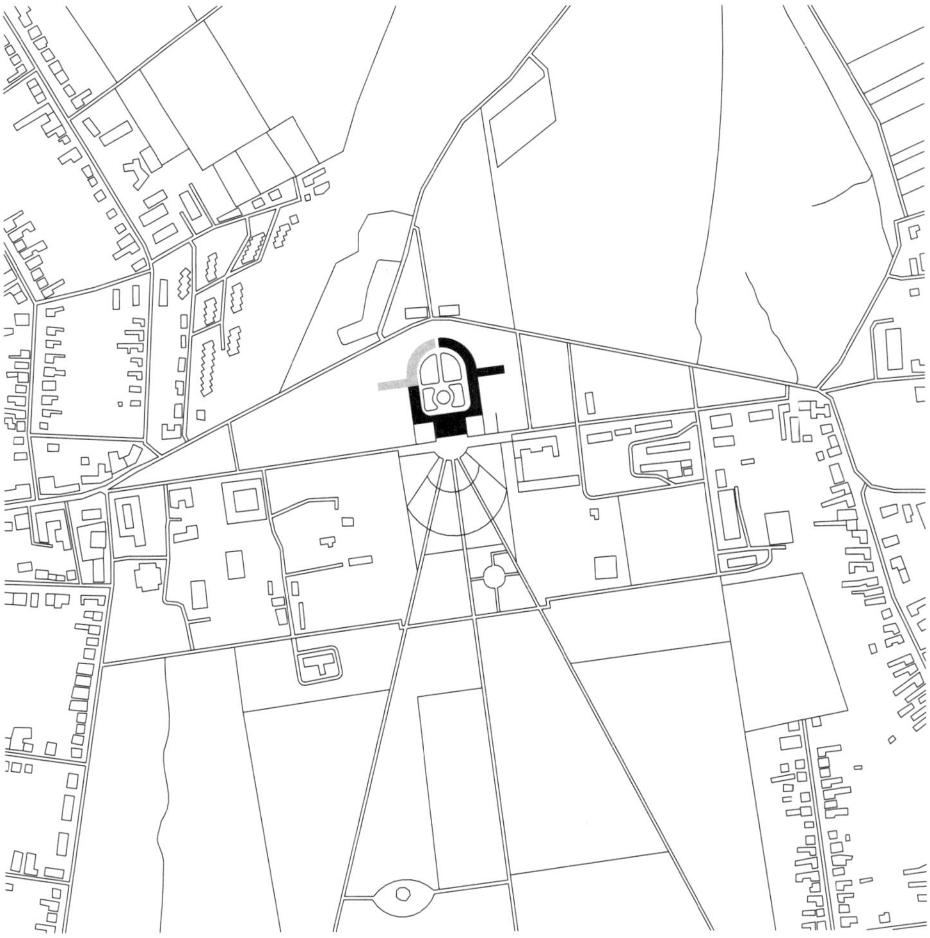

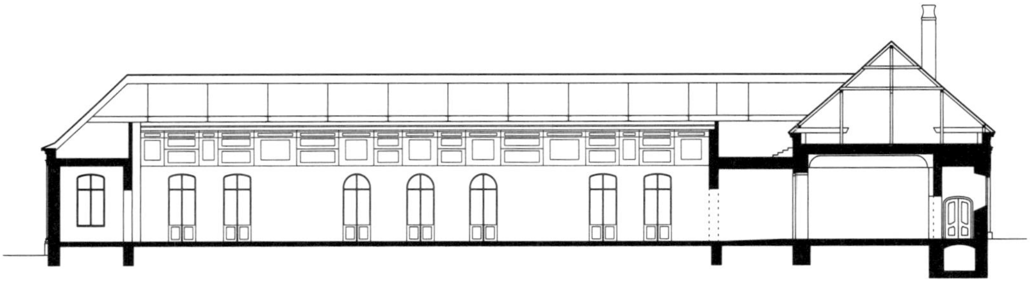

Longitudinal section through the picture gallery

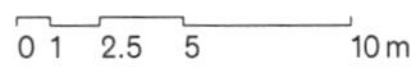

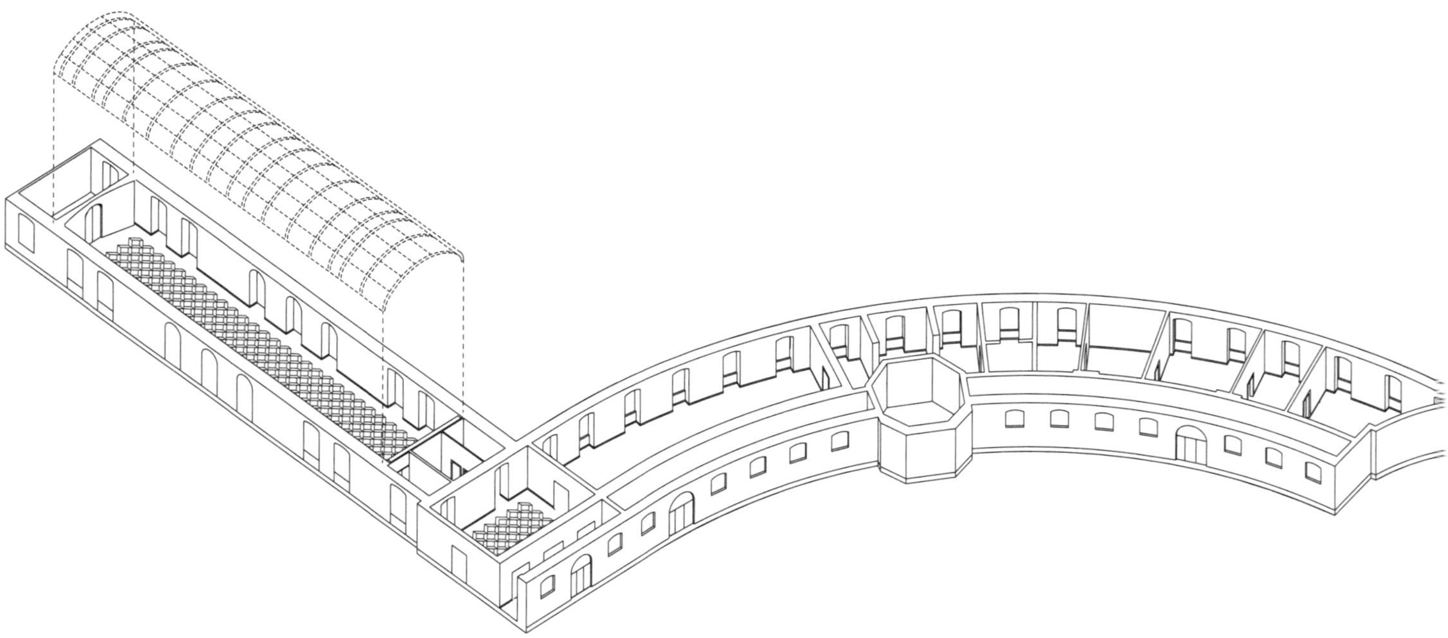

According to T. S. Eliot, history defines the present in advance in the same way as the present influences the perception of the past. No single serious work of art can be interpreted without this dialogue. If we look behind the meaning of these ideas, what is at stake is not only the interdependence of past and present, but also our relationship to an existing work – in this case to a building. More concretely, if we cannot interpret historical buildings from today's perspective and shape them in line with this interpretation, we not only miss an opportunity, we explicitly make a mistake, since we do not allow the voice of our times to be heard.

We kept these principles in mind when restoring the Esterházy Castle. The palace ensemble is one of the most important Baroque historical monuments in Hungary. The first impression visitors have is the feeling of unity and elevation when they see the grandiose inner courtyard or the central *risalit* coming into sight from the park on the other side. The spatial arrangement of the Baroque palace faithfully reflects the hierarchy of use at the time. The princely and royal suites in the middle *risalit* are more prominent than other parts of the building, partly due to their location within the building and partly due to their size and pomp.

We converted the far less ornamental ground floor of the western wing into an exhibition space: the western horseshoe wing originally accommodated the staff, while its lateral extension wing outside the central courtyard served as a secondary space for ceremonies and celebrations. The use of both wings has changed much over the years and a large part of the original walls and wall and ceiling painting can no longer be reconstructed. This freed us from some constraints in such a way that we were able to break away from a precise restoration of the past. Our plan abstracted and transformed the Baroque architectural elements and then refitted them into the design. During the process old and new elements were set in dialogue, sometimes a tense one, sometimes in agreement.

The reception of the new exhibition space was created by converting the former pool area, which had been constructed in the western horseshoe wing in the 1920s. Here, in order to approach it along its axis we opened up a new door in the inner courtyard façade, made to resemble the others. The cloakroom, the toilets, the suite of rooms for temporary exhibitions in this wing and the picture gallery are accessible from the courtyard with a newly installed reception area. Illusion is an attribute of the Baroque and frequently appears in a spatial way, often on the ceilings or floor coverings. We began to employ it consciously in the reception area. The spatiality of diamond shapes on the floor is reinforced by marble slabs polished in various ways. A refined, contemporary chandelier has been placed in the middle of the room, which illuminates both the ceiling and the floor through its ground prisms. The distorted image of the floor and the walls appears as reflections in the curving mounted surface of the new reception counter.

The picture gallery at the end of the lateral wing was once used as a gymnasium by the agricultural school that operated in the building after 1945. It was possible to reconstruct its original ground-plan with the help of the 1784 description of the castle and on the basis of how the walls stood. Yet there were no precise data about the nature of the ceiling, since only the walls were left after World War II and the ceiling was replaced by reinforced concrete. We reached back to historical precursors: the barrel-vaulted, coffered ceiling is a characteristic element of Baroque architecture. Its surface is divided into rectangular coffered panels where the sky often appears as the background in ceiling paintings. Pure white light behind the panelled *Barrisol* foil now symbolises the sky here. The panels stand out vividly from the vaulted surface. The gaps between them conceal the mechanical air supply and lighting busbar systems. The lighting panels were constructed on carriers of bent plywood, which hang down from steel holders. The space leading towards the western cabinet was closed with an irregular surface around the door, and ventilation has been resolved invisibly.

In the middle of the horseshoe wing the octagonal, irregular area of the former porcelain chamber was reconstructed following the line of the foundation walls. Thus, the suite of spaces in the wing towards the landscaped garden has been re-established. The walls of three of those rooms have been reconstructed on the basis of patterns we discovered during our research. A larger space next to the reception area was established in place of the former library.

However, our work did not end there. The redesigning of the three-storey building connecting the middle *risalit* to the wing has also already begun. Its chief embellishment will be the treasury on the first floor, which will be supplemented with a temporary exhibition space on the ground floor and storage space for art objects above. Since we are directly close to the historical middle *risalit,* the transcripts of spaces are perceptibly gentler.

Our design strategy, treating new and old as a unit, explicitly involves a pragmatic rather than theoretical approach. During our work we strove to continue telling the story begun by our predecessors, sometimes almost unnoticed. It is a kind of architectural narrative, which seeks the connection between the historical and the contemporary. If not in style or materiality, the added insertions assimilate to the old in their spatial concept and essence and thus form a unity. They certainly turn the listed monument back into a building for contemporary culture.

The complex, built between 1762 and 1766, was created by reconstructing and extending a hunting lodge that had previously stood here. Its appearance reflects the taste of Prince Nikolaus I, who favoured splendour.

In order to maintain the necessary air quality, visitors reach the picture gallery from the foyer through a double-door system.

The western chamber joins the other end of the picture gallery. Its intimate atmosphere is emphasized by the walnut cladding.

The picture gallery, the space for temporary exhibitions and the cloakroom can be accessed from the newly installed reception foyer. The use of materials recalls the playful illusions of the Baroque and the Rococo.

The appearance of the reinterpreted picture gallery is based on the powerful overall image of the ceiling and floor. All technical elements have been concealed in the new structures.

The windows looking out onto the courtyard enable light to reach the corridor on the ground floor of the horseshoe wing. Its arched layout and changing light add mystery to this route.

The gallery's ceiling is a reinterpretation of Baroque coffered ceilings. Surface lighting has been installed in the new panels in place of the former depiction of the sky.

The octagonal porcelain chamber, of which only the exterior walls had survived, has been reconstructed. It fulfils its original function again. Its interior walls with the new openings in the walls present a unique spatial situation in the flow of the exhibition.

The various epochs amalgamate in the transformed wing of the castle. The photograph shows the newly reconstructed wall coverings dating from the 18th century to the beginning of the 20th century.

Spaces of Water

Király Thermal Baths, Budapest 2017–

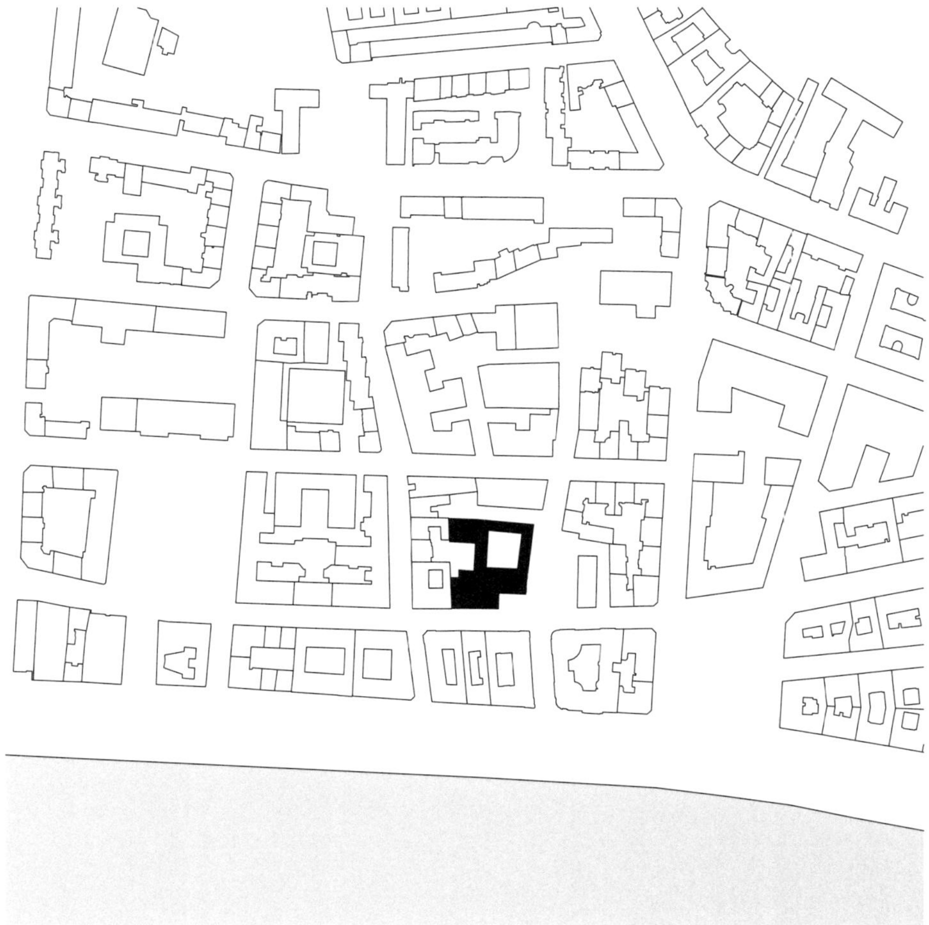

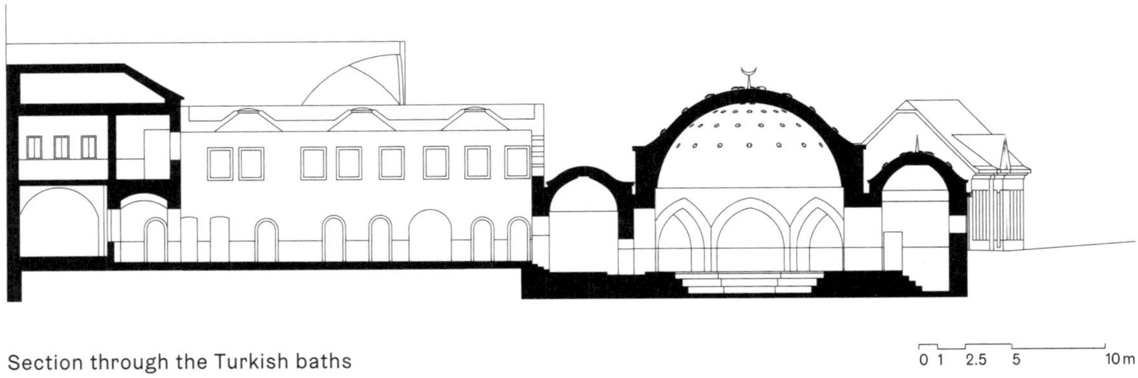

Section through the Turkish baths

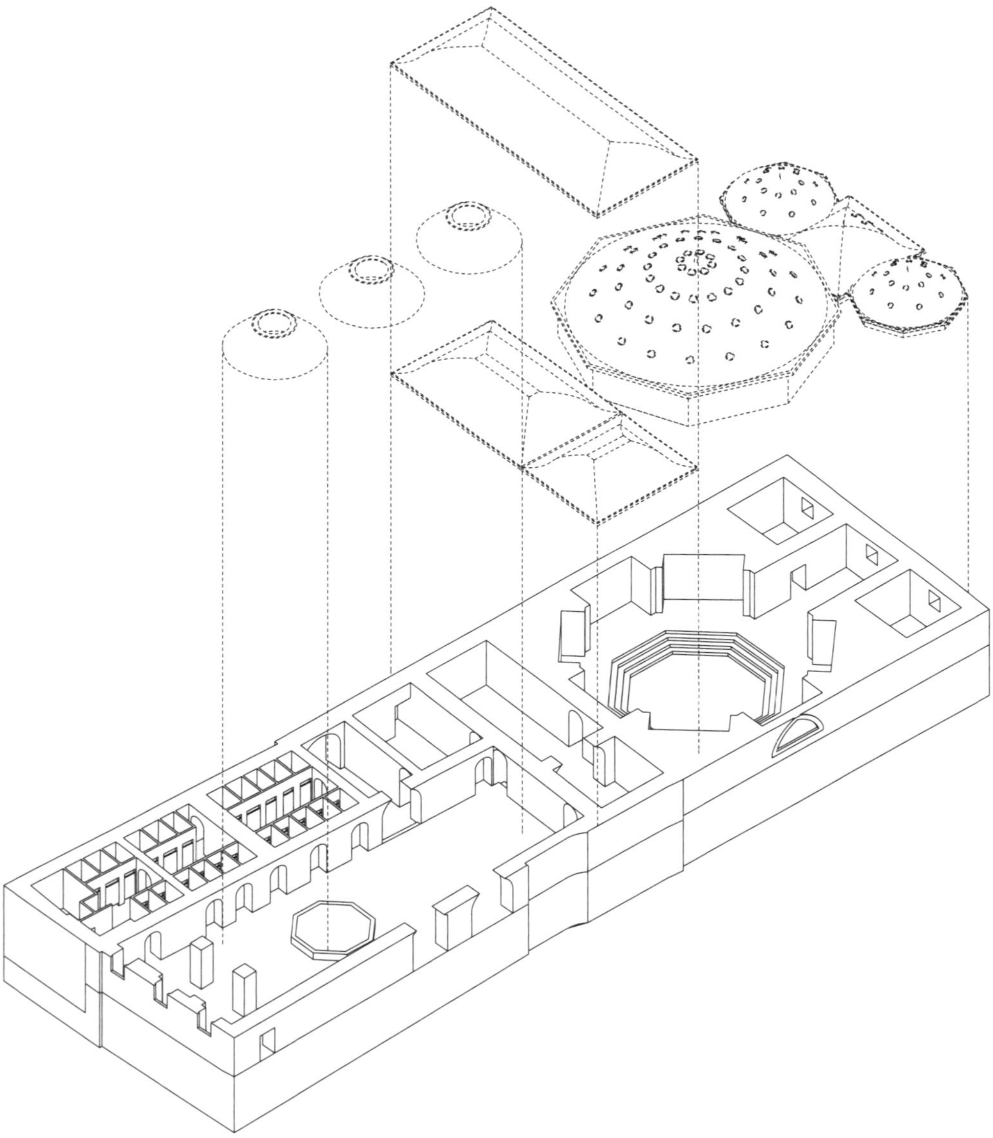

Water as a meditative medium has always attracted us in our work. The refurbishment of the Király Baths provided the perfect pretext for studying water as an element that influences the psyche and also for recognising how forceful the cultural aspect of bathing is. Besides the experience of spatial structure and architectural elements, this building constantly supplies us with a number of defining and subconscious stimuli. Here, water is simultaneously present in a variety of forms and is accompanied by a variety of scents and physical states: water vapour, steam and hot water itself are mixed in various spaces, joined by the distinctive aroma of thermal water and the flickering light created by the waves in the mysterious interior.

We believe that the ritual of bathing should not be a superficial experience, but rather a deep, profound and holistic one. The atmosphere of the Turkish bath commanded our way of thinking: instead of the loud, spatial and material experiences of today, we were drawn towards a meditative ambience. Besides water, light is another mystical element in a Turkish bath, it always enters the space from above and the rays penetrate deep into the bath. The bath itself evokes the image of a cave offering safety and cleansing.

Király Baths is one of the most authentic baths of the Ottoman era in Budapest. Its unique appearance is the result of the layers of different historic periods. The oldest part from the Ottoman era is joined by a Baroque building in the south, which in turn is flanked in the west by a classicist courtyard, its cloister and a succession of rooms. The seemingly random development is complemented by a courtyard in the south. The building as a whole can be regarded as a collage of prints from different times that meet in the present. One responds to the other, and the later integrates the earlier.

With this apparently ad hoc group of buildings, we aimed to restore the original sequence of spaces in the baths. The frigidarium, the original cold room, had been demolished and its place taken by the Baroque courtyard. By covering it over, we reinstated the classic sequence of rooms: frigidarium – tepidarium – caldarium. The inner lighting of the atrium is suitably subdued and is similar to that under the domes, with light entering through small openings. The inside mantle of the truncated, cone-shaped skylights is clad with Iznik tiles. The atrium is also equipped with an octagonal heated stone bench that matches the shape o f the central pool.

By contrast, the porches on each side of the classicistic courtyard are open. According to our plans, this complete openness is reduced in the new pool area. Here the light also gets in via other means: along both of the pool's long walls, it is filtered through from the top; this light also illuminates the storey of the changing rooms. The pool area opens up to the courtyard through a curved arch; light penetrates the space through a sequence of similar arches around the pool. The several historic periods and the layers they left behind create strict spaces and, at the same time, all the more dramatic views.

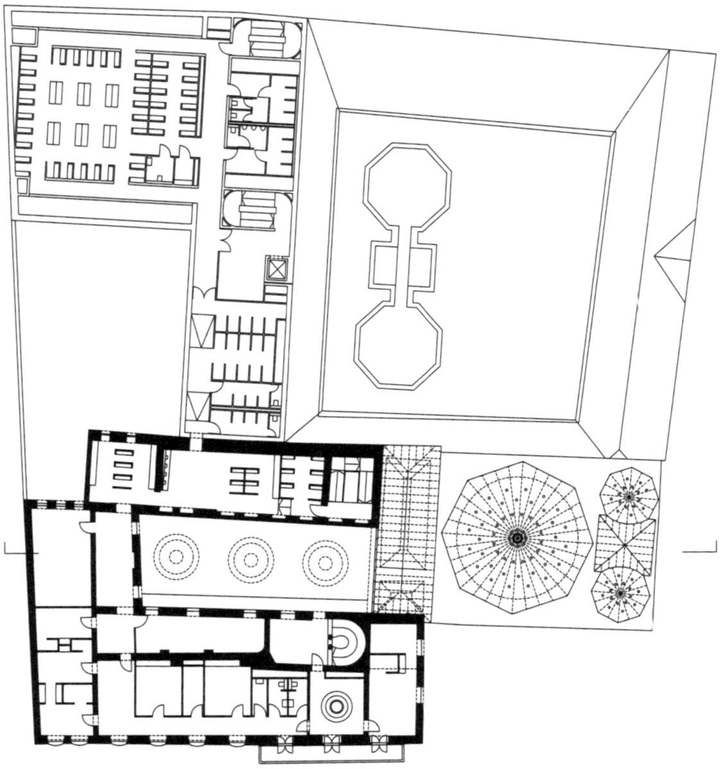

First floor plan

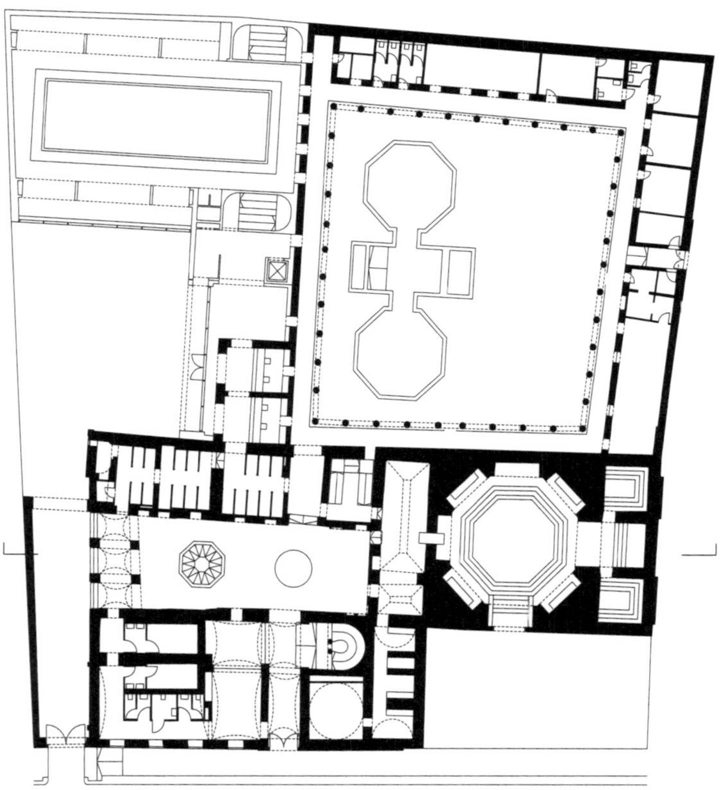

Ground floor plan

The new part of the building occupies the site of the former boiler house, while maintaining the double courtyard character. Turkish, Baroque, classicist and contemporary architecture are all present in the new complex, complementing one another.

The antechamber of the original Turkish baths no longer exists. Covering over the Baroque courtyard, surrounded by various volumes, has created a space that recalls the spirit of the original Turkish baths with light domes and Iznik tiles.

Light penetrating through the dome openings lends a special atmosphere to the old baths. Both the light and the framed views of nature play an important role in the new baths.

"[…] for it was the approaching dawn that held him in its spell, that 'promise kept each morning' that the earth, along with the town and his own person, would emerge from beneath the shadow of the night, and that the delicate glimmer of dawn would yield to the bright light of day …"

— László Krasznahorkai, *The Melancholy of Resistance*

Space and Light

39-40°C
" VIZHŐFOK 40°C "
JAVASOLT FÜRDÉSIDŐ
MAXIMUM 5 PERC
40°C medence
" egyidejű befogadó képessége 2 fő. "

HARCOS

NSFORMATOR
ENDSZER
Ü.SIN
T.SI

We Need Places that Radiate a Certain Tranquillity

A Conversation with the Architects Katalin Csillag and Zsolt Gunther with Claus Käpplinger

Claus Käpplinger 3h architects are based in Budapest. You are both Hungarians who spent several years in Austria after the fall of the Iron Curtain and then made the conscious decision to return to your homeland. What significance does it have today for you and your architecture that you are Hungarians and have lived and worked in Budapest since 2006?

Zsolt Gunther If you take a walk around Budapest, you see many irrational situations. Many streets and squares are a collage of disparate buildings that make little attempt to interact with one another. While there are some very elegant and beautiful works of architecture, there are also many mediocre buildings, especially those that were built in periods of transition when power was shifting from one system or ruler to the next. Because Hungary lies at the junction between East and West, it has often been the site of struggles between very different cultures. The history of Budapest and of Hungary is therefore full of new beginnings under radically different conditions. In these transitional periods, neither building clients nor their architects knew quite what direction to take. As a result, many projects were not a great success, but there are few that are really charming and even inspiring.

Budapest possesses an enormous range of architecture from these interim periods, buildings that vary in style and epoch but that never really reached maturity. For example, there was a form of Stalinism in Hungary called Socialist Realism, which at the time was prescribed by the authorities. The Hungarian architects made something quite different out of it and created an architecture that fused local characteristics with Scandinavian classicism. Four to five years later, however, after Stalin had died, Modernism returned in full force. In Hungary, therefore, it is hard to plan for the long term, and that is still the case today. For this reason, there have not been "pure" styles or co ncepts, and that has without doubt influenced our architecture. [Fig. 1]

Katalin Csillag We were born and live here, which of course has an influence on our architecture. History is always present in Hungary and in Budapest, even when we are not always conscious of it. There is a very refined, sophisticated quality to culture here, especially in architecture. But sometimes one finds oneself in a completely different context, where practicalities dominate, and decisions are made quickly and spontaneously. One sees this in an abundance of opposites, like compactness and expansiveness, restriction and openness or chaos and order. Today, our horizons are broader, and our borders are open. We have greater freedom, for example with respect to ornament and decoration, or collage-like architectural constellations, because nowadays such manifestations are possible and already exist here. There are, however, some limitations. Here in Hungary, much like in Portugal, high-tech architecture makes little sense because we don't have the same technological possibilities as the nations of the West.

Claus Käpplinger The Slovenian philosopher and globalisation critic Slavoj Žižek has repeatedly discussed the specific experiences of Eastern European countries and argues that their experiences of dysfunctional social and economic systems continue to influence contemporary society. Socialism and neo-liberalism have bred a distrust of broad plans and big promises. For this reason, today's Eastern Europe is characterised by a culture of improvisation: instead of grand schemes and ambitious goals, people prefer improvised solutions that can be achieved with limited resources and in the context of rapidly changing political and economic contexts. Does that also apply to your work and your experience of Hungary?

Zsolt Gunther The culture of improvisation in Hungary, and perhaps also in much of Eastern Europe, is without doubt a very important point. Today, we are often faced with the situation that we don't know how far a project will progress and what will become of it. Projects can be halted, and we are not sure when they will restart. We are always under great pressure to adapt to new developments. Our architecture is certainly not one of improvisation, but the circumstances in which they evolve can change abruptly and that has made us much more flexible.

Katalin Csillag We have learned that changes no longer mean the end of the world. We are prepared for the fact that we may have to alter or rethink certain aspects. Modifications are not unusual, and that is something we learned to deal with from our early days in the countryside, where a flexible step-by-step approach with different levels of detail was the only way to work. The villages and small towns of western Hungary were rarely conceived as pre-planned ensembles. Instead, they had very long plots to which successive buildings were added over time with little coordination: first the house, then various ancillary buildings as they became necessary. This additive approach has certainly informed our architectural concepts, and the flexibility this affords can be seen in our buildings. [Fig. 2]

Claus Käpplinger A large proportion of your work at 3h architects involves the extension and conversion of existing buildings. What is it that interests you especially about this work? After all, much is already given, and the architect has to take more account of the existing building substance.

Katalin Csillag It's strange: when we were young, we weren't at all interested in these kinds of projects. We were eager to create completely new architecture. Today, we love dealing with the many layers of old buildings. Old buildings provide the opportunity to develop quite specific and unique dialogues. To reach that point, however, one has to ask many questions and embark on a long process of reading and understanding a building's layers of time. To begin with, for example, we found Szeged Cathedral rather ugly. But with the commission, a very stimulating process of discovery and understanding started. There, as in the Esterházy Castle in Fertőd, one is confronted in particular with the aspect of ornament, which is very characteristic of Eastern Central Europe. In the past, we stayed away from ornamentation. Today, we see it more as a vital element that enriches our architecture.

Zsolt Gunther In Hungary, there is a great fear of emptiness, of unadorned space. For that reason, you see ornaments and decoration almost everywhere you look. Often they are quite exuberant, and often they do not match, resulting in all kinds of discontinuities. Ornamentation is an expression of something irrational that evades logic, but it also gives us surprising freedom in our design and above all is also a way of making connections. Our work is always more than just renovation. Renovation alone would be too little, and others are certainly better at it.

What appeals to us about working with old buildings is the luxury of space they afford. In most cases, the old buildings have lost their original use and their spaces rarely correspond rationally to the planned new uses. The programme of spaces and uses is one aspect, but often the focus lies on the architecture and its spatial impression. They have a surprisingly large number of spaces with no particular purpose. [Fig. 3]

Claus Käpplinger What strategies and goals do you pursue with your architectural interventions, especially when the conservation restrictions applying to historical monuments and to institutions mean they are confined to the interiors? In many cases, one sees little of your projects from outside. One might call them "projects without façades".

Zsolt Gunther Yes, there are often projects, or rather buildings, without façades, in which the structure plays a stronger role and our interventions are more limited but are also clear and decisive. This is something we learned from Lacaton & Vassal, despite our quite different architectural expressions. Often they are interventions that appear at first glance to make only a small change but achieve a great deal. Existing buildings are often stimulating intellectual puzzles, and spectacular interventions are very rarely a good idea. Much of what we do is often not immediately visible and leaves visitors and users guessing, which is part of what makes them interesting. In the case of the visitor centre for the cathedral in Szeged, for example, we eliberately went underground in order to make the existing building stand out more.

Katalin Csillag Of course, old buildings do not exactly meet the requirements of their new uses. There are always residual areas or high spaces, which for us provide a welcome opportunity to work with their spatial qualities and surfaces. Sometimes we find structures that we could not build in the same way today. The underground remnants of the church in Szeged, for example, which were made entirely of brick. [Fig. 4] Or the old reinforced concrete ribs of the existing building of the MOME campus, which have a large mass and are sometimes incredibly thin and sometimes incredibly thick and consequently stimulate our perception and allow us to see the space differently.

Claus Käpplinger Your work frequently makes intensive use of light, and especially natural light. Given the current trend towards very controlled, immaterial light atmospheres, your evident preference for natural light, which is generally hard to control, is surprising. Why do you clearly prefer daylight to artificial light? What role does light play in your architecture?

Zsolt Gunther If we look back in history, the first artificial light was the light of a fire. Our current most recent innovation in this field is the LED. How do they differ? The first, like a candle, is always alive, shaped by wind, temperature and space. LED light, on the other hand, is predictable, precisely replicable, even repetitive. You can, of course, use LEDs to create vibrant atmospheres, but more through programming than architecture. We are much more interested in the unpredictable quality of natural light.

Katalin Csillag My interpretation is slightly different from Zsolt's. When you consider some of the most important buildings of the past, buildings like the Pantheon in Rome, natural light always comes from above. Its attraction is because the sun shines from above. We are, however, more used to light shining in from the side, through windows. Light from above is more natural, more sensual and makes objects appear more natural. That's why we so often create spaces where light can shine in from above. [Fig. 5]

We also try to develop light in combination with the construction or influenced by it to bring it out more clearly or to make it legible in the first place. The underground entrance to the cathedral, for example, was very dark, which is why we deliberately employed the medium of light. The concrete beams are intentionally placed at close, regular intervals as structural elements, and their pattern is brought out using concealed artificial lighting strips. We achieved something similar with natural light, too, by making precise incisions to allow natural light to penetrate into the entrance areas with varying degrees of intensity.

At Esterházy Castle we continued exploring the interplay of light and construction in the picture gallery. To recall the notion of a Baroque-inspired coffered ceiling, we first replaced the existing flat ceiling with a barrel vault. In the space above the new, high ceiling, we incorporated indirect artificial light, so that the entire surfaces of the individual coffers are illuminated. The new supporting structure with its sculptural panels of light makes an abstract reference to Baroque precursors, and in its articulation thus fluctuates between the technoid Modern and painterly Baroque.

Claus Käpplinger There is a particularly haptic sense to the way you use light in that it brings out the qualities of a space and its respective materiality. There are many situations in your buildings where the source of light is not evident, or it enters from another, adjoining space. I'm thinking here of the steps of the square at Szeged or the entrance areas of MOME, where light enters the space through incisions and perforations in the building volume. [Fig. 6]

Zsolt Gunther Yes, our use of natural light often has a spatial quality, because for us light has to do with space and its elements. Artificial light, by contrast, we often conceal or use indirectly. The light circles in MOME are deliberately set apart from the light source. The light connects with the space and emphasises its spatial quality even more.

With natural light, too, we often favour openings through which light enters rather than windows. A window always regulates natural light so that it takes on its form. The window is part of the wall, which establishes a clear boundary between inside and outside.

An opening is something quite different. There is more continuity to the way natural light enters a building. Inside and outside are more closely linked, and the light touches the surfaces of the space. In the Turkish baths in Budapest, we used side openings through which the light can enter almost unhindered. The alternation between the mass of the wall and the void of the opening creates a completely different spatial tension.

Claus Käpplinger So, in your use of light you make a distinction not only between natural and artificial light but also between windows and openings to achieve different spatial atmospheres? What is also apparent is that you use light in conjunction with mass and body and not just space. You employ different means to materialise light in your projects, treating it not just as immaterial light waves but as a kind of haptic force. It must overcome resistance. One sees that it has been wrought, refracted and directed before it alights on a surface.

Katalin Csillag Openings in the form of perforations produce a quite different effect. We see openings as perforations in Romanesque churches. Conceptually, they are almost always subtractive: they are cut out, sliced or hollowed out. We see that light has made its way into the building. This way of treating light impresses us greatly. Usually light serves to convey a sense of lightness, but sometimes its effect can be reversed, as with the subtractive perforations: light takes on a sensual quality, amplifying the sense of gravity. Space becomes multifaceted, even enigmatic. [Fig. 7]

Light that enters through such openings, as in the main pool of the Turkish baths in Budapest, creates a sense of mystery. One has the impression that the light is separated into individual rays. The surface of the pool transforms them into ever-changing patterns of light, partly reflected into the room, partly refracted as they penetrate the water's surface. Light and space merge into a sensual, transformational whole, turning the space into an experience that changes with the seasons, time of day and the weather, an experience that is always new with every visit.

Zsolt Gunther For our design for the House of Hungarian Music competition, we also employed the "physical" quality of light, but in a different way. Here, openings in an organically formed roof canopy, into which organically shaped light channels are cut, allow light to permeate the interior of a pavilion without walls. Its emphatic architectural form and mass ties in lucidly with the surrounding urban woodland of the City Park, where the sunlight breaks through the dense treetops and illuminates the ground. The pronounced curvature and varying thickness of the roof canopy produces constantly changing circles of light in the interior, while throwing strong shadows at the edge of the canopy roof. In their expression of physical mass and material, these shadows relate to, but are very different from those of the nearby trees at the woodland's edge. [Fig. 8]

In another smaller project in the countryside, we used light to visually enhance its specific spatial geometry with its many irregular surfaces and fragments. The otherwise quite archetypal detached house has a fragmented ceiling landscape through which light tumbles as if into a ravine. Although not very large, the detached house acquires, through this surprising passage of light, a quite unexpected sense of space and drama. So, working with light, and especially with the changing quality of daylight, does play a significant role in our architecture. [Fig. 9]

[Fig. 1] The urban realm in Budapest

[Fig. 2] Traditional villagescape in Western Hungary

[Fig. 3] Undefined space in the undercroft, Szeged Cathedral

[Fig. 4] Brick pillars of the undercroft under Szeged Cathedral

[Fig. 5] Space with skylight in the Blues Centre, Notodden, design competition, 2014

[Fig. 6] Light circles in MOME's foyer staircase

[Fig. 7] Cistercian abbey church in Bélapátfalva

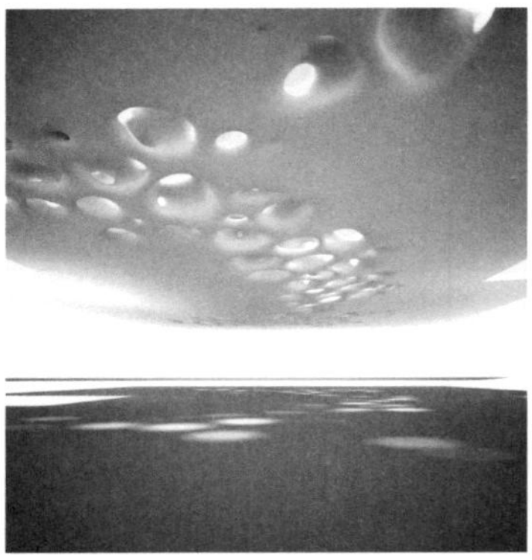

[Fig. 8] Roof canopy of the House of Hungarian Music

[Fig. 9] Model of a detached house

[Fig. 10] Backlit, perforated steel panels, Szeged Cathedral

[Fig. 11] The main staircase of the renovated MOME building

[Fig. 12] Picture gallery, Esterházy Castle in Fertőd

[Fig. 13] Staircase in MOME, BASE building

[Fig. 14] Access tunnel, Szeged Cathedral

Claus Käpplinger You very often employ the architectural means of space, material and light in a purist and contrasting way. Instead of radical experiments, you favour a sensitive approach, courageously picking up and continuing existing buildings using modern means. You examine what you find and transform it through your architecture, often in a striking way. Colour, however, tends to take a back seat in favour of clearly stated contrasts of materials.

Katalin Csillag Yes, we tend to use materials and colours in a restrained way in our projects. We use them to create contrasts that make clear references to a building's past or its location. In Szeged, for example, we found a lot of terrazzo flooring, a material that was commonly used in the 1920s and '30s. All the floors of the liturgical spaces were made entirely of terrazzo. So, we developed an entirely new vertical application of terrazzo, which one sees around the elevator or on the counter. It invites visitors to touch it, to sense the particular qualities of a material to which one rarely pays much attention.

Zsolt Gunther The other material we used was sheet steel as a means of enclosing or wrapping, particularly for the tower from the 13th century. We perforated it with numerous holes of successively smaller diameter to provide an indication of the brick masonry behind it. The brick wall is worn and badly damaged because it was repeatedly exposed to groundwater. We used artificial light in the form of strip lights to illuminate the space between the sheet steel and the masonry and draw attention to the historical scarred surface of the brickwork. The effect is virtual, but also very haptic, making visitors aware of the materials the cathedral is made of and how vulnerable they can be. [Fig. 10]

Katalin Csillag In MOME, too, what was already there played an important role. We wanted to preserve many elements of the old building, so that it would retain its original historical depth. We managed to ensure that its terrazzo surfaces, rosettes and railings were preserved. The rough wooden surface of the handrails and wrought iron balustrades reveal the craftsmanship that went into them. For the new additions, on the other hand, we deliberately introduced new elements that distance themselves conceptually from the historical details of the old building. For the main staircase, for example, we designed smooth handrails made of artificial stone.

The exposed concrete ceiling in the new building is a further example. Its rough surface was not intended but came about due to the sometimes rather inexact construction work. In the end it was a happy accident because the different aggregate states of the materials reflect the respective workmanship of the times in which MOME was created. They have been left visible intentionally as an integral part of the building complex's character: we see it as a strength and not a weakness. [Fig. 11]

It is not a disaster when occasionally a surface doesn't turn out as expected or cannot be perfectly restored. We make the best of it. Mistakes can ultimately contribute to the vitality of a project. Not everything needs upgrading to perfection: the combination of the surfaces we actually find and abstract additions sets up a stimulating tension or a disconcerting frisson that encourages engagement with the building and thereby also stimulates appropriation processes.

Claus Käpplinger I'm interested in the intellectual basis behind your architecture, in your architectural convictions. A theme that recurs in your writings is making links, disjointed histories, giving something back along with more intellectual ideas such as "transcripts", "narration" and "metamorphosis". One has the impression with your architecture that you wish to piece together a world that is becoming increasingly unmanageable, that you would like to pick up the loose ends of history with your projects and weave them into a new grand narrative in which past, present and future coexist. Narration, the joy of telling the story of different times and linking them together, is without doubt a characteristic of Postmodernism. But your narrative also seems strongly driven by a romantic view of the world, by the conviction that one can put the parts back together to form a whole. How do you see this?

Katalin Csillag While we live in a fragmented world, it cannot be our goal to reproduce this in our architecture. We need places that radiate a certain tranquillity. Rather than the broken, we need a sense of harmonious unity around us. It may be that this is a romantic approach.

The Ukrainian composer Valentin Silvestrov has determined that we are surrounded by too much noise. People have no need for noise or for fragmentation. They prefer instead to strive for completeness. As such, when we work with a situation as found in one of our projects, we try and develop something whole out of it. We are, after all, not autonomous beings, we are always in close contact with other people and other times. We are communal beings who seek proximity and shelter. What we seek in our buildings a sense of completeness, and this is also what informs our work.

Zsolt Gunther For me, narration is a further layer that I like to think spans a building invisibly. It is closely linked to its atmosphere. You could, perhaps, call this romantic, but I prefer to think it has to do with our history.

Our intention is to make history visible. We want to foster an understanding of it, albeit from the standpoint of the present day. Inevitably, we are therefore paraphrasing it to some degree. We use this idea of an architectural paraphrase very often. A good example of this is the project for the House of Hungarian Music, where we designed a pavilion in Budapest's City Park, which for us paraphrases the pavilions of Mies van der Rohe. When one develops narratives and makes connections, one cannot ignore these intellectual levels and historical references – after all, architecture is part of the arts and always also represents a link to the past.

Claus Käpplinger The idea of the heroic Modernist architect as the inventor of a new world has all but disappeared today. Postmodern writers have conclusively deconstructed the old linear order of texts. They present a world view that is multicentric and pluralistic and do that most earnestly and from many different perspectives. In recent decades, however, some former protagonists of Postmodernist literature and music, such as Hans Werner Henze and Péter Eötvös, have returned increasingly to traditional composition methods, in part to reach audiences better and also to relate their work more strongly to a point in history. Does that have parallels with your work?

Zsolt Gunther We do indeed have a strong affinity with writers and composers who strive to make connections to the past. That needn't necessarily be nostalgic or romantic. It's also one reason why I am sceptical of equating narration with romanticism. Our narration is not one of repetition or replication, it is instead frequently abstract, transforming the historical into something both familiar and unfamiliar. The picture gallery in Esterházy Castle in Fertőd, for example, makes very deliberate reference to the Baroque style of the original building, but the new coffered ceiling of illuminated panels maintains a definite distance to the historical past through its modern construction and materials, its use of light and not least its abstract white colour.

Katalin Csillag Architecture always has something to do with order. For example, the statics are an order that one cannot ignore. For us, Postmodernism means we have the freedom to decide which aspects we choose to focus on and which we want to tie into. The most important thing for us is a connection to function and place. Today, however, we are free to choose the means, qualities or narratives to achieve this. Our goal is to create architecture that strives to take things to a new level, to enrich the place and the experience. Our K4 project aims to give the citizens the space to rediscover and appropriate the city. As a result, something quite unique has evolved that is intimately connected to its location. Similarly, very normal people are struck by the overwhelming impression of the picture gallery in Esterházy Castle. It appeals not just to experts, architects or conservationists. [Fig. 12]

Claus Käpplinger "Spaces of Intensity" is the title of this book, and many of your buildings do indeed have a special intensity that does not fail to make a lasting impression and that is often not immediately apparent at first glance. Intensity can, however, also be perceived as exhausting, as a negative emotion, in that you have no choice but to react to a space that might actually be a neutral setting for activities. What do you associate primarily with intensity? Is it something individual or communal? What do people gain by engaging with your spaces and your architecture?

Katalin Csillag Indifference, blandness and neutrality are the more pressing problems facing contemporary society and blighting its architectures. Many of today's buildings lack a sense of permanence, continuity and physical presence.

For me, intensity has a lot to do with sensory experience, with situations that stimulate us to feel, sense and perceive more clearly. Our buildings, the atmospheres they create and the images they convey are designed to be experienced not from a single viewpoint but rather through movement in space. Movement, for us, does not automatically imply acceleration but rather the opposite: to slow down, to decelerate. Above all, human beings need moments of peace and tranquillity and buildings that create the best conditions for that. Architecture is very much about existential matters, about shelter and comfort, and these are what spaces of intensity provide. [Fig. 13]

Zsolt Gunther

Intensity also has to do with essence, with evoking essential qualities that stir something within us and move us. It has a certain richness, an unmistakable density that is often tied to a sustained quality, with archtypes, with the permanence of materials and a concentration of sensory impressions. On a more pragmatic level, intensity is most readily experienced by people on a small scale and for this reason we try and create ever smaller spaces within larger spaces to achieve the desired degree of complexity. This complexity is often produced through the deliberate use of orthogonality and spaces with a specific mass, as seen for example in Islamic architecture or Romanesque buildings in which light, materiality and atmosphere are distinctly palpable.

Katalin Csillag

Spaces can, of course, be experienced as intense and stressful when they trigger a reaction or compel one to respond. I don't have a problem with that when intensity moves something within us. There are occasionally also spatial situations in our buildings that are intense in the negative sense in that they don't invite one to linger. The tunnel-like connection between the foyer and the subterranean old church in Szeged is one such situation in which one is confronted by a relatively narrow conduit of skewed surfaces that transition from the flat-beamed ceiling of the foyer to the barrel vaults of the old crypt. In this sequence of spaces, forces of contrasting momentum come together with a tangible dynamism. [Fig. 14]

Geometria and its atrium is another example: here we were able to develop very intensive spatial experiences through a series of hung and cantilevered compartments of varying permeability that cause the light to fall into the atrium quite differently, stimulating the inhabitants to move and change their position. Here there are boxes hanging in the air! Ultimately, human experience is still primarily physical and not digital. Is it not better to turn our attention to real things, to make the world more tangible? To create more spaces and situations where people can simply sit and be, without doing anything special other than to see and feel and listen? We believe that people need today more of these spaces.

Dense Voids

Geometria Office Building, Budapest 2010 – 2013

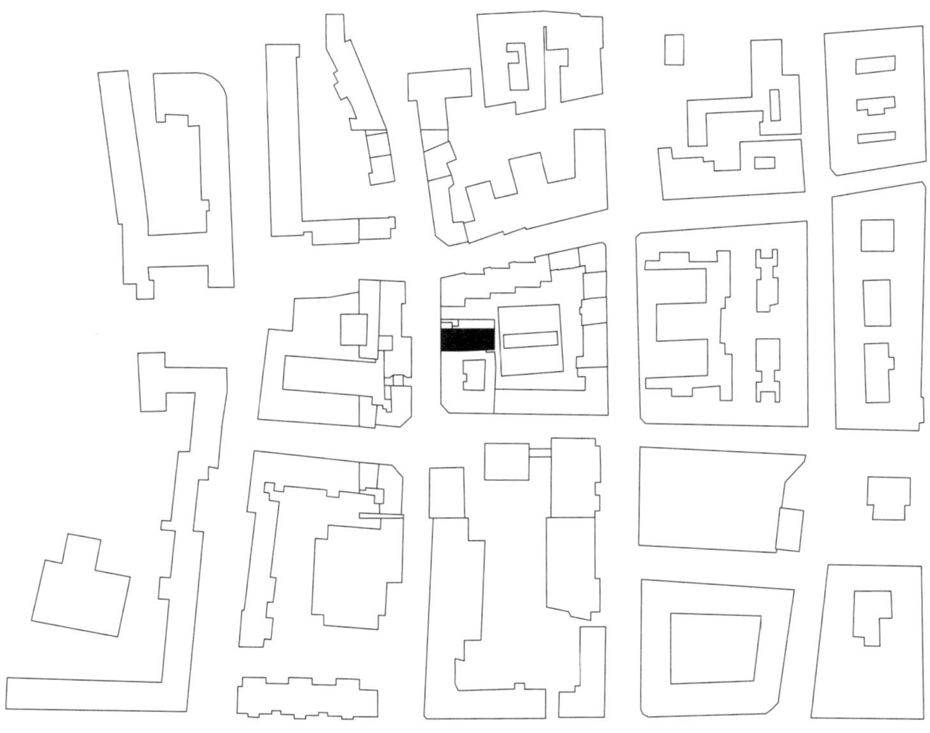

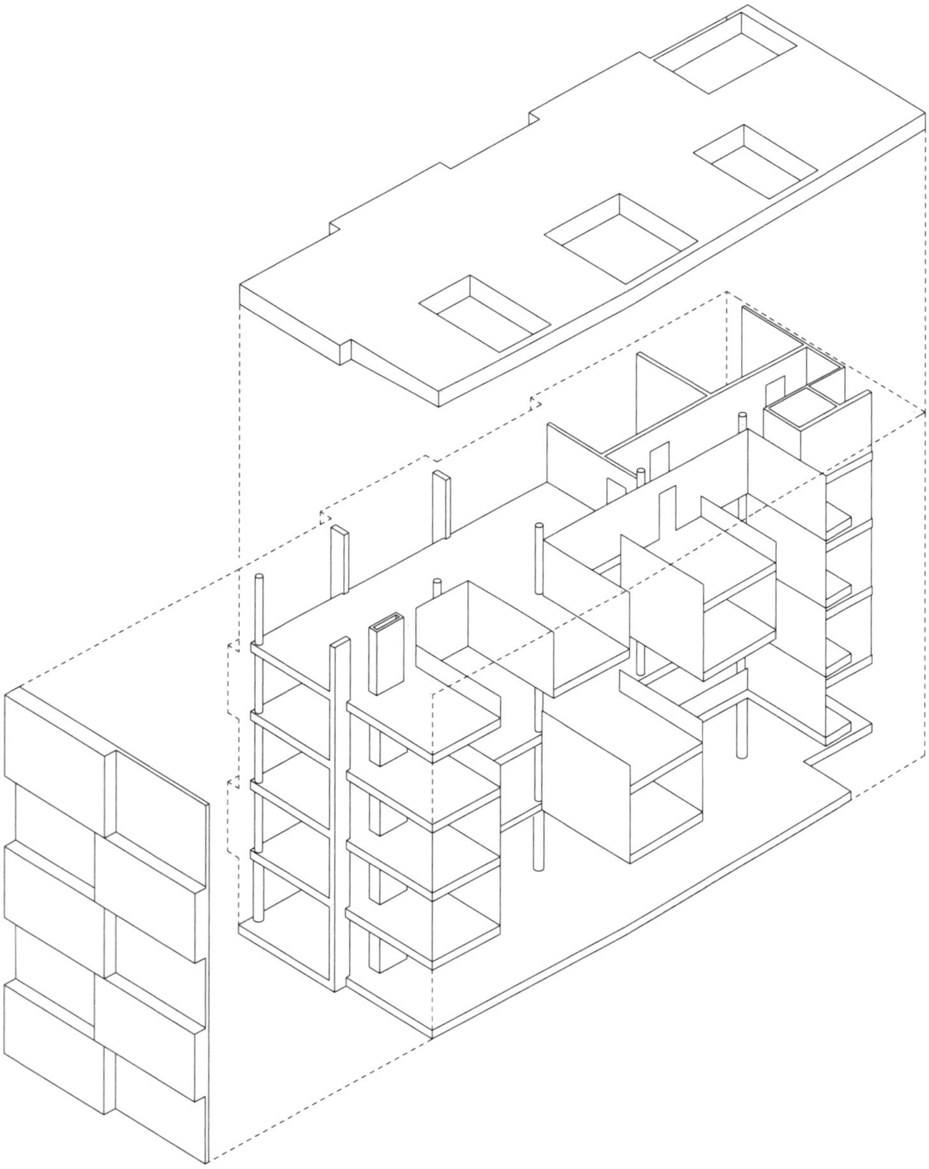

This small office building is situated close to the Danube in a densely built part of Buda. The cityscape is mixed, with contemporary, modernist and historicising buildings alongside each other. The streets are rather narrow, yet the courtyards of the buildings are sometimes surprisingly airy. The urban fabric opens up irrationally in several places, and thus space, light and air penetrate the narrow streets.

Streets with blocks and vacant plots, alternating building heights as well as the stylistically heterogeneous streetscape make it necessary to rethink adjustments necessary. Our building is situated in such a vacant space – between two buildings. Its volume disregards the building height of the next block, yet it is at the same height of the ridge of the firewall. We designed a simple rectangular prism next to the adjacent firewall, which forms a dialogue with the residential building on the other side of the gap between the two buildings. That is a clinker-brick block with a flat roof and tight proportions. The composition of rectangular prism – pause – rectangular prism creates a new form of adaptation. The created unity points beyond the triviality of neighbourhood relations; it is based far more on the rhythm of the pulsating urban fabric.

The building seemingly follows a strict formula, which helps maintain consistent geometrical thinking. Protruding and inset surfaces at each floor level, arranged like a chessboard, characterise the building. At the corners the boxes are shifted in their alignment to each other, thereby emphasising the building's plasticity. The fact that two distinct planes appear in different ways further varies the basic concept. The exterior plane has a screen pattern of grid points. This pattern is deliberately expressive and recalls the pop culture of the 1970s.

This formula becomes invalid in the interior, the irrationality of which overwrites the exterior's logic: the regular exterior glides into a pulsating interior. Here, glass boxes, which protrude into the atrium, float in a very tight, yet airy space. You may be reminded of Piranesi's infinite spaces, which resonate here on a smaller scale. The spaces in Piranesi's drawings make one restless. Why? Because they suggest the infinite nature of space, and the architectural elements that protrude into the space do not hide it: on the contrary, they draw the viewer's attention to it, which is similar to our small atrium. Thus, architectural space takes the lead role.

Only as much as is needed. Nowadays, naked glass surfaces have become commonplace in office architecture. Excessive transparency bares a building, opens up its secrets and, in the absence of a natural environment, makes its contents trivial. In our case the building's transparency is deceptive: it is not primarily about connecting the exterior with the interior; glass becomes far more the instrument of ambivalent divisions. Another attribute of glass becomes important: the vertical surface as a huge mirror becomes the means of virtual multiplication.

The building steers clear of the stigma of transparency with a simple gesture: grid points appear on the exterior glass surfaces. Ornamentation returns where it is the least expected: on the smooth, brutally plane surface of the glass – a pop-art, abstract ornamentation whose spatial appearance is enhanced by the in-and-out movement of the box-like surfaces.

Irrelevant office typology? Using the constraints of the plot, we made a virtue out of necessity. The absolutely economical, double-tract office system gives way to a work and a recreation zone, which is divided into two by a concealed passageway. Despite the recreation zone's restricted space it is a luxury, since it appears to be floating accidentally here and there in empty space, whereas the open-space offices become dense.

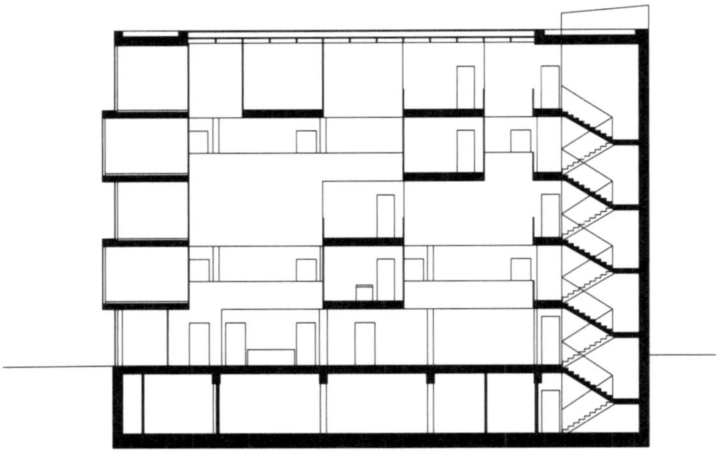

Longitudinal section

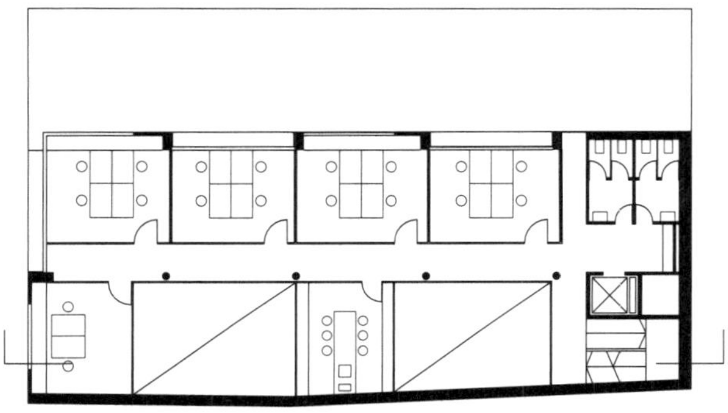

First floor plan

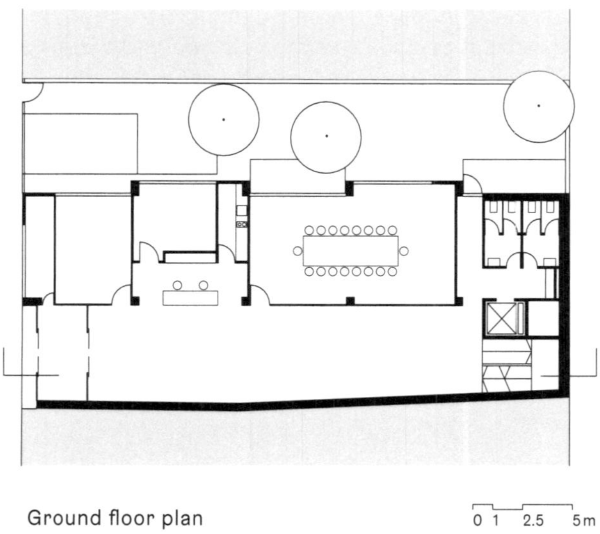

Ground floor plan

So that the boxes stacked on top of each other would appear as clearly as possible, the details were developed over a long period of time.

On entering, visitors are surprised by the airiness of the light-filled atrium, which is as high as the building and lit from above.

The spatial impressions constantly shift, as perceived when moving around. Open-plan and cellular offices alternate on each floor.

The space of the atrium offers sequences of varying density and of openings by using variably arranged "boxes". These accommodate a range of activities and function as kitchenettes, team or meeting rooms.

The façade responds to the brick-built block on the other side of the gap between the two buildings, albeit in different dimensions. Here, the exterior appearance is provided by elements with transparent walls of single-storey height.

A Resonant Body

House of Hungarian Music, Budapest 2014

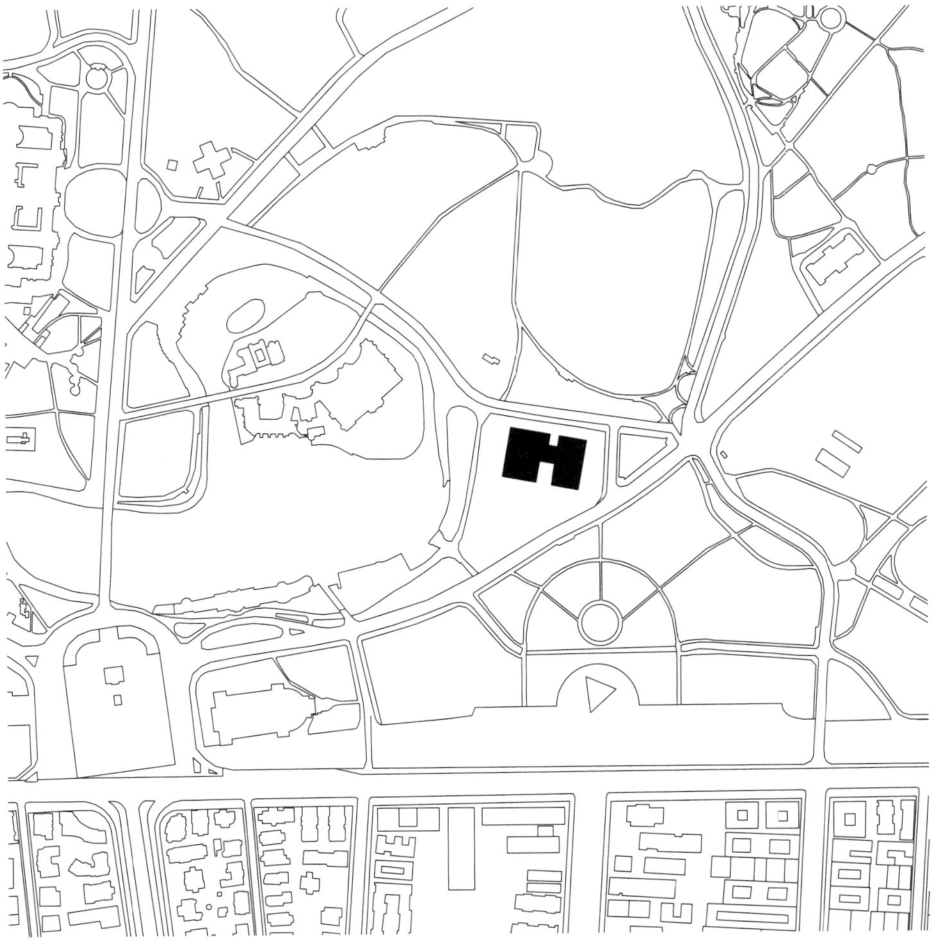

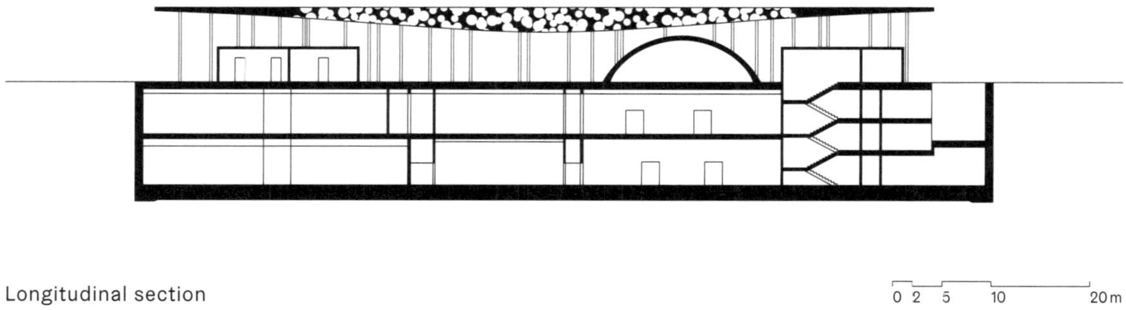

Longitudinal section

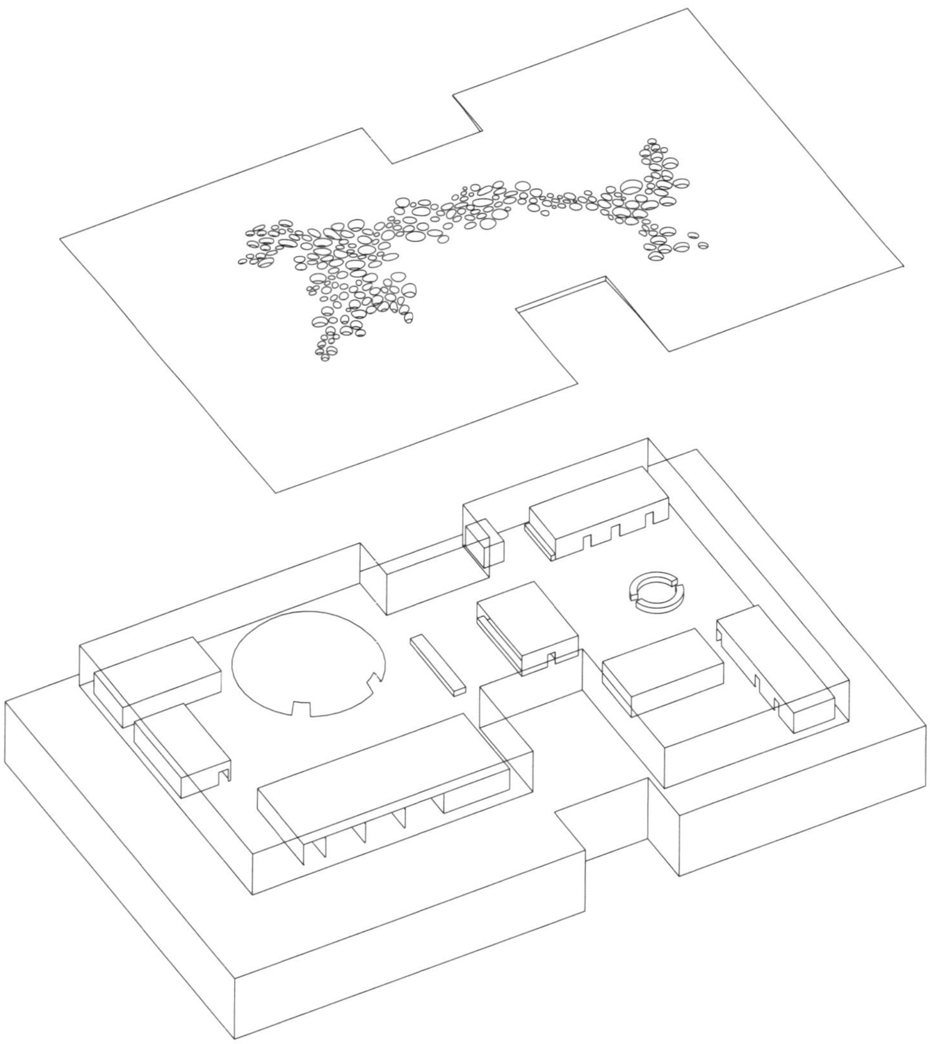

Budapest's City Park is a very popular urban forest. Escaping from the crowded city centre, we feel that natural elements dominate here. The most diverse associations arise within us with regard to the park: a haze envelops its lower-lying parts. The rustle of trees drowns the noise of the city. The leaves filter the city's dust. Walking among the fallen leaves, a pleasant scent permeates, and twigs crack underfoot.

These associations direct our attention not to composed music, but to its origin: the ancient nature of sound as a vibrating air column and rhythm come to mind. All this creates an atmosphere. So perhaps this is why it is important that the new museum or house of music dissolves in its surroundings and is linked to them in as many ways as possible.

Similarly to nature, music can be perceived as a flowing medium that permeates our bodies into their very insides. Can one pursue a design that follows this flow's atmosphere? Can architecture be created that does not appear as an obstacle to the flow, but rather as a helping hand? Can architecture be fashioned such that it increasingly disappears in tree trunks and leaves?

Unfolding this train of thought, our design defines a music pavilion from the point of view of the urban fabric, a type of building that has always been characterised by the relativity of openness and the state of being closed. A music pavilion is not a concert hall, where every built element serves to enhance the listener's experience, making it as undisturbed and pure as possible. It is something akin to a place where the invisible space of music is directly connected with the spaces of the outside world (the world of sounds). Instead of purity, it is governed by fusion, continuity and the plurality of perception.

It would be obvious to presume this relationship via the pavilion's glass membrane. Instead, it is the roof that becomes the material and symbolic connecting element between nature and the interior musical space. We have imagined a roof that hovers in the park, supported by thin columns that appear not to serve the purpose of bearing weight. Placed at irregular intervals, they follow the dynamics of the shape. This hovering concrete roof structure with its bulges and perforations is itself able to function as a giant musical instrument. This instrument is "filled" with sounds passing through the resonant body.

If the glass membrane bordering the pavilion is not for mediating between the inside world of music and the outside, what is the essence of its transparency? In line with our intentions, this and the interior world of the pavilion can be perceived rather as a fundamental *topos* of classical Modernism, as a paraphrase of flowing spaces. The spatial elements that limit full transparency, the semiglobe of the *music dome,* always only partially hide the surroundings. Thus, the interplay between the columns supporting the floating roof and the tree trunks results in random concurrences. An extensive project had to be carried out beneath the pavilion's restricted ground-floor space. The main straight-flight stairs lead to a special space under the building. The slightly descending, ribbed, suspended ceiling suddenly turns upwards at the end of the space, radiating light to the underground area via the slope. This place is a communication and assembly point between the exhibition spaces and the room where special concerts can be held due to its splendid acoustics.

Let us return from the underground world to the main floor of the pavilion and examine the floating roof again, not as a musical instrument, but as an important attribute of contemporary music. Music has always been concerned with cosmic scales. The pavilion opens up towards the sky through the cavities between the layers of the roof. An enormous cosmic dimension emerges in the roof. The image that appears on its interior surface symbolises the sky, as light penetrates in varying strength. The spectacle is especially impressive at night, when the stars and the moon shine through the roof's cavities.

Large spaces with enclosed walls have been placed underground. Natural light breaks through with elementary force beyond the slanting, slightly curved ceiling in the foyer of the underground concert hall.

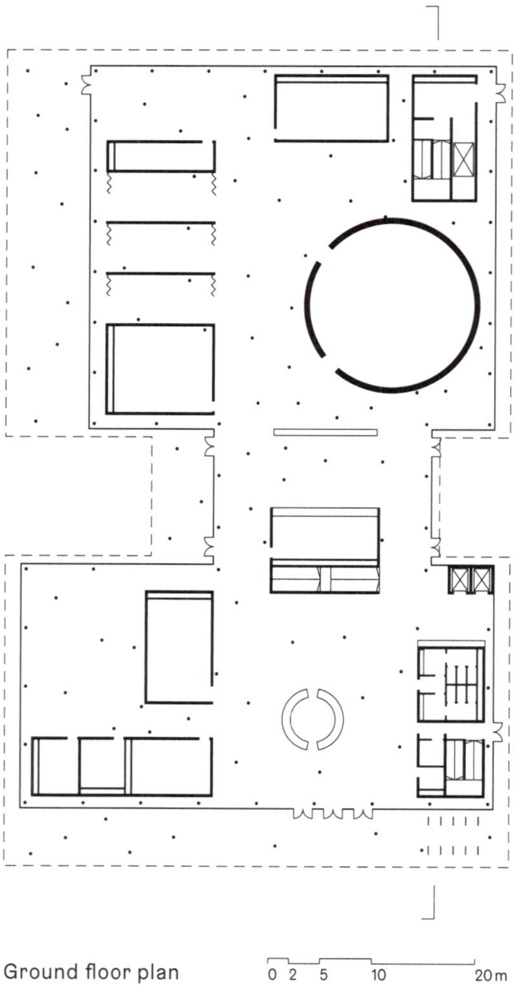

Ground floor plan

The enclosed spaces under the sculpted roof do not constitute an interconnected system,
but appear as independent objects. The roof itself is a resonating body with perforations, an experimental “musical instrument”.

The building is intended to appear as light as possible, with a hovering roof emphasising its dominant three-dimensional character.

The Power of Softness

Concert Hall,
Pécs
2007

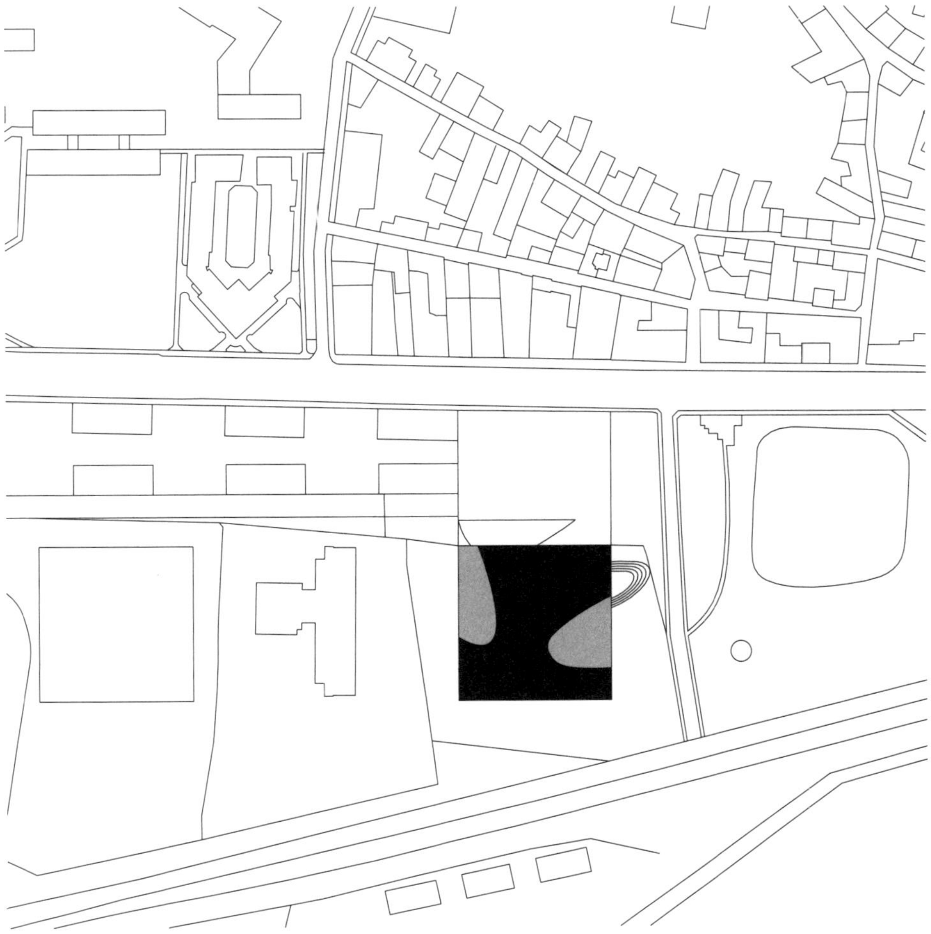

Façade detail

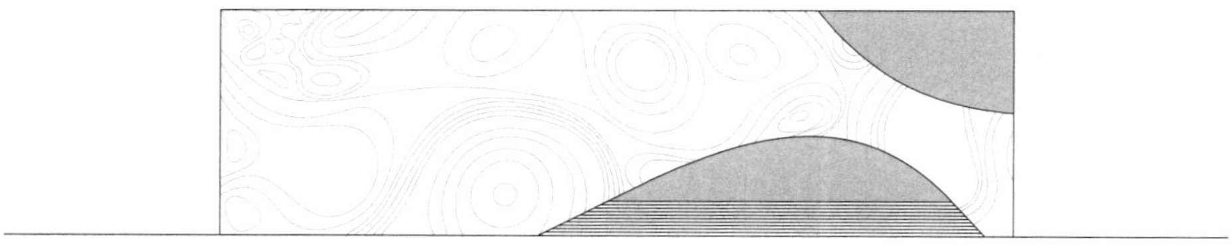

Northern elevation

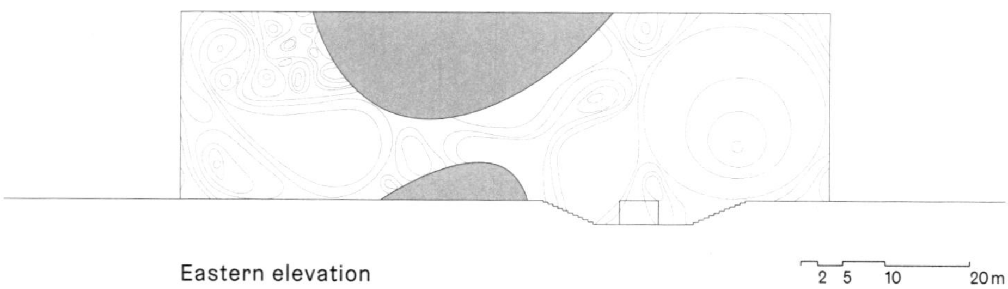

Eastern elevation

The composition of a concert hall is a lyrical work – one that evokes emotions as well as associations. It is determined by the relationship of lightness and heaviness and the concentration of material and emptiness, just as music is defined by rhythm, silence and sounds, which together create a tune.

The concert hall came into being at the intersection of music and architecture and it can be interpreted as a musical transcript. Both the building and music have a dual orientation: they simultaneously present the starting and end points of the concert hall interpretation. Its spatial world represents an essential factor in intensifying the musical experiences.

As regards the form of our building, it could stand anywhere. The built cube, neutral at first sight, is linked to the town of Pécs by simple gestures: the sophisticated amorphous incisions turn the concertgoers' attention towards three prominent points in the town. One is its most picturesque peak, Tettye. Another is the Zsolnay porcelain factory, whose history is closely connected with that of Pécs. The third is the park of the nearby Balokány Grove, one of the city's most important green areas.

The design of the volume is defined by a regular cube and the irregular, soft incisions that cut into it. The hardness and the generality of the concert hall's glass façade are broken up by the "melting" glass pattern, which is transparent and without distortion in the more important directions. The design of the façade surfaces was inspired by the Hungarian and Art Nouveau patterns of the famous Zsolnay factory. Their energetic curves unfolded from these. They can be seen on the seemingly neutral surface of the glass, often transforming the original motifs, making them partly unrecognisable. Two main volumes can be perceived behind the translucent membrane: the concert hall and the rectangular prism of the areas that serve the Philharmonic Orchestra. The intervening spaces are sliced out from the curving ceiling layers above one another, cut out in different ways. The spaces thus created are soft yet energetic and full of vivid tension.

The building accommodates a concert hall for 1200 people, the headquarters of the Pannon Philharmonic, with rehearsal rooms of different sizes, as well as the institution's directorate. The ground-plan and the building's spatial organisation ensure the separation of the spaces for the audience and the operational units. Visitors arrive via the promenade, while the catering establishments open towards the Balokány Grove. Due to its acoustics, the concert hall is suitable for holding symphony orchestra and jazz concerts, organ recitals and operetta performances as well as conferences.

The chief compositional element is music, through which we reach an unknown space. This theme inspires and at the same time has a calming effect. In constructional terms, softness becomes prominent in the building, which presumes the absence of force and compulsion. The foyer's genteel curves, the sensitive incisions into the rectangular prism, are imprints of the complexity and softness of the musical space here. Due to its tenderness, the building has a special atmosphere – one that is sensitive, we could say, atypical, unlike the dominant determinants of our world. The concert hall cube is present in the foyer as a dark, immaterial and almost transcendent mass. This gesture suggests the shift: the opposite of the outside transparent world appears inside the concert hall. Everything has been subordinated to the sound. Intimate density can be perceived in the classical shoebox-shaped space. Besides achieving maximum acoustics, the relief-like alignment of the wooden elements reinforces the aesthetics of the interior.

When designing the building we often listened to the compositions of the Ukrainian composer Valentin Silvestrov, who expressed his creed in an interview. "There is no need to map the noises of the world in music," he asserted, "because we hear that as music automatically. In addition, we must forsake a dark attitude and strive for faith, beauty and good things. Music should calm you and give what is missing in life ... To put it in a sentence, I would say that the new task of contemporary music is for man to sound in it." Silvestrov's thoughts encouraged us when we placed the human being in focus while composing the concert hall. We aimed to create spaces that enrapture the audience and enhance the experience that music can provide in a timeless and appropriate way.

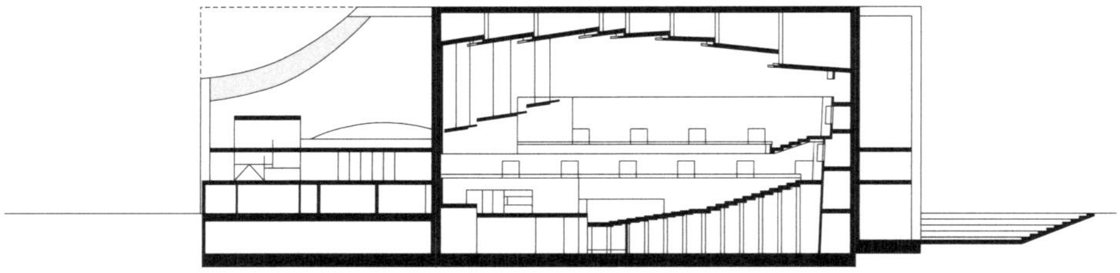

Longitudinal section through the concert hall

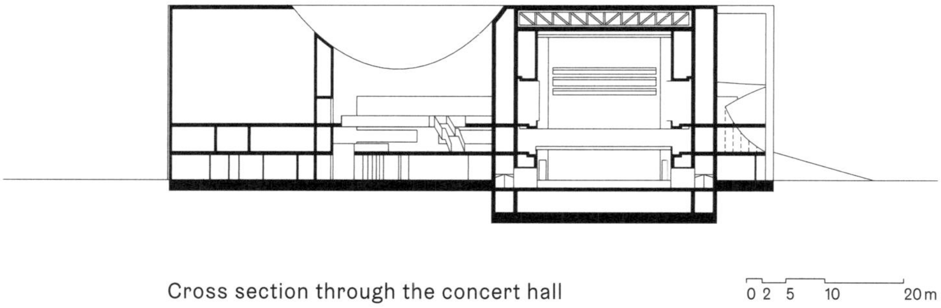

Cross section through the concert hall

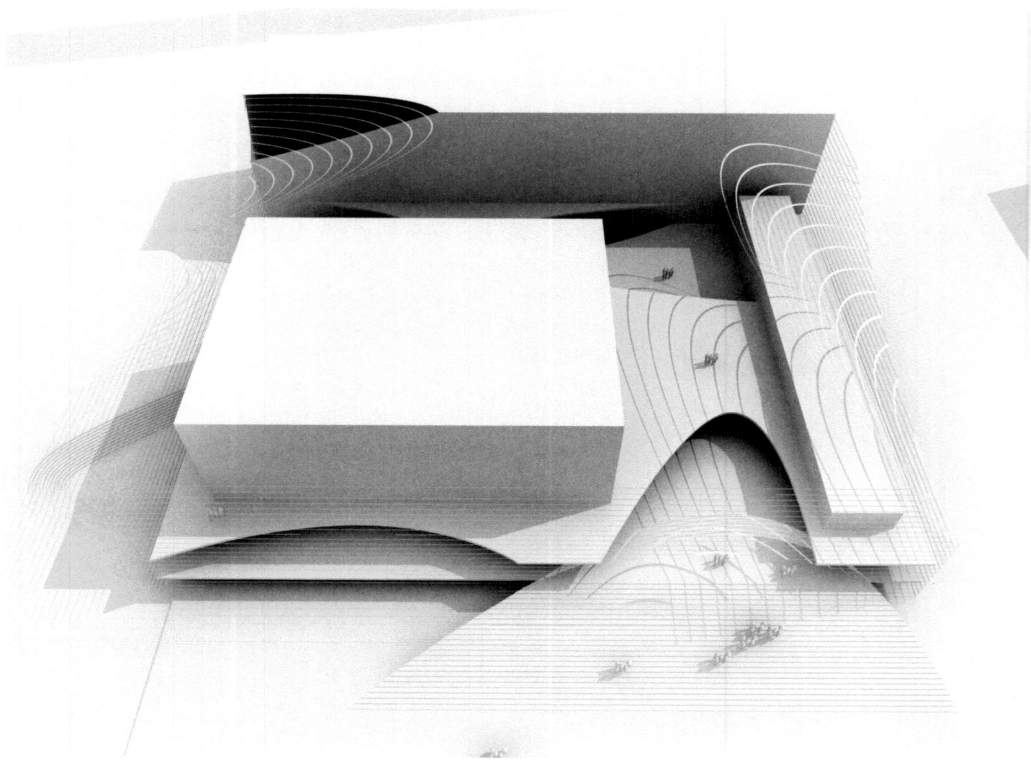

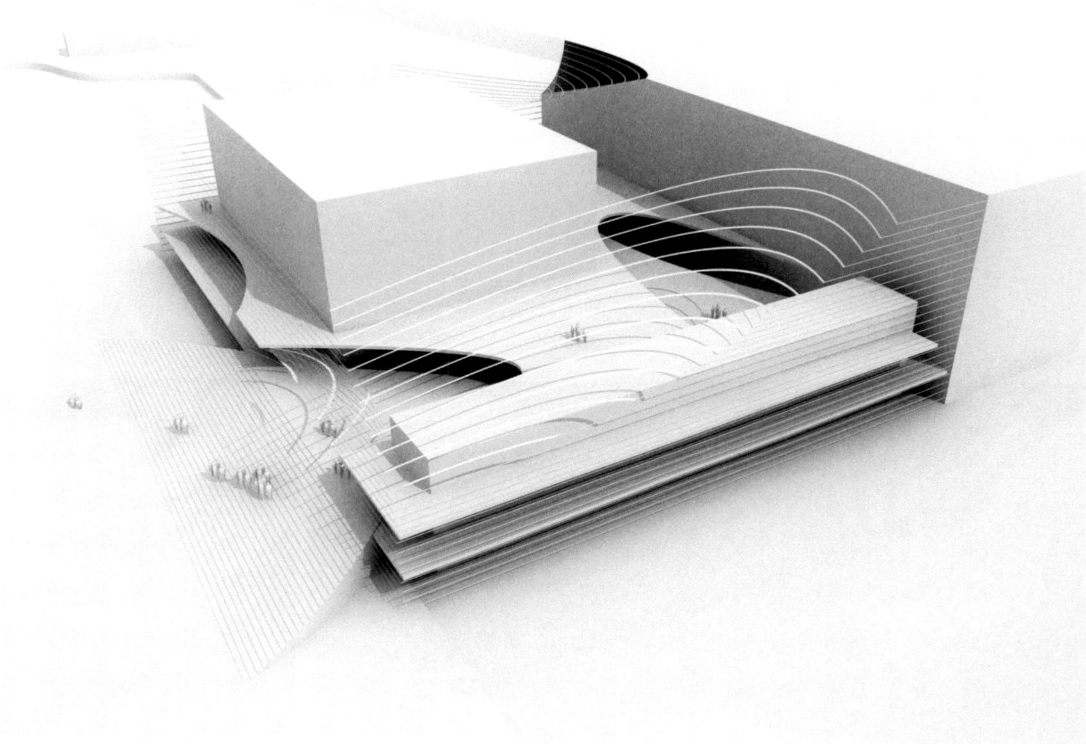

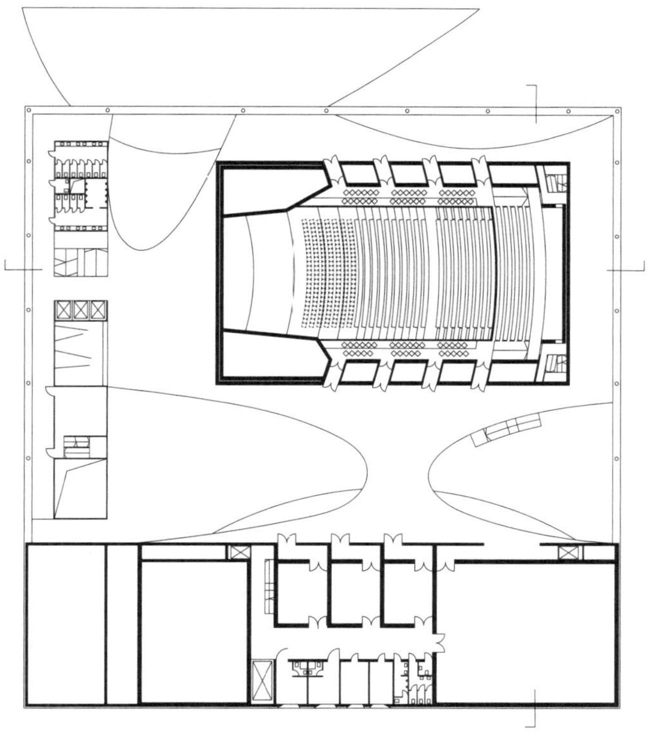

First floor plan

The plasticity of the building, resonating with the various landscape elements around it, highlights the duality of the design. The cube's austerity is counteracted by the softness of the fountain's pool, by the undulating benches and the broad sweep of the main stairs.

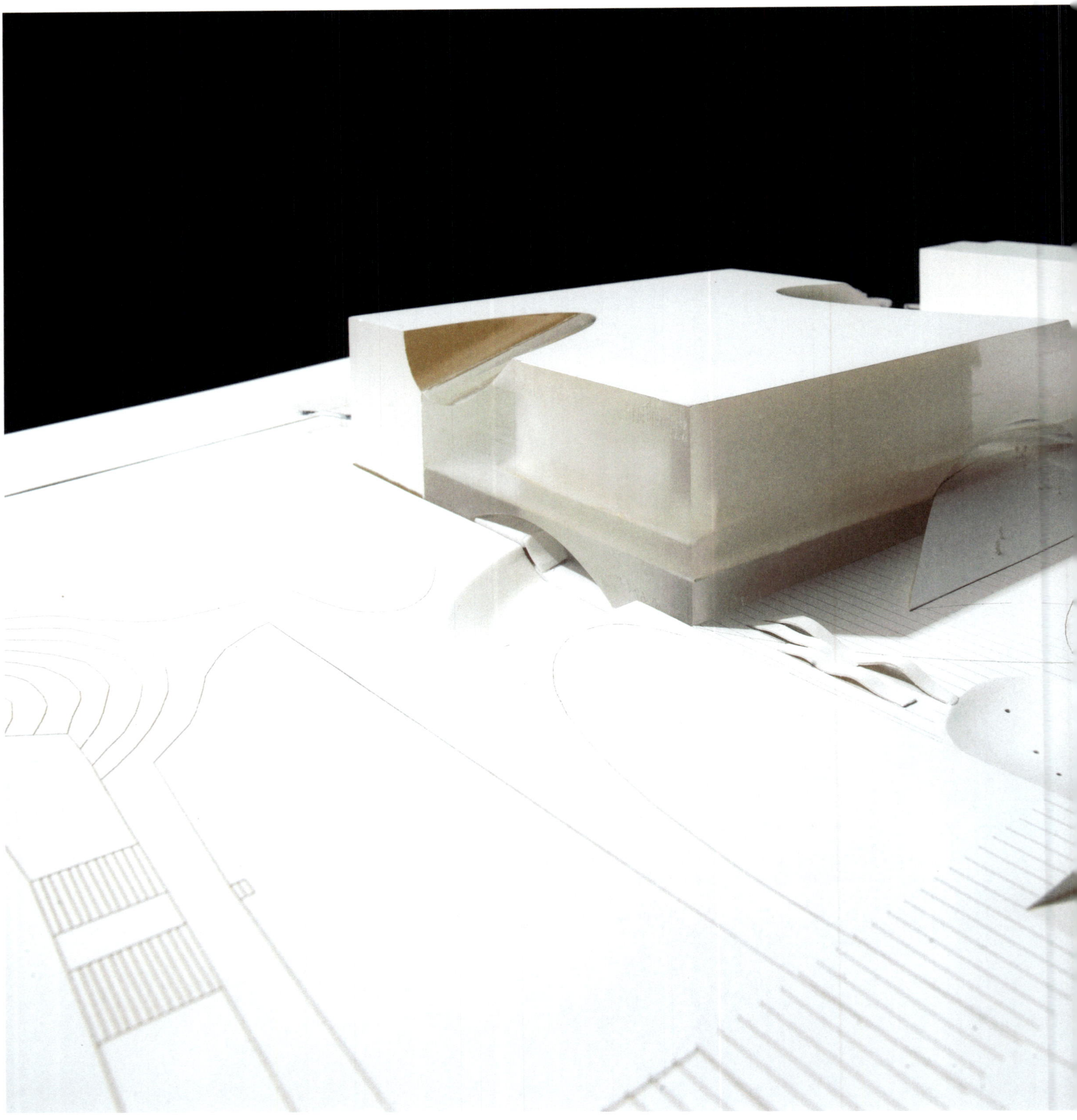

The depiction in winter is deliberate. The image created by the sculpted glass can indeed be compared to a crystalline cube.

Between Heaven and Earth

Benedictine Church
and Bell Museum,
Győr
2014 –

The precious wooden structure of the Baroque attic and the barrel vault can be seen in the loft space above the church.

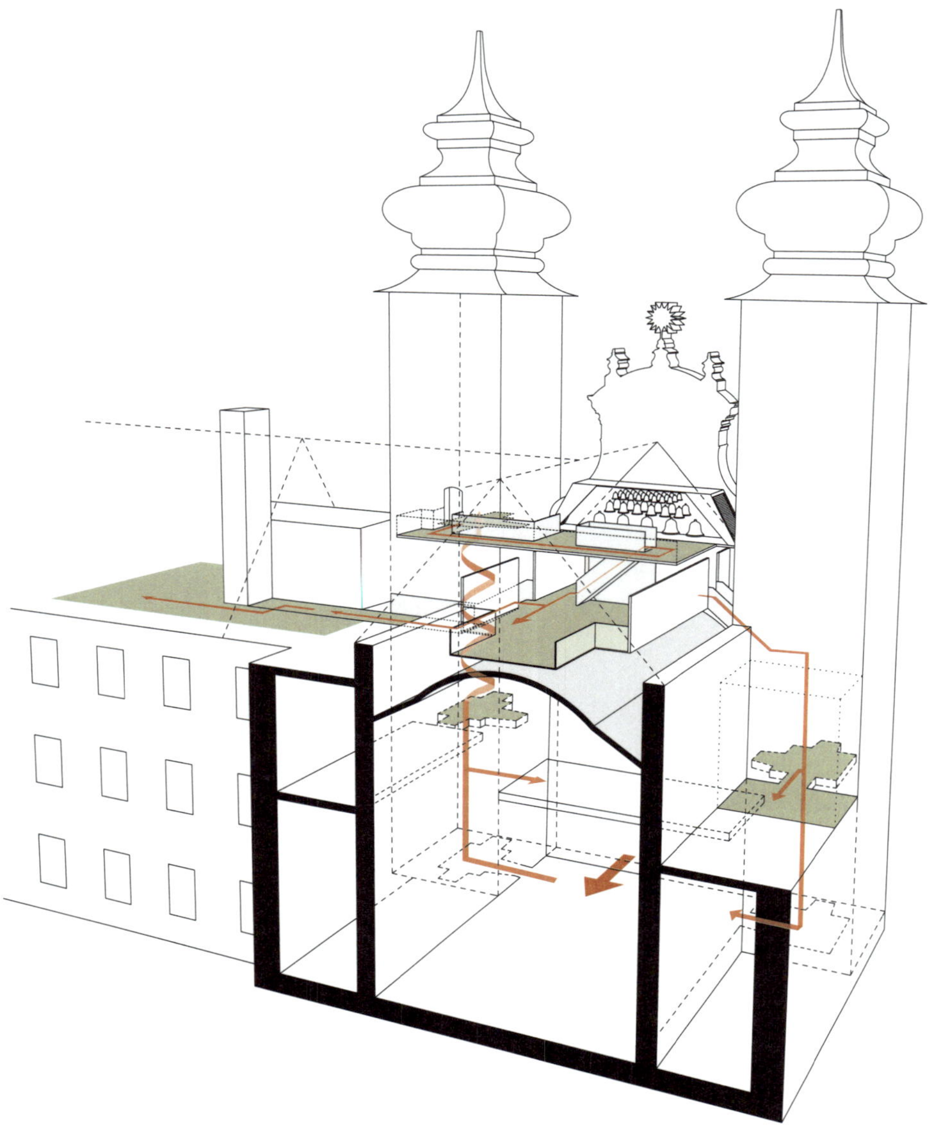

It is no exaggeration to say that this Benedictine church has become part of our lives. When we lived in Győr, we passed it every day. As the venue for our wedding celebration and the christenings of our children, not to mention the Sunday masses, it became the backdrop for our family celebrations. The fact that the church has played an important part in our lives makes all the difference when dealing with it. The deeply entrenched mental image of the building calls into question the need for change and intervention.

The Benedictine church of Győr is the oldest Baroque church in the country, preserving the earliest heritage elements of this period of Hungarian art history in original form dating back to 1641. Following the devastation left behind by the Turks in the 16th century, the town witnessed a considerable revival: the church, with its school and monastery, became a prominent place for education, culture and science under Jesuit ownership and later, since 1802 it has been run by the Benedictines.

Standing in the Baroque church space, probably very few people spend time wondering what kind of "secret" world is hidden above the church's ceiling fresco. Above the barrel vault, the Baroque roof structure and attic are realms of twilight, where the sound of the organ and the hymns sung by churchgoers can be heard well, even though this part of the church is a closed world situated halfway up to the bells. It is this mystical atmosphere that we wanted to preserve in our project. This mysterious levitation between heaven and earth has inspired the idea of the bell museum.

The deterioration of the roof supports required an urgent renewal of the roof, which in return enabled us to put on display the world above the church space. By making the whole attic area accessible, we wanted visitors to experience the rare roof space and enjoy the view of the barrel vaults from above. The Baroque roof structure is characterised by density and the presence of material. By introducing the museum function and making the upper, hidden world visible we continued the story that began in the Baroque era.

By using a steel structure that braces the walls and supports the visitor's route, we will correct the church's structural flaws, thus eliminating the tension stress of the barrel vault on the walls. The attic space will house an exhibition of bells, offering an insight into their history, highlighting the important role they played in the life of the community. In addition to the roof of the church, that of the monastery – flanking a large town square – will also be renovated and will showcase the history of Benedictine education in Győr. The display design is adapted to the attic atmosphere, with implanted "storage boxes" in the form of permeable chimneys beneath the roof.

In both spaces, we sought to enhance the memories of the attic by analysing its morphology and structures. Large wooden beams do not create a feeling of lightness; on the contrary, they give the sense of fullness. The wood feels rough to the touch and its scent is detectable close up. The spotlighting of the exhibits, the dimness of the rest of the space and the mysterious appearance of the barrel vaults evoke the empty spaces of abandoned roofs. The chimney walls rising from the middle wall of the monastery together with the exhibition chambers as their chunkier counterparts display objects from the treasures of the school. Material presence and twilight dominate everywhere, evoking the atmosphere of a generous, but sometimes tight attic space.

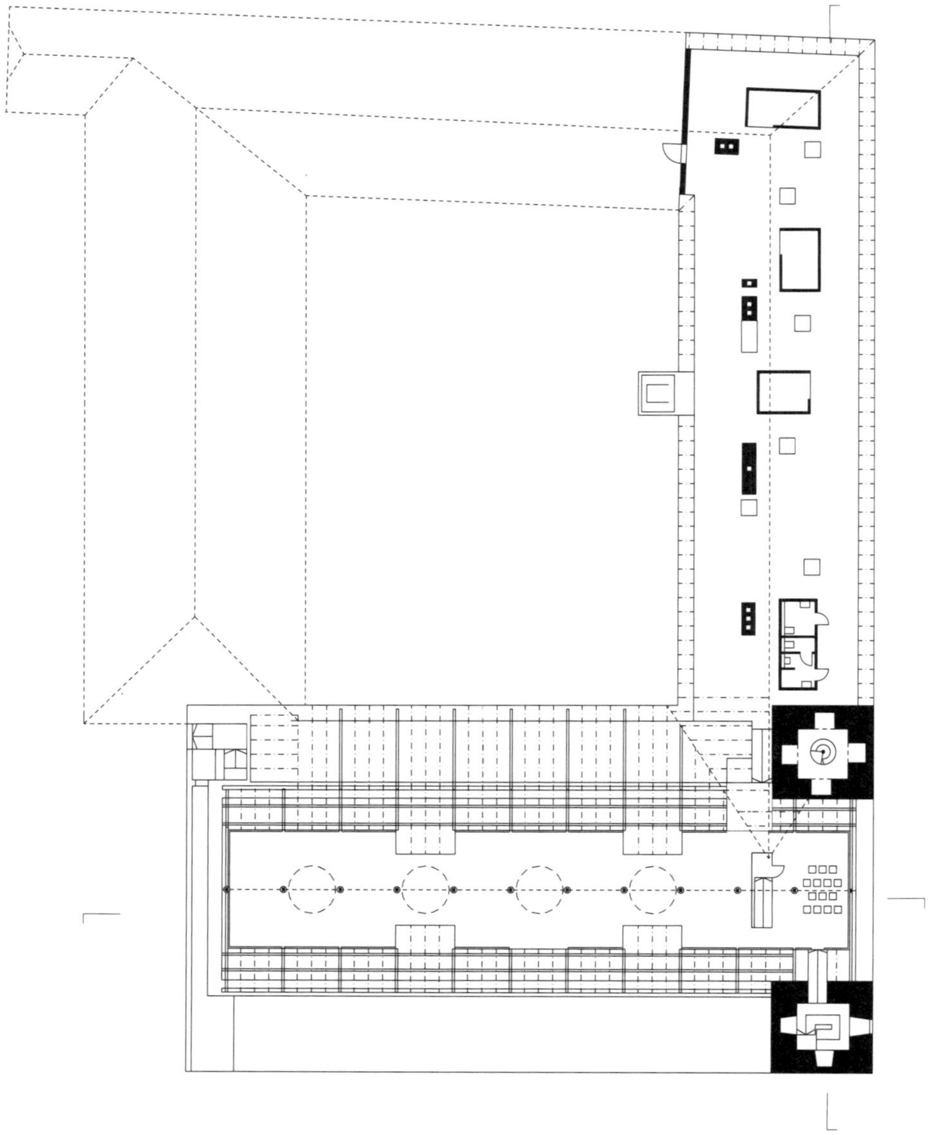

Roof level floor plan

Longitudinal section

Cross section

Large, colourful display spaces in the shape of illuminated chimneys are installed in the Baroque attic space. They contain many objects and aspects of Benedictine education through the past centuries.

Biographies

Katalin Csillag

was born in Győr in 1967. She gained her degree in architecture at the Budapest Technical University in 1992. Here, Tamás Karácsony was her mentor; she learnt much from how he meticulously customised his buildings exactly like a tailor. Besides accepting natural inconsistency, this also involved scope for moderate innovation. She began her career in Graz where she worked in several studios, including one where she worked alongside Helmut Zieseritsch for over two years.

Zsolt Gunther

was born in Budapest in 1964. He gained his degree in architecture at the Budapest Technical University. From 1986 to 1988 he attended the Master's course at the University of Applied Arts in Vienna as a student of Hans Hollein and François Burkhardt. He regards them and Zoltán Farkasdy, who taught in Budapest, as his mentors. He started his career as an urbanist working with Béla Nagy in Budapest and then worked abroad for a number of years: in the office of Mecanoo in Delft in 1991, later in Graz working with Volker Giencke in 1992, and with Ernst Giselbrecht from 1993 to 1994.

On their return to Hungary, Katalin Csillag and Zsolt Gunther founded their studio in their west Hungarian hometown, Győr, under the name of 3h architects, the reference being to the hardness of a pencil. Having become established, they worked primarily with the help of competition projects. Very early on they won prizes in international competitions, for example at Expo '96 Vienna and Europan 3. In 1997 their joint design with Árpád Ferdinánd won the first prize at Europan 4 in Graz. Their first major successes came with buildings designed for Audi AG industrial development in Győr, while in the same period their school in Csorna was built. With their designs often stretching architectural archetypes to their limits and with their own rational assessment of each situation, they remodel and rethink traditional approaches.

Combining an appreciation of concept and context was already important at the beginning of their careers. After the fall of the Iron Curtain, the rapid social, cultural and spatial changes in Hungary led them to search for concepts that are rather connected to the existing, for concepts that build bridges between past, present and future, but also among the different cultures that had shaped Hungary so much at the interface between East and West. So the purity of ideas was supplemented and enriched by the determination of context – the texture, the lighting, the location and the resulting narrative, and later on also the ornamental speech of architecture. As commissions grew, in 2006 they moved their office to Budapest, where the bustling, metropolitan environment resulted in new challenges. Themes such as density, scale, public spaces and the transformation of architectural heritage have since gained importance.

In 2009 Zsolt Gunther completed his doctoral studies at the Moholy-Nagy University of Art and Design. The title of his thesis was "Inverse Tradition – Provincial Architecture of the Future". The aim was to reintroduce the provincial in contemporary culture and theoretical discourse, and prevent the loss of traditional architectural values, given that in Hungary the emerging domination of information culture was marginalising the culture of the provinces.

Throughout their careers they have received various accolades. Both have been awarded the Ybl Prize, the most prestigious award for architects in Hungary. Zsolt received it in 2005, Katalin in 2019. Their buildings have been acknowledged by nominations for the Mies van der Rohe Award, the Piranesi Award and the World Architectural Festival, not to mention various Hungarian national prizes. Both of them are involved in teaching at different universities: Prague, Wiesbaden and Budapest. Katalin is also currently teaching at the Hungarian Master School, a postgraduate school for architects.

Team

Tamás Békesi

Born in 1970, studied at the Budapest Technical University between 1993 and 1998 and gained his degree in architecture. He worked in various architects' offices from 1998. In the period 2006 to 2008 he underwent training on a postgraduate course of monument preservation. Since 2008 he has been a project architect of 3h architects and since 2016 a senior partner. His works include K4 and Corvin 5 Office Buildings, the MOME Campus among others.

Gábor Kállay

Born in 1980, studied architecture at the Faculty of Architecture of Budapest Technical University between 1999 and 2006. There he participated in a postgraduate course in building energetics. From 2006 he worked in several Hungarian architects' offices. Since 2015 he has been working as a project architect and since 2017 as a junior partner in 3h architects. He has worked on a number of key schemes including the MOME Campus, the reconstruction and extension of the Király Thermal Baths and various successful competition projects.

Collaborators 1994–2020

Glória Apáti, Ábel Bálint, Emese Balogh, Réka Bánkuti-Tóth, Balázs Baranyai, Gergely Barcza, Gabriella Bárdos, András Márk Bartha, Cecília Bartos, **Tamás Békesi,** Júlia Boromissza, Lajos Börzsei, Csaba Bukta, **Bence Czirják, Tamás Csépke,** Tamás Döbrönte, Anett Eisenberger, **Ádám Farkas,** Zsombor Fehér, Zsolt Gall, **Dorottya Garay-Kiss,** Orsolya Gáspár, András Gerzsenyi, Orsolya Glavanovics, János Gyuricza, Anikó Hajdú, **Zsolt Henczel,** Zsófia Hoffmann, Mátyás Holló, Roberta Horváth, **Gábor Kállay,** Lilla Kántor, László Kara, Bence Kertész, Anna Sára Kiss, Blanka Klenk, Bence Komlósi, Krisztián Koós, Attila Kovács, Rita Madarasi-Papp, Mariann Mokos, **Kristóf Molnár,** Ádám Nagy, Arnold Németh, Tamás Németh, **Veronika Novák,** Soma Oszlányi, Norbert Paskó, Orsolya Pataj, **Zsolt Péteri,** Viktor Pósa, **Sarolta Rab, Lilla Radván,** Petra Reményi, Judit Repcsényi, Krisztián Sallai, Ádám Schiller, Sándor Sebestyén, Tamás Simon, Kinga Szabó, Kristóf Szabó, Tímea Szarka, **Tamás Szász, Anna Mária Szőgyi,** Anett Szternák, Krisztina Tari, Tamás Tavaszi, Annamária Tóth, Györgyi Tóth, Lili Tóth, Áron Török, Balázs Turai, Julianna Vajda, Janka Vizdák
(Bold denotes current staff)

Selected Works

Expo '95 Vienna
Vienna, Austria
International competition, 1st prize
Client: EXPO VIENNA AG
In collaboration with Péter Balogh
and Tibor Stahl
1991

Bank and Residential House
Győr, Hungary
Client: private
Team: Györgyi Tóth
1996–1998

EUROPAN 4
Graz-Eggenberg, Austria
International competition,
1st prize
Client: EUROPAN
In collaboration with
Árpád Ferdinánd
1996

Sports and Recreation Centre
Budapest, district 5, Hungary
Competition
Client: Belváros-Lipótváros
Beruházó Kft.
Team: Csaba Bukta,
Krisztián Sallai
1999

Special School for Children with
Intellectual Disabilities
Csorna, Hungary
Competition, 1st prize
Client: Győr-Moson-Sopron Megyei
Önkormányzat
Team: Orsolya Glavanovics, László Kara,
Krisztián Sallai
2001–2004

Social Housing
Budapest, district 8, Hungary
Client: Józsefvárosi
Önkormányzat
Team: Krisztián Sallai,
Károly Vaczurka
2001–2004

Aquarium Matrix Conference
Hall
Budapest, district 3, Hungary
International competition
Client: Graphisoft SE
Team: Viktor Pósa,
Krisztián Sallai
2002

Block of Apartments, Futó utca
Budapest, district 8, Hungary
Client: OTP Ingatlan Zrt.
Team: Orsolya Glavanovics,
Gergely Milassin, Krisztián Sallai
2002–2005

"Red Poppy" Audi Forum
Győr, Hungary
Client: Audi Hungaria Motor Kft.
Team: László Áder,
Roberta Horváth, Viktor Pósa,
Ildikó Raffayné Molnár,
Krisztián Sallai, Tamás Simon,
István Somogyi, Tamás Szabó
2002–2003

Central Office Building,
Audi Hungaria
Győr, Hungary
Invited competition, 1st prize
Client: Audi Hungaria Motor Kft.
Team: Lajos Börzsei,
Roberta Horváth, Viktor Pósa,
Ildikó Raffainé Molnár,
Krisztián Sallai, Tamás Simon,
Sándor Tárkányi, Anna Villám
2002–2003

Accommodation for 22 People with
Intellectual Disabilities
Koroncó-Zöldmajor, Hungary
Client: Győr-Moson-Sopron Megyei
Önkormányzat
Team: Orsolya Glavanovics, László Kara,
Krisztián Sallai
2002–2003

Extension of Budaörs Town Hall
Budaörs, Hungary
Competition, 2nd prize
Client: Budaörs Város
Önkormányzata
Team: Roberta Horváth,
Krisztián Sallai
2003

Institute for Children with Physical
Disabilities
Budapest, district 14, Hungary
Competition, 1st prize
Client: Budapest Főváros Önkormányzata
Főpolgármesteri Hivatala
In collaboration with Anthony Gall
Team: Balázs Baranyai, Gergely Barcza,
Roberta Horváth, Krisztián Koós,
Gergely Milassin, Orsolya Pataj,
Viktor Pósa, Krisztián Sallai,
Kinga Szabó, Tamás Tavaszi, Áron Török
2004–2009
Piranesi Award 2011, nominee
Mies van der Rohe Award 2011, nominee
Media Architecture Awards – Audience
Prize 2010

Town Centre and Event Hall
Győrszentiván, Hungary
Invited competition, 2nd prize
Client: Győr Megyei Jogú Város
Polgármesteri Hivatal
Team: Roberta Horváth, Krisztián Sallai
2004

High Court of Győr
Győr, Hungary
Competition, 3rd prize
Client: Győr Megyei Jogú Város
Polgármesteri Hivatal
Team: Péter Bach, Roberta Horváth,
Krisztián Sallai
2004

Church in Kismegyer
Győr, Hungary
Invited competition, 1st prize
Client: Magyar Bencés Kongregáció
Pannonhalmi Főapátság
Team: Krisztián Sallai
2004

Cultural Centre, Dísz tér
Budapest, district 1, Hungary
Competition
Client: Budai Várgondnokság
Kht.
Team: Dávid Baló, Sándor Rácz,
Krisztián Sallai, Gergely Sipos
2004

Design Centre
Budapest, district 5, Hungary
Competition, 2nd prize
Client: Központi Szolgáltatási Főigazgatóság
Team: Anett Eisenberger, Roberta Horváth, Viktor Pósa, Krisztián Sallai
2005

Sports Centre and Swimming Pool
Budaörs, Hungary
Competition, runner-up
Client: Budaörs Város Önkormányzata
Team: Anett Eisenberger, Roberta Horváth, Krisztián Sallai
2005

Learning Area for Children
Pannonhalma, Hungary
Client: Magyar Bencés Kongregáció Pannonhalmi Főapátság
Team: Krisztián Sallai
2006

Moorland Restoration and Visitor Centre
Keszthely, Hungary
Client: Pannon Egyetem Greorgikon Kar
Team: Balázs Baranyai, Gergely Barcza, András Gerzsenyi, Orsolya Pataj, Kinga Szabó
2006

Family House
Paloznak, Hungary
Client: private
Team: Ildikó Raffayné Molnár, Tamás Tavaszi
2006

Extension of Lővér Winery
Sopron, Hungary
Client: Sopvin Kft.
Team: Orsolya Pataj, Tamás Tavaszi, Áron Török
2006–2011

Concert Hall
Pécs, Hungary
Competition
Client: Pécsi Önkormányzat
Team: Orsolya Pataj, Kinga Szabó, Áron Török
2007

Árkád Shopping Centre
Szeged, Hungary
Invited competition, 2nd prize
Client: ECE Budapest Kft.
Team: Tamás Békesi (project architect), Glória Apáti, Péter Bach, Emese Balogh, Zsolt Bánhegyi, Tamás Döbrönte, Mátyás Holló, Lilla Kántor, Bence Kertész, Csaba Kisgergely, Anna Sára Kiss, Ádám Langer, Orsolya Pataj, Tímea Szarka, Tamás Tavaszi, Lili Tóth
2007–2011
Building Industry Award for Excellence 2012
DGNB (Deutsche Gesellschaft für Nachhaltiges Bauen) Gold Award 2011
Resource Property Award "Project of the Year" 2011

Kelenföld Railway Station and its Surroundings
Budapest, district 11, Hungary
Urban design competition, 1st prize
Client: Budapest Főváros Önkormányzata Főpolgármesteri Hivatala, Budapest XI. Kerület Újbuda Önkormányzata Polgármesteri Hivatala
In collaboration with MŰ-HELY Zrt.
Team: Orsolya Gáspár, Mátyás Holló, Gergely Schöff, Áron Török, Balázs Turai
2007

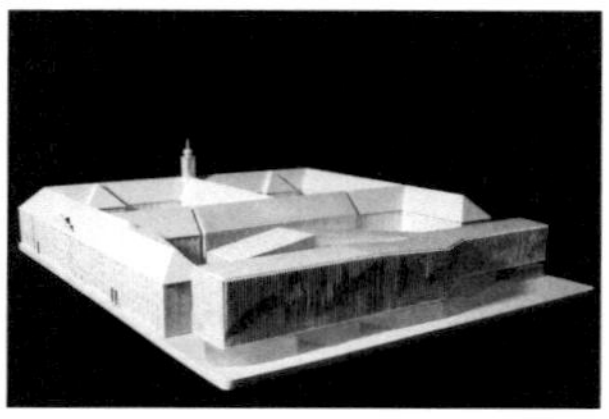

Extension of Budapest City Hall
Budapest, district 5, Hungary
Competition
Client: Főpolgármesteri Hivatal
Team: Emese Balogh, András Márk Bartha, Orsolya Gáspár, Mátyás Holló, Ádám Nagy, Orsolya Pataj
2008

Development and Modernisation of Hospital
Szeged, Hungary
Competition, runner-up
Client: Szegedi Tudományegyetem
Team: Mátyás Holló, Ádám Nagy, Orsolya Pataj
2008

Agora Pólus Interactive Exhibition Centre
Győr, Hungary
Competition, runner-up
Client: Győr Város Önkormányzata
Team: Tamás Döbrönte, Orsolya Gáspár, Mátyás Holló, Roberta Horváth, Albert Lovas, Ádám Nagy, Orsolya Pataj
2009

National Museum
Oslo, Norway
International competition
Client: Statsbygg
Team: Tamás Döbrönte, Mátyás Holló, Orsolya Pataj, Tímea Szarka
2009

Museum of Natural Sciences
Copenhagen, Denmark
International competition, runner-up
Client: University of Copenhagen
Team: Tamás Döbrönte, Mátyás Holló, Eszter Kovács, Orsolya Pataj, Tímea Szarka, Domonkos Újfalusi
2009

N41 Office Park
Budapest, district 12, Hungary
Client: Biggeorge's-NV 4. Ingatlanforgalmazó Befektetési Alap
Team: Tamás Döbrönte, Mátyás Holló, Orsolya Pataj, Tímea Szarka
2009

Extension of the Medicinal and Thermal Baths of Pápa
Pápa, Hungary
Client: Pápai Termálvízhasznosító Kereskedelmi és Szolgáltató Zrt.
Team: Tamás Döbrönte (project architect), Mátyás Holló
2009–2011

S House
Budapest, district 11, Hungary
Client: private
Team: Tamás Békesi (project architect), András Márk Bartha, Bence Kertész, Orsolya Pataj
2010–2012

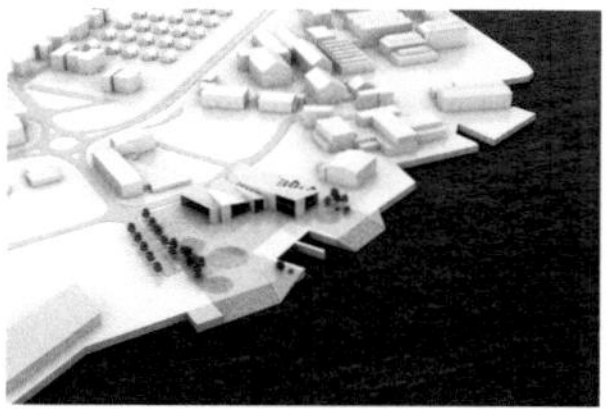

Blues Centre
Notodden, Norway
International competition
Client: Nottoden commune
Team: András Márk Bartha, Mátyás Holló, Tímea Szarka
2010

320° Art Centre
Siófok, Hungary
Competition
Client: Siófok Város Önkormányzata
Team: András Márk Bartha, Orsolya Pataj, Tímea Szarka
2010

Museum of the Second World War
Gdańsk, Poland
International competition
Client: Muzeum II Wojny Światowej w Gdańsku
Team: András Márk Bartha, Attila Fábri, Bogdán Funk, Mátyás Holló, Orsolya Pataj, Tímea Szarka, Mária Thuróczy, Dániel Vincze
2010

Geometria Office Building
Budapest, district 2, Hungary
Client: Geometria Kft.
Team: Orsolya Pataj (project architect), Zsombor Fehér, Lilla Kántor, Bence Kertész, Rita Madarasi-Papp, Tímea Szarka
2011–2013
Architectural Award for Excellence 2015
Building Industry Award for Excellence 2013

K4 Office Building (Vision Towers)
Budapest, district 13, Hungary
Clients: Futureal Development Holding Kft., KPMG
Team: Tamás Békesi (project architect), András Márk Bartha, Zsombor Fehér, Lilla Kántor, Bence Kertész, Anna Sára Kiss, Tamás Németh, Orsolya Pataj
2011–2014
Building Industry Award for Excellence 2015

Barn Conversion Apartment House
Győrszentiván, Hungary
Client: Casa del Grano Ingatlanforgalmazó és Hasznosító Kft.
Team: Anikó Hajdú
2011

National and University Library II
Ljubljana, Slovenia
International competition
Client: Zbornica za arhitekturo in prostor Slovenije
Team: András Márk Bartha, Attila Csóka, Klára Hegedűs, Krisztián Jager, Attila Lakomcsik, Lilla Kántor, Szabolcs Molnár, Eszter Móricz, Zoltán Paczolay, Orsolya Pataj
2012

Renovation of Szeged Cathedral
Szeged, Hungary
Client: DÓM Fejlesztő- és Turisztikai Szolgáltató Szervezet
In collaboration with Váncza Művek Architect Studio
Team: Tamás Békesi (project architect), Orsolya Pataj (project architect), András Márk Bartha, Zsombor Fehér, Dorottya Garay-Kiss, Tamás Németh
2012–2015
AIT-Award – public building category special mention – 2018
2A Europe Architecture Award 2017 – category "Old and New", 1st prize

L House
Győr, Hungary
Client: private
Team: András Márk Bartha, Lilla Kántor, Tamás Németh, Orsolya Pataj
2012–2015

Detached Holiday House in the Region of Lake Balaton
Lovas, Hungary
Client: private
Team: András Bartha, Tamás Békesi, Anna Sára Kiss
2012

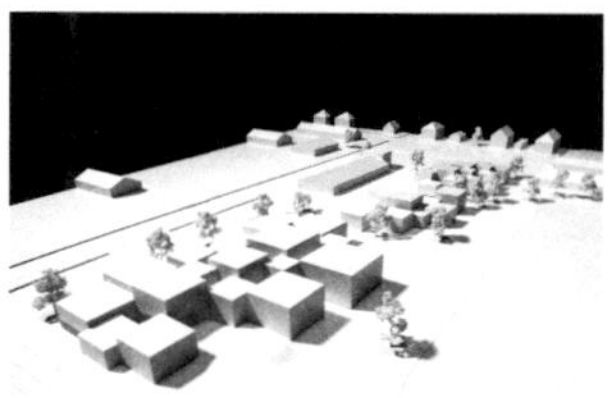

Waldorf School
Tartu, Estonia
International competition
Client: Tartu Free Waldorf School Association
Team: András Márk Bartha, Dorottya Garay-Kiss
2012

Extension of Pedagogical College
Salzburg, Austria
International competition, runner-up
Client: Big Bundes Immobilien Gesellschaft
Team: András Márk Bartha, Dorottya Garay-Kiss, Lilla Kántor
2013

Intermodal Transport Centre
Debrecen, Hungary
Competition
Client: Debrecen Megyei Jogú Város Önkormányzata
Team: Tamás Békesi, Zsombor Fehér, Dorottya Garay-Kiss, Orsolya Pataj
2013

House of Hungarian Music
Budapest, district 14, Hungary
International competition, shortlisted
Client: Liget Zrt.
Team: Zsombor Fehér, Dorottya Garay-Kiss, Soma Oszlányi
2014

Benedictine Church and Bell Museum
Győr, Hungary
Client: Magyar Bencés Kongregáció Szent Mór Perjelség
Team: Ádám Farkas, Anna Sára Kiss, Kristóf Molnár, Lilla Radván, Kristóf Szabó, Krisztina Tari
2014–

Reconstruction of the West Wing of the Esterházy Castle, Phase I
Fertőd, Hungary
Client: Eszterháza Kulturális, Kutató- és Fesztiválközpont Nonprofit Kft.
Team: Anna Sára Kiss (project architect), Tamás Békesi, Dorottya Garay-Kiss, Blanka Klenk, Veronika Novák, Soma Oszlányi
2014–2019
World Architectural Festival 2019 – Finalist in category "Completed Buildings: New and Old"

Corvin 5 Office Building
Budapest, district 8, Hungary
Client: FUTUREAL New Ages Ingatlanfejlesztő Kft.
Team: Tamás Békesi (project architect), Réka Bánkuti-Tóth, Júlia Boromissza, Ádám Farkas, Emese Galamb, Gábor Kállay, Zsolt Péteri, Tamás Szász, Krisztina Tari
2015–2020

Moholy-Nagy University of Art and Design
Budapest, district 12, Hungary
International competition, 1st prize
Client: Moholy-Nagy Művészeti Egyetem
Team: Tamás Békesi (project architect), Gábor Kállay (project architect), Ábel Bálint, Balázs Baranyai, Júlia Boromissza, Ákos Dobrányi, Ádám Farkas jr., Ádám Farkas, Emese Galamb, Dorottya Garay-Kiss, János Gyuricza, Borbála Parizán, Zsolt Péteri, Petra Reményi, Krisztina Tari
2015–2019

Renovation and Extension of the Cloister in Városmajor utca
Budapest, district 12, Hungary
Client: Szent Keresztről Nevezett Irgalmas Nővérek Közép-Európa Tartomány
Team: Tamás Békesi (project architect), Gábor Kállay, Mariann Mokos, Veronika Novák, Annamária Tóth
2015–

Development and Extension of Kós Károly Vocational School
Érd, Hungary
Invited competition, 1st prize
Client: Érd Megyei Jogú Város Önkormányzata
Team: Ádám Farkas (project architect), Veronika Novák (project architect), Júlia Boromissza, Tamás Csépke, Dorottya Garay-Kiss, Petra Reményi, Sarolta Rab, Krisztina Tari
2016–

Residential Building, Jakab József utca
Budapest, district 13, Hungary
Client: OTP Ingatlan Zrt.
Team: Gábor Kállay (project architect), Julianna Vajda (project architect), Cecília Bartos, Tamás Csépke, János Gyuricza, Blanka Klenk, Norbert Paskó, Sarolta Rab, Zsolt Péteri
2016–

Sports Centre
Budapest, district 9, Hungary
Competition
Client: Budapesti Corvinus Egyetem
Team: Tamás Békesi, Tamás Csépke, Krisztina Tari
2017

Reconstruction and Extension of the Király Thermal Baths
Budapest, district 2, Hungary
Competition, 1st prize
Client: Budapest Gyógyfürdői és Hévizei Zrt.
Team: Gábor Kállay (project architect), Cecília Bartos, Júlia Boromissza, Zsófia Hoffmann, Lilla Radván
2017–

Renovation of the Abbey Church and its Immediate Surroundings
Bélapátfalva, Hungary
Client: Érseki Vagyonkezelő Központ
Team: Tamás Békesi (project architect), Tommaso Laezza, Veronika Novák, Lilla Radván, Krisztina Tari
2018

Creative Centre of Brno
Brno, Czech Republic
Invited international competition, 3rd prize
Client: Kancelář architekta města Brna
In collaboration with Stempel & Tesar
Team: Júlia Boromissza, Tamás Csépke, Tomasso Laezza, Veronika Novák, Lilla Radván
2018

Budapest South Gate
Budapest, Hungary
Invited international master plan design competition, 3rd prize
Client: KKBK Kiemelt Kormányzati Beruházások Központja Nonprofit Zrt.
Team: Tamás Csépke, Ádám Farkas, Kristóf Molnár, Lilla Radván, Kristóf Szabó, Krisztina Tari
2018

New Museum of Transport
Budapest, district 10, Hungary
Invited international competition
Client: Magyar Műszaki és Közlekedési Múzeum
Team: Gábor Kállay, Zsófia Hoffmann, Lilla Radván, Kristóf Szabó
2019

Reconstruction of the West Wing of the Esterházy Castle, Phase II
Fertőd, Hungary
Client: Eszterháza Kulturális, Kutató- és Fesztiválközpont Nonprofit Kft.
Team: Tamás Csépke, Zsófia Hoffmann, Krisztina Tari
2019–

Sports Complex – Swimming Hall and Ice Rink
Kazincbarcika, Hungary
Clients: Kazincbarcikai Sport Központ "Delfin" Vízisport Klub, Kazincbarcikai Ördögök Sportegyesület
Team: Tamás Békesi (project architect), Tamás Csépke, Kristóf Molnár, Zsolt Péteri, Sarolta Rab, Kristóf Szabó, Krisztina Tari
2019–

About the Authors

Olaf Bartels

was born in 1959. He is an architect, author, editor, curator, moderator and lecturer who lives in Hamburg. He studied architecture at the Academy of Fine Arts, Hamburg (Diploma 1987). He has published many books and journal articles and has conducted research on contemporary architecture and urban development, the history of architecture, urban history, and urban development in Germany and Turkey. He has taught at universities in Berlin, Braunschweig, Hamburg, Istanbul and Ankara and is a member of the German Academy of Urban Development and Regional Planning (DASL).

Balázs Danyi

was born in 1985. He received an MSc degree in architecture from Budapest University of Technology and Economics (BUTE). He works as a freelance photographer specialising in our built environment. In his work he is in constant search for simplicity and clarity. As a trained architect he has a sensitive understanding of the essential conceptual message of built works – one that he intends to reveal through his photographs. His works are regularly published in renowned international and local magazines, books and exhibitions.

Zsolt Gunther

was born in 1964. He is an architect and founder of 3h architects – see biographies on pages 276–277.

Claus Käpplinger

was born in 1963. He lives and works as a freelance architecture and urban critic in Berlin. He has authored numerous publications in Germany and writes regularly for international architecture magazines such as "Architektur Aktuell" /Vienna or "De Architect"/The Hague. His books include "Young French Architects", "Dictionnaire de l'Architecture du XXe siècle", "Hansen+Petersen" and "Grüntuch Ernst Architects" (ARCA). In 1993–96 he organised the German-Austrian architectural initiative "Berlin und seine Zeit" and in 1998–2005 the interdisciplinary discussion group "Stadtsalon" in Berlin (since 2007 the BDA-Stadtsalon) on questions concerning the city, architecture and perception. He has taught at different universities and since 2013 typology at the Institute for Design and Architectural Strategies at the Technical University Braunschweig.

Holger Kleine

was born in 1962. He lives and works in Berlin. He studied architecture and musicology in Berlin and New York and with his office has realised numerous prizewinning buildings, among them the German Embassy in Warsaw, the Schreibhaus am Steinhuder Meer and the housing project "Jules et Jim". In 2010, he was appointed Professor of Design at RheinMain University of Applied Sciences in Wiesbaden. In 2014, he published the book "New Mosques" and in 2018 "The Drama of Space", introducing a set of terms that helps people reflect on their experience of architecture and the delight and appreciation this brings. He lectures widely on the topic, holding seminars in Europe, Asia and America, most recently in Mexico, Bangladesh, Jordan and the USA.

Ákos Moravánszky

was born in 1950. He studied architecture at the Technical University in Budapest between 1969 and 1974. From 1977 he studied art history and historic preservation at Vienna University of Technology, where he received his doctorate in 1980. Between 1983 and 1986, he was Editor-in-Chief of the magazine of the Hungarian Union of Architects, "Magyar Építőművészet". From 1986 until 1988 he was a Research Fellow at the Zentralinstitut für Kunstgeschichte in Munich. Between 1989 and 1991 he was invited to the Getty Center for History of Art and the Humanities as a Research Associate. From 1991 until 1996 he was appointed Visiting Professor at the MIT. In 1996 he was invited to teach the Theory of Architecture at the Institute gta of the ETH Zurich, where he has been Titular Professor since 2005. He has organised international conferences such as "Freedom – Free Time: Fleeing from the Everyday in Eastern & Western European Architecture 1960–1980" at the ETH Zurich in 2007 and "Experiments: Architecture between Natural Sciences and Art" in Gut Siggen in 2008. He has been President of the editorial board of the Swiss architectural journal "Werk, Bauen+Wohnen" and serves on the editorial board of the journal "tec21", and the advisory boards of "Footprint" and "Prostor".

Image Directory of the Photo Essays

Section	No.	Image
Context	1	View of Budapest
	2	Winter ploughland, western Hungary
	3	Arable land at Lake Neusiedl
	4	Rural house, Cigánd
	5	Rural house with courtyard on a narrow plot, Fertőrákos
	6	Country road at Lake Neusiedl
	7	North Vehicle Repair Station of the Hungarian public railway network (MÁV), Kőbányai Street 30–36, Budapest
	8	Roofscape in the city centre, Budapest
	9	Near the Danube on the Pest side of Budapest
	10	Firewalls in the city centre, Budapest
	11	Detail of the Liberty Bridge (Szabadság híd), Budapest
Intermediate Spaces	1–2	Béla Hofstätter and Ferenc Domány, Block of flats belonging to the Factory Pension Fund of the Manfred Weiss Companies, Margit Boulevard 15–17, Budapest
	3	Gedeon Gerlóczy, Arcade, block of flats on the corner of Petőfi and Párizsi Streets, Budapest
	4–5	Zsigmond Quittner, Former Hungarian Journalists' Retirement Institute, Alkotmány Street 16, Budapest
	6	György Kővári, Southern Railway Terminal, Budapest
	7	András Ivánka, Hospital Clubhouse, Zrínyi Street 13, Győr
	8	György Szrogh, Headquarters of the Union of Mining Workers, Városligeti City Park Lane 46–48, Budapest
	9	Ignác Alpár, Former Headquarter of Anker Life and Annuity Insurance Company, Anker Alley 1–3 and 2–4, Budapest
Ornamental Perception	1	Gyula Rimanóczy, "R" building of the Technical University of Budapest, Műegyetem Quay, Budapest
	2	UVATERV, BKV Traffic Control Centre, Üllői Street 12, Budapest
	3	Béla Lajta, detail of the Trade School, Vas Street 9–11, Budapest
	4	Imre Platschek, block of flats of the Trust Pension Society, Margit Boulevard 29, Budapest
	5	Staircase detail in the city centre of Budapest
	6	Flóris Korb and Kálmán Giergl, Academy of Music, Liszt Ferenc Square 8, Budapest
	7	Béla Lajta, detail of the Trade School, Vas Street 9–11, Budapest
	8	Artúr Sebestyén and Ármin Hegedűs, Hotel Gellért and Gellért Bath, Gellért Square 1, Budapest
	9	Béla Lajta, detail of the Trade School, Vas Street 9–11, Budapest
	10	Béla Rerrich, Ferenc Gál College, Dóm Square, Szeged
	11	Artúr Sebestyén and Ármin Hegedűs, Hotel Gellért and Gellért Bath, Gellért Square 1, Budapest
	12	Rural house, Main Street, Fertőszéplak
	13	Gyula Wälder and György Kardos, Madách Houses, Madách Imre Square 3–4, Budapest
Space and Light	1	Király Baths, Fő Street 84, Budapest
	2	Church of the Cistercian Monastery, Bélapátfalva
	3	Ádám Clark, Buda Castle Tunnel, Alagút Street, Budapest
	4	István Szabó, reformed parish church of outer Kelenföld, Ildikó Square 1, Budapest
	5–6	Alajos Hauszmann, attic of the Museum of Ethnography, Kossuth Square, Budapest
	7–8	Kálmán Reichl and Virgil Borbíró, Kelenföld Power Station, Vízpart Street, Budapest
	9–10	Metallurgical Plants, cooling towers, Gyár Street, Ózd
	11	Csaba Virágh, National Electric Power Distribution Station in Buda Castle, Nándor Street 5, Budapest

Illustration Credits

Every effort has been made to trace the copyright owners of the images contained in this book and we apologise for any unintentional omission.

Photos

Olaf Bartels 167 (Fig. 1), 167 (Fig. 6)

Tamás Bujnovszy 10 (Fig. 6), 11 (Fig. 8), 11 (Fig. 13), 11 (Fig. 14), 18 (Fig. 15), 21 (Fig. 16), 21 (Fig. 20), 103 (Fig. 3), 103 (Fig. 5), 114, 119, 120, 121, 122–123, 124–125, 131, 132 (middle), 132 (bottom right), 134 (top right), 134 (bottom right), 138–139 (left), 140 (top left), 148–149 (right), 167 (Fig. 5), 168 (Fig. 9), 168 (Fig. 10), 168 (Fig. 11), 177, 179, 181, 182, 183 (bottom left), 183 (top right), 185, 188–189, 190–191, 192–193, 194, 198–199, 200, 201 (top left), 201 (bottom right), 202, 203, 204–205, 206, 207, 236 (Fig. 10), 236 (Fig. 11), 236 (Fig. 12), 236 (Fig. 13), 236 (Fig. 14), 240, 245, 246, 247, 248, 249, 250–251, 278

Csaba Csathó 73 (top left), 73 (middle), 73 (bottom right)

Balázs Danyi 15 (Fig. 4), 15 (Fig. 7), 21 (Fig. 17), 21 (Fig. 19), 24–25, 26–27, 28 (top left), 30 (bottom left), 30–31 (right), 32–33 (left), 33 (bottom right), 34, 35, 36–37, 66, 71, 75, 76 (top left), 76 (bottom right), 77, 78–79, 87, 88 (bottom left), 88–89 (right), 90, 91, 92–93, 94, 95, 96–97, 98–99, 103 (Fig. 6), 126, 132 (top left), 133 (top right), 133 (middle), 133 (bottom right), 134 (middle), 135, 136–137 (left), 137 (right), 139 (right), 140 (bottom right), 141, 142, 143, 144, 145, 146, 147, 148 (left), 151, 152, 153, 154, 155, 156 (top left), 156–157 (bottom right), 157 (top), 158, 159, 160–161 (left), 161 (right), 162–163, 167 (Fig. 3), 167 (Fig. 4), 172, 178, 180, 184, 186–187, 217, 218, 219, 220–221, 226, 227, 228–229, 235 (Fig. 1), 235 (Fig. 2), 235 (Fig. 3), 235 (Fig. 6), 235 (Fig. 7)

Cemal Emden 168 (Fig. 7), 168 (Fig. 8)

Zsolt Gunther 10 (Fig. 5), 11 (Fig 10), 15 (Fig. 2), 18 (Fig. 8), 18 (Fig. 11), 18 (Fig. 13), 64, 235 (Fig. 4)

Copyright: HMA MPDC Hungarian Museum of Architecture, Photographer: Andrea Häider, Häider Archive 10 (Fig. 4), 46, 52, 53

Gábor Máté 11 (Fig 9), 11 (Fig. 12), 15 (Fig. 3), 15 (Fig. 5), 18 (Fig. 10), 18 (Fig. 12), 18 (Fig. 14), 21 (Fig. 21), 51, 54–55, 56, 61, 62–63, 65, 72 (top right), 72 (middle), 72 (bottom right), 74 (middle), 74 (bottom right), 103 (Fig. 1), 103 (Fig. 2), 106, 111, 112 (bottom left), 112 (top right), 113, 236 (Fig. 9), 266–267, 276

Ákos Moravánszky 10 (Fig. 1), 11 (Fig. 11)

Tamás Thaler 168 (Fig. 12),

Csaba Villányi and Zalán Péter Salát 28–29 (bottom right), 97, 222, 223, 224–225 (left), 225 (right)

Ute Zscharnt 167 (Fig. 2)

3h architects 15 (Fig. 6), 84 (bottom left), 230 (middle), 230 (left), 230 (bottom right)

Computer renderings

3h architects 18 (Fig. 9), 21 (Fig. 18), 21 (Fig. 22), 21 (Fig. 23), 80, 84 (top right), 85, 168 (Fig. 13), 208, 213, 214, 215, 235 (Fig. 5), 236 (Fig. 8), 252, 256 (top), 257, 258–259, 260, 264 (bottom right), 265 (top right), 267 (right), 268, 274–275, 279, 280, 281, 282

Acknowledgements

We owe our gratitude to all those who have helped in the creation of our book. Without the commitment of our colleagues in the office, the expertise of our co-designers and the patience of those who commissioned the buildings included in this book, it could not have been realised.

Our thanks are due to the project leaders, especially our partners, Tamás Békesi and Gábor Kállay, who ensured the quality of the designs even amidst the hectic periods of everyday life. We learnt much from those who commissioned the buildings – in connection with our early designs, Pál Nádas, principal of the institute for children with physical disabilities, gave us useful advice, as did others. Later, our designs were shaped during very positive consultations with Tibor Tenke (Geometria), the Benedictine Order and the MOME Lab, especially with Gábor Kopek in connection with the MOME project.

We are grateful to the authors of the essays, who devoted a lot of energy towards understanding and interpreting our designs and ideas. We were engaged in a dialogue with Ákos Moravánszky for a long time. Holger Kleine and Olaf Bartels represented a fresh attitude, which helped to clarify our work from a different perspective.

The imagery used by László Krasznahorkai is very close to ours; so we borrowed the quotations for the picture essays from him. His thoughts support the atmosphere of the images suggestively, yet faithfully at the same time. The initial intention was reinforced by an accidental encounter in the Jedermann Café in Budapest. The themes recalled by Balázs Danyi's sensual photos reflect the buildings and situations which are very important for our architecture. We also thank Tamás Bujnovszky, Andrea Haider and Gábor Máté for their splendid architectural photography.

Our intention was not to make a traditional book about architecture, since Hungary's context cannot be interpreted automatically in relation to contemporary architecture. Our editor, Claus Käpplinger, devoted much effort to making the context understandable. That was how the book's structure emerged, with the groups of picture essays, essays and projects repeated rhythmically. Zalán Péter Salát created the book's final design. We experimented with him a great deal in order to create a unique book. We are grateful to him for his patience and creativity. Finally, many thanks are due to Henriette Mueller-Stahl and Amelie Solbrig, working for Birkhäuser, who contributed their advice to the editing of the book.

Katalin Csillag and Zsolt Gunther

The publication was kindly supported by nka National Cultural Fund of Hungary